25 . xii . 1994

Anne and Tony

Happy Christmas

Love from Nick

Page 54 gives you an idea of what I get up to at work!

CHRISTIE'S

Review of the Season 1994

CHRISTIE'S
Review of the Season 1994

Edited by
FRANCIS RUSSELL

Assisted by
OPHELIA JAMES

CHRISTIE'S

Copyright © Christie, Manson & Woods Ltd., 1994

A CIP catalogue record for this book is available from the
British Library

ISBN 0–903432–45–5

Printed and bound by Watmoughs, Bradford and London

Cover illustration:
A gypsum bas-relief Wall-Slab from Room C, the north-west
Palace of Ashurnasirpal II at Kalhu (Nimrud)
883–859 B.C.
72 × 46 in. (183 × 117 cm.), $2\frac{1}{2}$ in. (6.4 cm.) thick
Sold by order of the Governors of Canford School
London, 6 July 1994, £7,701,500 ($11,891,116)

Frontispiece:
Attributed to PIERRE GOUTHIÈRE (French, 1732–1813)
A Pair of Louis XVI ormolu-mounted Chinese aubergine
porcelain Ewers supplied to Marie-Antoinette for the Cabinet
Intérieur de la Reine at the Château de Versailles, circa 1783
19 ins. (48·5 cm.) high: 11 in. (28 cm.) wide
Sold by the Luton Hoo Foundation
London, 9 June 1994, £1,046,500 ($1,579,169)
Record auction price for French ormolu-mounted porcelain

These ewers are discussed in an article by Charles Cator on p. 132.

**All prices include the buyer's premium where applicable.
The currency equivalents given throughout the book are
based on the rate of exchange ruling at the time of sale.**

CONTENTS

FOREWORD

by Sir Anthony Tennant

Christie's have offered outstanding works of art from many distinguished collectors this last season. Our sale from the Collection of Hubert de Givenchy in Monaco will long be remembered for its beauty and quality. Other memorable occasions have been the sale of Orientalist pictures collected by Malcolm Forbes, that of furniture and designs by Charles Rennie Mackintosh assembled by Dr. Thomas Howarth and the Barbra Streisand Collection of 20th Century decorative and fine arts.

The Ryohei Ishikawa Collection of United States Stamps sold at Christie's in New York provided the highest total for a single-owner collection of stamps. A private cellar of magnificent wine achieved the highest total for an auction of wines from a single source. Other collections have included those of Sir Michael Sobell and Mary, Viscountess Rothermere, highly important printed books from Beriah Botfield's Library and the second sale of Italian Maiolica from the Arthur M. Sackler Collections.

Christie's sales have achieved many new record prices, for furniture made by Chippendale from Brocket Hall, for a portrait by El Greco, a picture by Henri 'Douanier' Rousseau, for any piece of silver – the Hanover Chandelier from the Givenchy Collection – and for a photograph, a carpet, an Oriental textile, a Korean work of art, an Islamic work of art, a violin by Guarneri, a book by Steinbeck, a teddy bear and a European fan as well as for Old Master and 19th Century pictures.

Many remarkable discoveries have been made at Christie's this year. Among the most impressive was that of the fascinating royal provenance of a pair of Louis XVI ormolu-mounted Chinese porcelain ewers (*frontispiece*) which through research initiated by Christie's were found to have belonged to Queen Marie-Antoinette and which she had consigned for safekeeping at the beginning of the French Revolution. These became the most expensive French decorative objects to be sold at auction when they reached £1,046,500 in London.

Another discovery was that of a three thousand-year-old Assyrian relief (p.214), once thought to be plaster cast, found in a school tuck shop in the South of England and identified as a missing wall slab from the north west Palace of the Assyrian King Ashurnasirpal II (883–859 BC). The relief sold for £7.7 million, a record for any antiquity and any sculpture. Christie's also sold two Fabergé eggs, thought to have been lost until we brought them to auction in May.

One of the most extraordinary objects ever to be auctioned was a so-called 'unicorn's horn', actually a narwhal horn (p.118), one of only two surviving examples carved in England in the twelfth Century; it achieved £441,500 in London. From the twentieth century Christie's East sold a collection of original Walt Disney storyboard drawings found in an attic. Further superb works of art included a group of Sèvres plates providing a panorama of early nineteenth-century French history from the Service des Arts Industriels bought by King Louis-Philippe (p.200).

It has been a lively year for collectibles at Christie's South Kensington and Christie's East in New York. The Britains Archive (p.195), a unique accumulation of over 3,000 toy soldiers and figures attracted international interest and was 100 per cent sold. The Golden Era of Hollywood featured large at Christie's East this year with memorabilia from the Estates of Clark Gable and Vincent Price.

We conducted a number of country house sales in America and in the United Kingdom. The Collection of Mr. and Mrs. George W. Scott Jr. of Lancaster, Pennsylvania was 100 per cent sold, while a sale of the contents of Mere Hall, Cheshire in England (p.308) offered an unusual glimpse of the heritage of the Grand Tour in Europe. The sale at Mere Hall was the highest totalling Christie's house sale since West Dean in 1986 and a painting by Sir Nathaniel Dance at £243,500 attained the highest price ever paid at a country house sale.

The last year has seen further expansion for Christie's both geographically and in the range of sale categories offered. We recently marked the opening of our first office in China with an exhibition of Oriental and Western works of art in Shanghai, attended by over five thousand people. We now hold twice-yearly exhibitions of works of art in Korea and have held our second series of sales in Singapore and Taiwan. This year also saw our most successful auctions to date in Hong Kong, which included, for the first time, a sale of Western jewellery and watches.

In South America we have strengthened our representation in Argentina, Uruguay and Chile, and mounted regular exhibitions in Mexico. We are now holding auctions in Greece and, for the first time, recently held an auction in Tel Aviv. In New York we have substantially improved the facilities for clients by adding extra floor space.

The art market like any other is affected by economic strength or weakness, but works of art of respected provenance and great quality and beauty have continued to appreciate in value over time. Christie's clients are and will continue to be well placed to benefit from this.

SALES TO THE NATION

by Edward Manisty

In the United Kingdom, sales to the Nation, or 'negotiated sales', are achieved in two ways. By private treaty sale to a public museum or institution. Alternatively by offer in lieu of tax, whereby the Nation acquires the object in satisfaction of a liability to capital taxation faced by the owner, and allocates it to an appropriate institution. In any such transaction the owner forfeits the opportunity of testing the open market, and as some recompense is rewarded with what is known as the 'douceur'. Effectively this means that the benefit he obtains is enhanced by a bonus equal to a quarter of the tax liability that he would have faced had he sold on the open market at the agreed value. In recent years, with reductions in the penal rates of tax applicable on death in the past, it has become strongly arguable that a 25% douceur no longer affords a sufficiently attractive incentive to owners to renounce the temptations of the marketplace for a negotiated sale. With this qualification, the concept of the negotiated sale as a means of securing objects for the Nation is a sound one, potentially conferring benefits both on the owner who must dispose of his property, and the institution, and thus the general public, which acquires it. However, if the concept remains good, the method of funding now attached to it and the machinery associated with it are long overdue for radical reassessment. Such a reassessment might be carried out in the wider context of a review of tax incentives available to those engaged in forming new collections and those attempting to preserve old ones: a theme developed at the end of this essay.

Before turning to what the future might hold, what has it been possible to achieve within the existing framework over the past season? The variety of objects acquired by the Nation through Christie's agency is considerable, as is the price range involved. At one end of the spectrum a small family archive was sold by private treaty to a County Record Office for a value before the douceur of £1,000, and at the other, Gainsborough's conversation piece, *Portrait of the Artist, with his Wife and elder Daughter seated in a Landscape* was accepted in lieu of tax at an agreed value of £1,750,000 and allocated to the National Gallery. The completion of this transaction fulfilled a wish expressed by Sybil, Marchioness of Cholmondeley that after her death a painting should be transferred from Houghton to the National Gallery to mark the tenure of office of her brother Sir Philip Sassoon as Chairman of its Trustees from 1933 to 1935. A more fitting tribute to two notable members of the Sassoon family and to the taste and energy of that family as collectors could hardly be imagined.

The strength of the ties that so often exist between major collectors and the museums of this country was demonstrated a second time when the Executor of the estate of Mary, Viscountess Rothermere, agreed – as a mark of Lady Rothermere's affection for Britain's heritage – to withdraw from auction a group of important seventeenth-century objects, and to sell them by private treaty to the Victoria and Albert Museum. The group, which had previously been on loan to that museum, included a spectacular Jacobean-style doublet (p.5) and a contemporary portrait, by an artist still unidentified, of Margaret Layton (d. 1641), the wife of Francis Layton, a Yorkshire landowner, who served the first three Stuart monarchs as Yeoman of the Jewel House, and who suffered for his devotion to the Royalist cause during the Commonwealth. The portrait, of about 1620, shows that the doublet has never been altered. It is believed to be one of only two pieces of domestic English dress depicted in a contemporary portrait that survives from the period before 1700.

A cabinet miniature of Queen Elizabeth's favourite Robert Devereux, 2nd Earl of Essex (1567–1601) was accepted in lieu of tax. The portrait shows Essex at the height of his favour as a courtier, at one of the tourneys that continued to be held in Elizabeth's reign, wearing the glove of his patroness, the Queen, tied to his arm. It is now accepted that this miniature is the work of Nicholas Hilliard (1547–1619), who enjoyed the patronage and protection of Essex. It has been allocated to the National Portrait Gallery.

Christie's has been instrumental in the acquisition for the Nation of two highly important horological instruments. The completion of these sales has been assisted by the recent ruling by the Inland Revenue that clocks and watches are not subject to Capital Gains Tax. The beneficiary in each case has been the National Maritime Museum at Greenwich, which includes the Royal Observatory, itself a foundation of the Stuart monarchs. In 1674, King Charles II appointed John Flamsteed (1646–1719) 'our astronomical observator' at the new found site of the Observatory on the hill above Greenwich. The Observatory was set up with the aim of facilitating the navigation of the British fleet, and in particular of resolving problems associated with measuring longitude for the purposes of pinpointing a position at sea. A key element in Flamsteed's work in this respect were the two clocks presented to him and made by Thomas Tompion (1638–1713). These, originally with 13 foot pendulums, hung above rather than below the movement, and enormous weights, were cased behind the skirting in the Octagon Room at the Observatory to reduce air friction and thus improve accuracy. Wound up only once a year, they are believed to be the oldest surviving English year clocks. The primary purpose of these clocks was to time the astronomical observations which gave birth to the navigational method involving the use of a sextant, a timepiece, and reference to the Nautical Almanac which endured as the basis of marine navigation for the next two hundred years. After the death of Flamsteed in 1719, both clocks were removed from Greenwich, with his other instruments, by his formidable widow, who successfully resisted Government attempts to purloin them. Subsequently they were converted into longcase form. One is now at the British Museum and the other found its way to Holkham Hall where it was included in the list of heirlooms left by Thomas Coke of Holkham, 1st Earl of Leicester (1754–1842), the great agriculturalist. It is from Holkham that the clock has come home to Greenwich.

A second private treaty sale to the National Maritime Museum was of an historic pocket marine timekeeper made in 1776 by

THOMAS GAINSBOROUGH (English, 1727–1788)
Portrait of the Artist, with his Wife and elder Daughter, seated in
a Landscape
oil on canvas
$36\frac{1}{2} \times 27\frac{7}{8}$ in. (91.3 × 69.5 cm.)
Accepted in lieu of tax by H.M. Treasury and allocated to the
National Gallery, London

John Arnold (1736–1799), known as 'Arnold No. 36'. While John Harrison (1693–1776) had perfected a chronometer a few years earlier, receiving the reward promised in an Act of 1714 to 'such person or persons as shall discover the Longitude', Arnold was in the forefront of the improvement of such instruments and their production on a regular basis. His timekeepers were bought by the East India Company for use on their vessels and were taken by explorers in the late eighteenth Century on their voyages around the Antipodes. A delightful but alas apocryphal story has it that Arnold No. 36 accompanied Captain Cook on his final voyage. Even if it did not enjoy this distinction, it served as the prototype for Arnold's development of the chronometer, undergoing its proving tests at the Royal Observatory, where over a period of 13 months the total error was only 2 minutes 33 seconds. Appropriately it now returns to the scene of its original trials.

25 April 1994 marked the 300th anniversary of the birth of Richard Boyle, 3rd Earl of Burlington (1694–1753).

To mark the anniversary of his birth English Heritage is undertaking a complete renovation of Burlington's suburban residence Chiswick House. Christie's has been able to play a small part in this ambitious project by negotiating a private treaty sale of five gilt-gesso open-arm chairs between his descendants and English Heritage for display at Chiswick House. This lavishly decorated folly designed by Burlington and built between 1725 and 1729 was modelled on Palladio's Villa Capra near Vicenza. It was embellished with works of art of all kinds intended as a mirror of its creator's taste, both to divert its owner when in residence at Chiswick, and to dazzle his literary and artistic friends.

The chairs were originally from a set of ten with two sofas, supplied to Lady Burlington in 1735 by Stephen Langley for the Garden Room, now the Summer Parlour, which served as her dressing room. This negotiated sale shows in a graphic way the capacity of available procedures not only to bring important items into public ownership but also to restore them to the building for which they were made.

The procedures also continue to ensure that important objects that have never left the house with which they are associated remain in situ there. A further offer in lieu of items from Nostell Priory related to a substantial group of drawings by Robert Adam and James Paine, with designs of furniture by Chippendale for the house, to remain there in the care of the National Trust.

It is particularly pleasing to record two transactions involving the National Museum of Wales the completion of which gave such satisfaction to both the owners and the Museum. It was in 1838 that Margaret Sandbach, granddaughter of the Liverpool banker and collector William Roscoe (1753–1831), travelled to Italy with her husband, Henry Sandbach. In Rome they visited the celebrated sculptor, John Gibson (1790–1866), who was to remain close to Margaret until her death in 1854. The Sandbachs commissioned Gibson to create a number of works for their new house, Hafodunos in Denbighshire, building a private gallery to house these. One of the most noted of these sculptures was that of the Goddess Aurora, the bringer of dawn. This had been lent for some sixty years to the Museum of Wales by the Sandbachs' descendants. It is gratifying that it will remain where it has been for so long. The second item, a rare English silver kettle and tripod stand, was accepted in lieu of tax, from the estate of Sir Philip Shelbourne. The kettle was made in London by Thomas Gladwin in 1719, apparently for George Treby (1684?–1742), MP for Plympton Erle and a Minister of the Crown in Walpole's administration. Treby was a major patron of silversmiths, commissioning a famous toilette service from Paul de Lamerie now in the Ashmolean Museum. The stand, made in London by John White, has a Welsh provenance, bearing the arms of Vaughan of Llwydiarth from which family it passed by marriage to the Williams-Wynn family in whose ownership it remained until 1935.

Sadly archives and family papers are items that seldom stimulate the popular imagination in the same way as important paintings or items of furniture. Their interest and importance is none the less for this. Such papers provide the historian with the structure on which he can hang the social history of this country and the manner in which our great collections were formed and sometimes disposed of. The sale by way of private treaty from the estate of Rosemary, Lady Ravensdale to the Hertfordshire County Council of the so-called Panshanger Archive is a reminder of this truth. The great house at Panshanger was demolished in 1953 and its contents dispersed, yet this particularly rich archive, long deposited on loan with the Hertfordshire Record Office, remains to constitute an extremely rich and varied picture of the talented family who lived at Panshanger for over 300 years. It is the record of the Cowpers, the Lambs and the Grenfells, and of their artistic and literary connections with Browning, Watts, Lord Leighton, Burne-Jones, Wilde, Henry James, Kipling, Siegfried Sassoon, as well as with major political figures over three centuries. A highlight is the personal papers of Lady Caroline Lamb (1785–1828), the wife of Lord Melbourne, with relics of the tempestuous relationship with Byron which caused such scandal and led to her separation from her husband. This archive, which includes Repton's Red Book for Panshanger, indeed constitutes a unique record of a house and those who breathed life into it.

The National Maritime Museum at Greenwich again benefited from the sale of the papers of Sir Charles Middleton, 1st Lord Barham (1726–1813), who served as First Lord of the Admiralty at the time of Trafalgar. Barham was then in his eightieth year, and if the Dictionary of National Biography is to be believed, was 'no longer fit to be at the head of the English Navy even in peace, still less during a great war'. Nonetheless his papers provide a fascinating insight into both administrative and operational matters relating to the Navy in the late eighteenth and early nineteenth centuries, including letters from Nelson to Barham, a memorandum in an unidentified hand reporting on the outcome of Trafalgar, and other memorabilia of the Battle.

A sale in a corner of the market which has come into the limelight lately was that of a gold Bronze Age torc or necklace to the County Museum at Lincoln. The torc, dating from about 1200 to 1000BC, was found in a field and awarded, by Coroner's Inquest, to the finder, who instructed Christie's to negotiate the sale to the Museum

With the increase in the use of metal detectors in the search for buried objects, the effectiveness of the ancient law of Treasure Trove governing finds such as this has become in recent years a matter of considerable debate. Dating as it does from the time of Richard I's crusading ventures, and constituting an ingenious method of filling the Royal coffers for such purposes, over the last 200 years or so the law in this area at best has been an amusing anachronism and at worst, an ass.

Lord Perth, working with the British Museum, has introduced a Bill to reform the law which, if enacted, will broaden the category of objects that constitute Treasure Trove and end the

A Bodice, worn by
Margaret Layton
(1579?–1641)
linen, with brightly
coloured silks and silver gilt
thread, gold lace and sequins
English 1610–20
Sold by private treaty to the
Victoria and Albert
Museum

necessity for Coroners and their juries to perform the mental gymnastics involved in deciding whether hundreds of years ago, an owner concealed an object with the intention of recovering it, when it would constitute Treasure Trove accruing to the Crown, or whether he simply abandoned it, when it would not accrue to the Crown. The Bill will not change the present system of paying a reward equivalent to the full market value of an object found to be Treasure Trove and retained by a museum. It will facilitate, however, the prosecution of those who uncover items that are potentially Treasure Trove and fail to report the discovery to the Coroner. Such reforms, so long overdue, should go a long way towards ensuring that the Nation is able to acquire valuable hoards intact, without disturbing the present arrangements whereby members of the public participating in such finds are fairly rewarded.

An experienced observer writing in an influential journal recently expressed the view that the completion of any negotiated sale 'must be something of a miracle'. The 'miracles' of the past season have indeed been achieved within a cumbrous and imperfect structure, in which lengthy delays often arise and where the sun of the Government's Citizens Charter has yet to rise. What of the future?

Until the early years of the this century the acquisition of wealth brought with it a desire on the part of the begetter to show a public face, which often involved the acquisition of beautiful possessions and their placement in suitable surroundings. The ambience created by Mr Melmotte in Grosvenor Square before his fall – enhanced, of course, by the presence of his lovely daughter – so shrewdly observed by Trollope in 'The Way We Live Now' – is but one entertaining, and not wholly fictitious illustration, of what drove the new merchant class to collect in days gone by.

However, the new, and it is to be hoped more durable,

Melmotte has so much to distract him from Boulle and Boucher. Perhaps today the BMW, with the bathroom and other 'fitted' benisons now available are more obviously redolent of the sense of security that he craves, than works of art. The firing of his imagination as a collector may need a fiscal stimulus, that perhaps, understandably, in the absence of the motor car and other modern distractions, with no capital gains tax and with income tax charged at two old pence in the pound, Mr Melmotte never needed to persuade him to set 'the south side of Grosvenor Square ablaze' in the 1870s.

That this is indeed so, and that the awarding of fiscal incentives to collect to its citizens, is one mark of the civilised state at the end of this Century is well recognised outside this country. For instance, in the United States the Clinton Administration has recently restored the full deductibility for income tax purposes to gifts of works of art to public museums. Again in the Republic of Ireland if a collector acquires an important work of art and allows it to be displayed for at least six years in a public museum he may thereafter dispose of it free of Capital Gains Tax.

The time has come for a wholesale review of the framework and funding of negotiated sales. This might profitably be extended to consider the tax incentives that should be offered by the State to stimulate the formation by its citizens of new collections, to secure the enhancement and preservation of existing collections, both old and new, and to facilitate the retention of important works of art in this country, whether in public or private ownership. Private collections provide the negotiated sales of the future, as the curators of our museums must be keenly aware. The implementation of such a review under the auspices of Government, involving wide-ranging public consultation, would with the advent of the National Lottery, help to shed much needed rays of light to dispel at least some of the shadows that have lengthened over the world of Sales to the Nation in the last few years.

THE MASTER OF THE CARRAND TONDO (Italian, active circa 1430)
The Madonna of Humility
tempera on gold ground panel
$28\frac{1}{2} \times 20\frac{1}{4}$ in. (72.5 × 51.5 cm.)
London, 8 July 1994, £496,500 ($764,610)

The artist takes his name from a *desco da parto* or birth tray of the *Judgement of Paris* in the Carrand Collection in the Museo Nazionale del Bargello, Florence. Acquired by the pioneering collector, the Rev. Walter Davenport Bromley, this Madonna fetched 16 guineas at his posthumous sale at Christie's in 1863: in 1937 it was acquired by Samuel Courtauld, best known for his interest in French Impressionists, and later bequeathed by him to Christabel, Lady Aberconway.

THE MASTER OF SAINT ANNA (Flemish, 15th Century)
A Triptych: The Virgin and Child with Saints Catherine of
Alexandria and Barbara
oil on panel
centre compartment $28\frac{1}{2} \times 19\frac{1}{4}$ in. (72 × 48.4 cm.);
wings $28\frac{1}{2} \times 8$ in. (72 × 20.3 cm.)
New York, 12 January 1994, $440,000 (£294,697)

The Master, named after the Saint Anna altarpiece in the
Historische Museum, Frankfurt, was active in Bruges in the late
fifteenth century and influenced by the Master of the Saint Lucy
Legend. The central panel is derived from a lost work by Hugo
van der Goes.

BERNARDO DI STEFANO ROSELLI (Italian, 1450–1526)
A Cassone Panel: The Triumphal Entry of Alfonso I into Naples
tempera on gold ground panel
$17\frac{1}{4} \times 66$ in. (43.2 × 167.6 cm.)
New York, 12 January 1994, $385,000 (£257,697)

This cassone front shows the triumphal entry of Alfonso I of
Aragon (b. 1395; King of Naples 1443–58) into Naples on
26 February 1443, the first Renaissance re-enactment of a
Roman triumph. Part of the notable group of Italian works formed
by Alexander Barker and sold at Christie's in 1879, it then
fetched 16 guineas.

MIRABELLO CAVALORI, called MIRABELLO DI
SALINCORNO (Italian, 1535–1572)
Isaac blessing Jacob
oil on panel
$22\frac{7}{8} \times 17\frac{1}{8}$ in. (58 × 43.5 cm.)
London, 8 July 1994, £397,500 ($612,150)

Cavalori is best known for the *Lavinia at the Altar* and *A Wool Factory*, which he contributed circa 1570–2 to the decoration of the Studiolo of Francesco I de Medici in the Palazzo Vecchio, Florence. This panel is datable 1569–70.

Sir (John) Charles Robinson (1824–1913), who sold the present picture with an attribution to Salviati at Christie's in 1885, was a major figure in the London art world in the second half of the nineteenth century. A subsequent owner was the notable connoisseur Charles Loeser.

DOMENIKOS THEOTOKOPOULOS, EL GRECO
(Spanish, 1541–1614)
Portrait of a young Lady
signed 'doménikos theotokópolis epoíei' (in cursive Greek)
oil on canvas
Sold from the Estate of Mary, Viscountess Rothermere
$19\frac{7}{8} \times 16\frac{1}{2}$ in. (50.5 × 42 cm.)
London, 10 December 1993, £1,706,500 ($2,547,805)

This picture is first recorded in the sale of General the Hon. John Meade at Christie's, 8 March 1851, when it fetched 3 guineas. It is generally dated to the 1590s and, as a portrait of a woman by the artist, is a considerable rarity.

The sitter's identity has given rise to much speculation. Sánchez Cantón thought that she might be Alfonsa de los Morales, first wife of the artist's son Jorge Manuel. Goldscheider suggested that the same model may have been used for the *Madonna of Charity* at Illescas and Lafuente noted a resemblance to several El Greco Madonnas: while Beruete considered her of less than aristocratic status, Vázquez-Campo claimed that she was the Infanta Catalina Micaele, daughter of King Philip II.

JOACHIM ANTHONISZ. WTEWAEL (Dutch, 1566–1638)
The Raising of Lazarus
signed 'IOACHIM WTEN WAEL FECIT'
oil on canvas
$30\frac{1}{4} \times 40$ in. (76.8 × 101.6 cm.)
New York, 12 January 1994, $770,000 (£515,395)

This notable discovery probably dates from soon after 1600, and
may be compared with the *Baptism of Christ* of 1607 in the
Hermitage, St. Petersburg.

Like Wtewael's other treatment of the *Raising of Lazarus* in the
Museé des Beaux-Arts, Lille, this picture is indebted to Abraham
Bloemaert. An engraving of the subject by Jan Muller of the mid-
1590s, probably after Bloemaert, also shows the crowd before an
arched architectural background with two striding men flanking
the group in ingeniously contrasting poses. The main figures are
similar in both print and painting.

Right:
SEBASTIAN VRANCX (Flemish, 1573–1647)
The Four Seasons (Autumn illustrated)
oil on panel laid down on panel
$20\frac{1}{8} \times 25\frac{5}{8}$ in. (51 × 65 cm.) a set of four
New York, 18 May 1994, $693,000 (£461,492)

AMBROSIUS BOSSCHAERT I (Dutch, 1573–1621)
A Tulip, a Pot Marigold, a Peony, Roses, a Columbine, a Stock,
Forget-Me-Nots, a Wild Violet and a Hyacinth in a glass Jar with
a Butterfly and a Caterpillar on a Ledge
signed with monogram 'AB'
oil on copper
$6\frac{1}{2} \times 4\frac{5}{8}$ in. (16.5 × 11.6 cm.)
London, 8 July 1994, £309,500 ($476,630)

The pot marigold and the white rose on the left are identical to
those in the flower piece of 1609 by the artist in the
Kunsthistorisches Museum, Vienna. Formerly in the Constantine
collection, the picture was sold at Christie's on 14 May 1971 for
17,000 guineas.

Left:
OSIAS BEERT I (Dutch, circa 1580–1624)
A Pear, Apples and Apricots on a *Wan-li* Dish, Plums, Walnuts, Hazelnuts, Apricots, Grapes, Pears and Mulberries on pewter Plates, *Fraises-de-bois* in a *Klapmuts*, a Nautilus Cup, Roses and Tulips in a blue and white Chinese Vase, *façon de Venise* wine Glasses, a Knife, Hazelnuts and Twigs with four Butterflies – a Peacock, two Whites and a Red Admiral – on a wooden Table
signed 'O.BEERT.f'
oil on panel
$25\frac{1}{4} \times 45\frac{1}{2}$ in (64.2 × 115.5 cm.)
Amsterdam, 11 May 1994, Fl. 1,610,000 (£575,000)

Little is known about Osias Beert, an Antwerp trained artist whose career was, to a degree, overshadowed by that of Jan Bruegel I, but whose merits were certainly recognised by Rubens who collaborated with him on one occasion.

JAN DAVIDSZ. DE HEEM (Dutch, 1606–1683/4)
Oysters, Cobnuts, a peeled Lemon and an Orange on a pewter Plate with a Plum and Grapes on a partially draped Table
signed 'J.De heem'
oil on panel
$9\frac{1}{2} \times 13\frac{3}{8}$ in. (24.3 × 34 cm.)
London, 10 December 1993, £243,500 ($363,546)

Above:
TOMAS HIEPES (Spanish, circa 1610–1674)
Bunches of Grapes on a Vine in a Manises ceramic Vase, with Pomegranates, Quinces, Pears and other Fruit on a wooden Table and African Marigolds growing in a Manises ceramic Vase on a window Ledge
signed and dated 'ORIGINAL DE TOMAS HIEPES, EN Vç 1654..'
oil on canvas
$43\frac{1}{2} \times 53$ in. (110.5 × 134.6 cm.)
New York, 12 January 1994, $781,000 ($522,758)

Little is known about Hiepes, who was active from the middle of the seventeenth century in Valencia. Such was his reputation in that city that Antonio de Orellana, the biographer of Valencian painters, wrote 'one did not see baskets of fruit, nor flowers, etc., nor biscuits, nor pates, nor cheeses, nor tarts, nor meat pies, nor the furniture or accessories of the pastry shop or other objects of the same type, well executed conforming to nature, that one did not take it on the spot for a work of Yepes'.

This picture displays Hiepes' characteristic use of chiaroscuro and muted light-brown colours and his simplistic, planar sense of composition. The Manises ceramic vases are typical earthenware vessels from the province of Valencia, and appear in other pictures by the artist.

ISAACK KOEDIJCK (Dutch, 1617/18–1668)
A Barber Surgeon tending a Peasant's Foot
signed 'I Koedijk'
oil on panel
$35\frac{3}{4} \times 28\frac{3}{8}$ in. (91 × 72 cm.)
London, 10 December 1993, £287,500 ($429,238)

Koedijck is believed to have been born in Amsterdam, and is documented as having lived alternatively in both that city and in Leyden until 1645.

This picture has been dated circa 1650, on the basis of the costumes and its relationship with *Empty Glass*, dated 1648, and *The Reveller*, dated 1650, in the Hermitage, St. Petersburg.

MICHIEL VAN MUSSCHER (Dutch, 1645–1705)
A Notary in his Office handing Deeds to a Man as a Youth
looks on
signed and dated 'Hiob Berckheyde 1672'
oil on canvas
$30\frac{7}{8} \times 24\frac{1}{2}$ in. (78.5 × 62.2 cm.)
London, 22 April 1994, £287,500 ($427,800)

The picture may well correspond with one recorded in a sale at
Amsterdam, 10 July 1742, lot 98 'Een Binnekamer met een
Notaris met zyn Klerken, door Musscher' (An Interior with a
Notary and his Clerks, by Musscher).

This exceptional record of one facet of life in seventeenth-
century Holland bears what purports to be the signature of Job
Berckheyde: the attribution to Musscher was first proposed by
Mr Willem van de Watering in July 1974.

JAN VAN HUYSUM (Dutch, 1682–1749)
Pink and white double Hollyhocks, Morning Glory, Marigolds,
Cockscombs, Passion Flowers and Forget-Me-Nots surrounding
a sculpted Urn, with a Melon and Plums in a wicker Basket,
Grapes, Peaches, Plums, a split Melon, Raspberries, Red
Currants, Walnuts, a Pomegranate, Apricots and other Fruit on a
stone Ledge, with a Cabbage White, Red Admiral and Painted
Lady Butterflies and other Insects
signed and dated 'Jan van Hüysum/Fecit 1730'
oil on panel
$30\frac{1}{2} \times 23\frac{1}{2}$ in. (77.5 × 59.7 cm.)
New York, 12 January 1994, $2,640,000 (£1,767,068)

This exceptional work by the artist was one of a pair from the
celebrated collection of Jan and Peter Bisschop of Rotterdam,
acquired with a pendant in 1771 by Jan and Adriaen Hope of the
distinguished banking family. The pictures were separated in the
posthumous sale of Adele, Lady Meyer at Christie's in 1930: this
panel fetched 750 guineas at Christie's in 1934.

JAN VAN HUYSUM (Dutch, 1682–1749)
Roses and other Flowers in a Basket on a marble Ledge
(illustrated); and Fruit, Hazelnuts and Hollyhocks on a marble
Ledge
both signed 'Jan Van Húÿsúm fecit' (the signature on the first
partially obscured by the auricula)
oil on panel
Sold by Sir Evelyn de Rothschild
$15\frac{3}{4} \times 13$ in. (40 × 33 cm.) a pair
London, 8 July 1994, £826,500 ($1,272,810)

This panel and its pendant are datable to the mid–1720s, and are
thus marginally earlier than the much larger and more ambitious
flower piece illustrated opposite. Their provenance is, however,
complementary: they were first recorded in 1835 in the
collection of Jonkheer Willem van Loon (1794–1847) of
Amsterdam which was acquired *en bloc* in 1878 by Baron Lionel
de Rothschild (d. 1879) of 148 Piccadilly and Gunnersbury Park,
Middlesex. The two subsequently passed to his third son,
Leopold de Rothschild of Ascott, Buckinghamshire.

EUSTACHE LE SUEUR (French, 1616–1655)
Christ on the Cross with the Magdalen, the Virgin and Saint John
the Evangelist
oil on canvas
Sold from the IBVM Charitable Trust, The Bar Convent, York
$42\frac{7}{8} \times 28\frac{7}{8}$ in. (109 × 73.2 cm.)
London, 10 June 1994, £397,500 ($599,430)
Now in the National Gallery, London

This is a variant of the larger canvas in the Louvre, from which it differs most notably in the head of the Virgin, which is not in profile in that picture. The Louvre version is said to have been in a Parisian church, possibly the Oratoire Saint-Honoré, until the Revolution. Both paintings were formerly regarded as the work of Simon Vouet, Le Sueur's master, whose style they strongly reflect. Pictures of this kind are poorly represented in English collections and it is not known who presented this example to the Bar Convent in York, probably in the 1870s.

NICOLAS DE LARGILLIÈRE (French, 1656–1746)
Portrait of François Pommyer and Yves-Joseph-Charles
Pommyer, playing with a King Charles Spaniel
oil on canvas
$29\frac{1}{2} \times 36\frac{1}{4}$ in. (75 × 92 cm.)
London, 10 December 1993, £529,500 ($790,544)

The sitters were the twin sons of Yves-Joseph Pommyer and
Marie-Marguerite Lefèvre. Like his father, François Pommyer
became *Trésorier général de France au Bureau des Finances d'Alençon*;
he married Elisabeth de Lorne, daughter of the *Secrétaire du Roi*
François de Lorne and of Anne Papillon. He succeeded to his
father-in-law's office on 2 March 1731 and died in 1779. Yves-
Joseph-Charles Pommyer was also *Écuyer* and *Seigneur de
Rougemont*. He became an *Avocat du Parlement* and died before
1777.

The picture is datable circa 1710 and formed part of the notable
group of portraits of members of the Pommyer family by
Largillière.

A CAPRICCIO BY CANALETTO

by Francis Russell

No season in the saleroom would seem complete without its quota of canvasses by Canaletto, for the simple reason that no major Italian topographical painter of the eighteenth century was so consistently productive as the Venetian. Each of his innumerable views of his native city has an inevitability of its own, and so, in a rather different way does the noble *Capriccio with the Scuola di San Marco* which was sold last April.

Canaletto is thought of above all as a view painter, indeed *the* view painter of the eighteenth century. But after he was honoured with membership of the Academy at Venice in 1763, he presented to that institution not a picture of the city, but his *Capriccio: a Colonnade opening on to the Courtyard of a Palace*, which is dated 1765. At the outset of his career Canaletto had worked as a painter of scenery for the stage, but his later *capricci* should be seen less as a return to the interests of his youth, than as evidence of his determination to be thought of as more than a mere painter of townscapes. No less an authority than Count Francesco Algarotti, the greatest Venetian connoisseur of the age, wrote admiringly in 1759 of Canaletto's *Capriccio: a Palladian Design for the Rialto Bridge, with buildings at Vicenza*, which he deemed to represent a new kind of composition, in which buildings and imaginary designs were transposed within a specific setting, in that case the Grand Canal.

When in England in the early 1750s, Canaletto executed three *capricci* for specific settings in the most advanced London mansion of the day, Chesterfield House in Mayfair. A larger group of *capricci*, formerly in the Lovelace collection, was probably commissioned by Thomas King, who in 1767 succeeded as 5th Baron King, presumably for the decoration of one, or perhaps two, rooms in his London house. Canaletto also painted a *capriccio* of monuments in Whitehall *en suite* with the series of views supplied in 1755 for another English patron, Thomas Hollis.

While this was very probably also originally intended for an English patron, the marginally earlier *Capriccio with the Scuola di San Marco* is, one might venture to suggest, rather closer in spirit to the picture Algarotti admired than the general run of the painter's architectural fantasies. It shows the west façade of one of the great monuments of Renaissance Venice, the Scuola di San Marco, from a specific view point, the loggia of the late medieval Ca'Grifalconi-Loredan (Canareggio 6359 in Calle de la Testa). The loggia itself is greatly enlarged in scale by Canaletto, who follows the design of the flight of steps on the left quite closely; but this also is increased in size. What is, in reality, a narrow yard assumes the scale of a *campo*, flanked to the right by a range of utilitarian buildings. These again are much more extensive than their models. The long, richly fenestrated façade of the Scuola, extended to the design of Jacopo Sansovino between 1533 and 1543, dominates the composition. Here also, however, Canaletto aspired to improve on reality. The whole building is raised on a ground floor of his imagination: the simple pediment of the bay on the left is crowned by the artist with three pinnacles - directly based on a section of the façade of the great church of Santi Giovanni e Paolo, the Zanipolo, which adjoins the Scuola.

Canaletto's intention was no doubt to provide a foil to the upper part of the main front of the Scuola, seen from the side, its silhouette emphasised by the suppression of the façade of the Zanipolo, that would, in reality have been within the viewer's line of vision. Fact and fantasy are thus perfectly balanced, in a composition in which the use of the arcaded loggia suggests a clear parallel with that of the centring of the arch in the Northumberland *London seen through an Arch of Westminster Bridge*, painted in 1746-7. Canaletto was always fascinated by the depiction of restricted space, as his views of so many of the Venetian *campi* and of Whitehall prove. The Scuola di San Marco *Capriccio* carries this process to a logical and definitive conclusion.

Canaletto paid particular attention also to the figures he introduced in the composition. The station of these is clearly defined: on the left a cloaked gentleman climbs the steps, observed by a woman from behind a curtain; a messenger with a wig - and a wig box - pauses by the column opposite a woman who has been sweeping. On the right a patrician child holds out a bone for a dog, a servant standing at his side. Further back a labourer draws water from the well, while beyond the watergate a man of consequence parleys with a boatman.

While the original purchaser of the picture cannot be identified, the picture is known to have been owned by Sir Thomas Neave, 2nd Bt. of Dagnam Park (1761-1848), who inherited or acquired a substantial collection of works by Canaletto. His father, Richard Neave, a Governor of the Bank of England who was created a baronet in 1795, was painted in 1751 by Zoffany and is known to have made the Grand Tour; while his mother, born Frances Bristow, was perhaps a relation of the William (Billy) Bristow who speculated in pictures and works of art acquired in Italy in the 1740s: his parents were painted together by Gainsborough. In 1810, before he succeeded as baronet, Thomas Neave ordered a family portrait from the young David Wilkie, whose papers suggest how demanding the commission proved. The nine Canalettos Neave owned did not constitute a series and were of varying date: one described simply as a *View in Venice* was lent to an exhibition at the British Institution in 1824. The fact that the collection included a view of Rome, *the Piazza del Campidoglio and the Cordonata*, which is a variant of one of the Hollis series, may explain the former identification of the *Capriccio with the Scuola di San Marco* as a view of the Palazzo Barberini. For whichever of the patrons of his London years the picture was supplied, it offers touching evidence of Canaletto's instinctive visual sympathies for the city of his birth.

GIOVANNI ANTONIO CANAL, IL CANALETTO
(Italian, 1697–1768)
Capriccio with the Scuola di San Marco, Venice, from the
Palazzo Grifalconi-Loredan
oil on canvas
$34\frac{1}{2} \times 54$ in. (87.7 × 137.2 cm.)
Sold by the Executors of the late Sir Arundell Neave, Bt.
London, 22 April 1994, £2,201,500 ($3,275,832)

GIOVANNI ANTONIO CANAL, IL CANALETTO
(Italian, 1697–1768)
The Grand Canal, Venice, looking East from the Campo S. Vio
oil on canvas
$18\frac{1}{2} \times 30\frac{7}{8}$ in. (47 × 78.5 cm.)
London, 10 December 1993, £1,211,500 ($1,808,770)

One of four pictures by the artist believed to have been acquired
by George Proctor in Venice in 1738–40, this remained with his
descendants until it was sold at Christie's in 1977.

GIOVANNI PAOLO PANINI (Italian, 1691/2–1765)
The Roman Forum and the Campidoglio seen from the Arch of
Constantine, with the Basilica Emiliana, the columns of the
Temple of Castor and Pollux and the Temple of Saturn and
Vespasian, the Arch of Septimius Severus, Santa Maria Aracoeli,
and the Dome of SS. Luca and Martina
signed and dated 'I.P.P. 1751'
oil on canvas
$22\frac{3}{4} \times 37$ in. (57.8 × 94 cm.)
New York, 12 January 1994, $638,000 (£427,041)

BERNARDO BELLOTTO (Italian, 1721–1780)
The Porta Santo Spirito, Rome, with the Via dei Penitenzieri and
the Campanile of Santo Spirito in Sassia (illustrated): and The
Arch of Titus, Rome, with the Wall and Gate of the Farnese
Gardens and the Temple of Castor and Pollux beyond, two
tourists in the foreground (a pair)
oil on canvas
$38\frac{3}{4} \times 29\frac{1}{2}$ in. (98.5 × 75 cm.)
Sold by the Executry of Manon, Countess of Lovelace
London, 10 December 1993, £1,761,500 ($2,624,635)

According to Bellotto's early biographer and friend Pietro
Guariento, the artist travelled to Rome 'to employ his talent in
drawing and painting the antique buildings and most beautiful
views of that city'. Several drawings survive from this visit
including a pen drawing of the Porta Santo Spirito. Such sketches
formed the working models for paintings, as with this pair of a
Corinthian classical arch and a Renaissance gateway of the
Tuscan order designed by Antonio da Sangallo, the Younger,
which would have been painted after the artist's return to Venice.
Indeed the sketches produced by Bellotto in Rome had such an
influence upon his uncle, Canaletto, that for many years he was
believed to have accompanied Bellotto to Rome.

CHARLES-ANTOINE COYPEL (French, 1694–1752)
Portrait of Madame Dupillé and her daughter (illustrated); and
Portrait of Monsieur Dupillé
signed, inscribed and dated 'MADAME / DUPILLE / AVEC /
SA FILLE / PEINT / EN 1733 / PAR / COYPEL / EN
HABIT / DE BAL'; and 'MONSIEUR / DUPILLE PEINT /
EN / 1733 / PAR Mr / COYPEL / EN ROBE DE /
CHAMBRE'
oil on canvas
57¾ × 38 in. (146.7 × 96.4 cm.)
Monaco, 19 June 1994, Fr. 2,886,000 (£341,054)

This pair of portraits has a distinguished place in the *oeuvre* of
Coypel. The architectural settings suggest his knowledge of
Dutch seventeenth-century prototypes.

JEAN-HONORÉ FRAGONARD (French, 1732–1806)
A Shepherdess seated with Sheep and a Basket of Flowers near a
Ruin in a wooded Landscape
oil on canvas
$28\frac{1}{4} \times 36\frac{3}{8}$ in. (71.8 × 92.5 cm.)
London, 10 June 1994, £287,500 ($433,550)

The young Fragonard's talent was spotted by François Boucher, in whose studio he is presumed to have worked for two or three years before he received the *Grand Prix* of the *Académie royale de peinture* on 26 August 1752. A number of pictures of the ensuing period are now believed to have been painted secretly for Boucher, and this example, with its pendant, are additions to the group. Their first recorded owner was Thomas Edmondson (1765–1836) of Baltimore, Maryland.

ANTONIO JOLI (Italian, circa 1700–1777)
A panoramic View of the City of London from the Thames near the Water Gate of Somerset House
oil on canvas
Sold from the Estate of Dame Merlyn Myer
$33\frac{3}{4} \times 50\frac{1}{2}$ in. (85.8 × 128.3 cm.)
London, 10 December 1993, £386,500 ($577,045)

Joli, the most widely travelled of the great view painters of the eighteenth century, arrived in London from Venice by way of Dresden in 1743/4 and left for Madrid in 1749/50. Between 1744 and 1748 he is recorded as a painter of theatrical scenery, and possibly also assistant manager, at the King's Theatre in the Haymarket. He also executed a number of decorative schemes, notably that which survives in the hall of the Richmond home of the theatre's manager John James Heidegger.

What was presumably a depiction of this view was among the first works executed by Joli in England. A 'piece of perspective ... painted ye Length ways of ye cloath ... per Traverso' showing a 'View of St Pauls ... a beautiful picture and veramente di buon gusto' is recorded having been painted for Richmond House, Whitehall, in 1744.

(detail)

LOUIS-LÉOPOLD BOILLY (French, 1761–1845)
A Carnival on the Boulevard du Crime
signed and dated 'Boilly 1832'
oil on canvas
24 × 42 in. (61 × 108 cm.)
New York, 12 January 1994, $937,500 (£627,510)

Boilly was the outstanding French exponent of genre painting in
the early nineteenth century and this exceptional work suggests
his range as a commentator on contemporary life.

ANTONIO ALLEGRI, called CORREGGIO
(Italian, circa 1489–1534)
Saint Benedict
red chalk, on pink prepared paper
$6\frac{1}{8} \times 4\frac{5}{8}$ in. (15.5 × 11.9 cm.)
New York, 11 January 1994, $101,500 (£68,029)

The drawing, previously attributed to Andrea del Sarto, is a study for Saint Benedict in Correggio's lost fresco of *The Coronation of the Virgin* formerly in the apse of the Benedictine Abbey of San Giovanni Evangelista, Parma. Correggio worked extensively in the church, most notably on the fresco decoration of the cupola and apse in the first half of the 1520s. The apse fresco was destroyed at the end of the sixteenth century when the Benedictines decided to extend the church to the east. Mindful of the quality of the fresco they preserved the central section of the original and commissioned Cesare Aretusi to paint a replica in the apse. The technique of the drawing is Correggio's favoured medium of red chalk on a background made pink by smudging chalk, probably with a wetted finger, onto the paper.

The pose of the figure, who stands to the left of the Virgin, is almost identical in the fresco, although the head was moved to a more frontal position. The finished nature of the drawing would suggest that the pose had already been established, and that the artist intended the Saint to be shown half-length as he appears in the fresco.

HENDRICK AVERCAMP (Dutch, 1585–1634)
An ice Scene with a Gentleman admiring an elegantly dressed
Woman skating, other Skaters, Kolfplayers and horsedrawn
Sledges beyond
signed with monogram 'HA'
black lead, watercolour and bodycolour, brown ink framing lines
$7\frac{3}{4} \times 12\frac{1}{2}$ in. (19.5 × 31.6 cm.)
Amsterdam, 15 November 1993, Fl.253,000 (£90,357)

SIR PETER PAUL RUBENS (Dutch, 1577–1640)
The Parable of the Vineyard, after Andrea del Sarto
numbered '14'
black chalk, pen and brown ink, brown wash heightened with
white on light brown paper
$10\frac{3}{8} \times 14\frac{3}{8}$ in. (26.5 × 36.5 cm.)
Sold from the collection of Mr. Alfred Normand
Monaco, 20 June 1994, Fr.666,000 (£79,032)

SIR ANTHONY VAN DYCK (Dutch, 1599–1641)
A Beach with a Ship, a wooded Ridge beyond
signed 'A: van dyck'
pen and brown ink
$7\frac{7}{8} \times 11\frac{1}{2}$ in. (19.8 × 29.1 cm.)
London, 5 July 1994, £73,000 ($112,420)

This drawing dates from the first half of the 1630s when the artist
spent much of his time in England. Although the site cannot be
identified it is possible that it is near Rye where van Dyck made a
celebrated group of drawings. Rye was the port from which boats
made the crossing to Dieppe, and van Dyck probably drew the
views of the town while waiting for a favourable wind. It is
impossible to be certain if the drawing is an English view because
van Dyck returned relatively frequently to Flanders in this period,
and there are two comparable landscape studies in the British
Museum, one dated 1634, which were probably drawn in his
native country. The practice of making *plein air* views, such as the
present one, was probably inspired by those of van Dyck's master
Rubens. The composition of the drawing with the motif of a
wooded ridge recalls Venetian landscape studies by Titian and
Campagnola, which van Dyck would have seen during his time
in Italy. The extraordinary economy and atmosphere of van
Dyck's pen and ink landscape drawings is only matched in the
seventeenth Century by those of Rembrandt some twenty years
later.

This drawing belonged to the painter Jonathan Richardson
Senior (1665–1745), who owned 13 of the 23 landscape and
plant studies now accepted as by van Dyck's hand.

REMBRANDT HARMENSZ, VAN RIJN
(Dutch, 1606–1669)
Studies of the Heads of four bearded Men in Hats or Turbans
pen and brown ink, brown wash, on light brown prepared paper
$5 \times 6\frac{1}{4}$ in. (12.6 × 15.8 cm.)
New York, 11 January 1994, $332,500 (£222,855)

This drawing probably dates from 1636. It is related, both in style
and subject, to a large sheet of studies in the Barber Institute,
Birmingham; both were drawn not with a specific painting in
mind, but rather as a type of model sheet which could be used at a
later date by Rembrandt and his pupils as points of reference for
compositions. Typically for the period, Rembrandt prepared the
paper with a light brown wash to create a warm, soft effect,
somewhat akin to the Japanese paper that he sometimes used in
his printmaking. The heads are drawn directly in pen and ink
with no preliminary underdrawing in chalk. The figure on the
left has been worked up in brown wash, including the masterly
depiction of his silhouette behind him.

MARCO RICCI (Italian, 1676–1729)
Two Travellers in a Carriage followed by a Rider on a Path at the
Top of a Hill
black chalk, pen and brown ink, brown wash
$14\frac{1}{2} \times 20\frac{1}{2}$ in. (37 × 52.2 cm.)
Monaco, 20 June 1994, Fr.643,800 (£76,397)

OLD MASTER PRINTS

REMBRANDT HARMENSZ. VAN RIJN
(Dutch, 1606–1669)
Christ crucified between the two Thieves: 'The Three Crosses'
drypoint with engraving
$15\frac{1}{8} \times 17\frac{7}{8}$ in. (38.5 × 45.4 cm.)
London, 30 June 1994, £133,500 ($206,258)

GIORGIO GHISI (Italian, 1520–1582)
The Vision of Ezekiel
engraving
$16\frac{1}{4} \times 26\frac{3}{4}$ in. (41.4 × 67.9 cm.)
London, 30 June 1994, £29,900 ($46,196)

FRANCISCO DE GOYA Y LUCIENTES
(Spanish, 1746–1828)
La Tauromaquia
set of thirty-five etchings
burnished aquatint, drypoint and engraving
$10\frac{7}{8} \times 15\frac{3}{8}$ in. (27.5 × 39 cm.)
New York, 9 May 1994, $90,500 (£60,576)

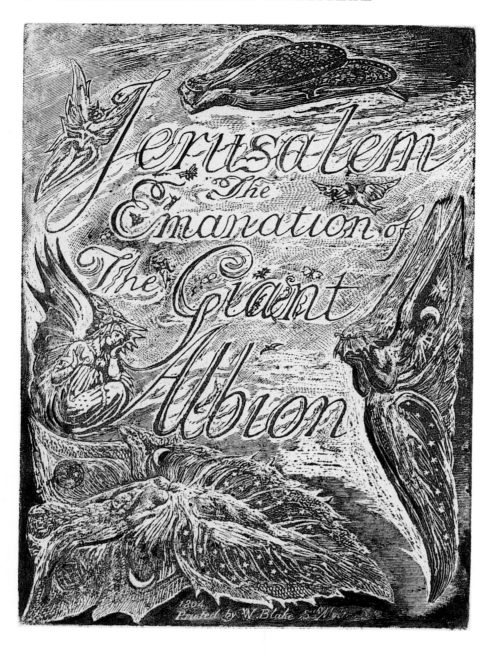

WILLIAM BLAKE (British, 1757–1827)
Jerusalem The Emanation of The Giant Albion
100 relief etchings with white-line engraving, printed in black,
frequent additions of black and grey wash with occasional touches
of ink and white heightening
$12\frac{1}{2} \times 9\frac{3}{4}$ in. (32 × 25 cm.)
London, 30 November 1993, £617,500 ($917,605)

Right:
WILLIAM BLAKE (British, 1757–1827)
Milton: Plate 38 (Albion on the Rock)
relief etching with white-line engraving, printed in
black, with grey wash additions
$5\frac{5}{8} \times 4\frac{1}{8}$ in. (13.5 × 10.5 cm.)
London, 30 November 1993, £62,000 ($95,790)

WILLIAM BLAKE (British, 1757–1827)
The Pastorals of Virgil
relief etching, printed in black ink
$6 \times 3\frac{1}{2}$ in. (15.3 × 8.7 cm.)
London, 30 November 1993, £59,800 ($88,863)

WILLIAM BLAKE (British, 1757–1827)
The Man sweeping the Interpreter's Parlour
white-line metal cut, printed in black ink
$3\frac{1}{8} \times 6\frac{5}{16}$ in. (7.9 × 16 cm.)
London, 30 November 1993, £58,700 ($87,228)

BRITISH PICTURES

THOMAS GAINSBOROUGH, R.A. (1727–1788)
Peasants Going to Market
oil on canvas
48 × 58 in. (121.9 × 147.3 cm.)
Sold by private negotiation on behalf of the Council of Royal
Holloway College, University of London, October 1993,
£3,500,000 ($5,250,000)

This magnificent landscape marks a high point in Gainsborough's
Bath period (1759–74). It is almost certainly the picture bought
by the banker Henry Hoare for 80 guineas in 1763 and hung at
Stourhead. It may also have been one of the two unidentified
landscapes exhibited by Gainsborough at the Royal Academy in
1771, which he referred to in a letter to a friend, the Hon.
Edward Stratford, as 'The best I ever did'. The picture was sold at
Christie's as part of the Stourhead heirlooms sale on 2 June 1883,
when it was bought by Thomas Holloway.

A shimmering early morning mist sets the ethereal tone of the
picture and suggests the influence of Rubens whose landscapes so
intoxicated Gainsborough in the late 1760s and early 1770s. The
group of peasants silhouetted against this backdrop of light, as
they appear over the brow of a hill on their way to market, both
emphasize and define the grandeur of Gainsborough's pastoral
vision.

The picture was sold for a record price. The proceeds of this sale
will be added to the endowment fund established to provide for
the maintenance, restoration and refurbishment of Royal
Holloway College.

THOMAS GAINSBOROUGH, R.A. (1727–1788)
Portrait of the Artist
oil on canvas
$24\frac{7}{8} \times 18\frac{3}{4}$ in. (63.2 × 47.6 cm.)
Sold from the collection of the late Sir Michael Sobell
London, 15 April 1994, £298,500 ($439,989)

Gainsborough painted several self-portraits, returning to the theme at different points in his career. This, one of his last attempts, relates to the self-portrait of circa 1786 in the collection of the Earl of Leicester, Holkham Hall. By coincidence Christie's was also responsible this year for arranging the negotiated sale of Gainsborough's *Portrait of the Artist with his Wife and Children seated in a Landscape* to the National Gallery on behalf of the Marquess of Cholmondely (see pages 2–3).

SIR NATHANIEL DANCE, R.A. (1735–1811)
Venus appearing to Aeneas and Achates as a Huntress
signed and dated 'N. Dance P. 1762'
oil on canvas
87 × 105 in. (221 × 266.8 cm.)
Mere Hall, 23 May 1994, £243,500 ($367,442)

Nathaniel Dance received three major commissions for historical paintings taken from Virgil's *Aeneid* while in Rome between 1754 and 1765. The subject of this picture comes from Book One of the *Aeneid*. Venus, Aeneas's mother, is seen disguised as a huntress guiding Aeneas and his companion Achates to Dido's palace after a storm had wrecked the Trojan fleet and washed them ashore near Carthage. It is one of Dance's most impressive historical compositions, particularly for the skillful portrayal of Aeneas's surprise and delight on recognising his mother, and the intensity of her motherly love for her son. This picture was commissioned by Sir Henry Mainwaring, 4th Bt. who was in Rome on the Grand Tour together with his friend and neighbour George Harry Grey, 5th Earl of Stamford (1737–1827). Both of them had already sat to Dance for a double portrait earlier in the year. Dance completed this picture in June 1762 and his gratification is suggested by a letter written in October 1761 in which his brother George considered that 'he had learned more in the study of the picture than he should have in painting twenty others in the common way'. Dance seems also to have held back the delivery of the picture so that he could show it to Richard Dalton, Librarian to King George III, who paid a visit to his studio in February 1763, the result of which was the Royal commission for *Timon of Athens*.

For further information about the Mere Hall sale, see page 308.

GEORGE DAWE, R.A. (1781–1829)
Portrait of Mrs. White (née Watford),
signed and dated 'G. Dawe Pinx 1809'
oil on canvas
$88\frac{1}{2} \times 54\frac{1}{2}$ (223.5 × 138.5 cm.)
Sold from the Collection of the late Sir Robert Abdy, Bt.
London, 15 April 1994, £177,500 ($261,635)

George Dawe began his career as a portrait painter in London at the Royal Academy schools in 1796. He went on to become an eminent painter of portraits and historical subjects many of which he exhibited at the Royal Academy to which he was elected in 1814. This painting is an essay in elegance and one of his most remarkable portraits. Dawe moved to Russia in 1819 at the initiation of Tsar Alexander I, where he became first portrait painter to the Imperial Court and was commissioned to paint over three hundred portraits of generals who had distinguished themselves in the Napoleonic Wars. These now hang in the Military Gallery at the Hermitage, St. Petersburg.

JOHN E. FERNELEY, SEN. (1782–1860)
The Great Match between *Clinker* and *Radical*
from Barkby Holt to Billesdon Coplow
signed, inscribed and dated 'J. Ferneley/Melton
Mowbray/March 31st/1826' and inscribed lower
centre '*Clinker*'
oil on canvas
$44\frac{1}{2} \times 63\frac{1}{2}$ in. (113 × 161.3 cm.)
Sold by Sir Arthur Collins, K.C.V.O.
London, 15 December 1993, £139,000
($206,832)

JOHN FREDERICK HERRING, SEN.
(1795–1865)
Duncan's Horses
signed and dated 'J. F. Herring. Sen./1842'
oil on canvas
$40\frac{1}{4} \times 52\frac{1}{8}$ in. (102.3 × 132.3 cm.)
London, 15 December 1993, £309,500
($460,536)

JOHN E. FERNELEY, SEN. (1782–1860)
The Quorn Hunt in Full Cry, with Lord Rancliffe, Mr.
Holyoake, Mr. Maxie on *Cognac*, Valentine Mayer, Captain
Horatio Ross, Mr. Ferneley and Squire Osbaldeston
signed, inscribed and dated 'J. Ferneley/Melton Mowbray/1825'
oil on canvas
$26\frac{1}{2} \times 87\frac{1}{4}$ in. (67.3 × 221.7 cm.)
London, 15 April 1994, £117,000 ($172,458)

JAMES WARD, R.A. (1769–1859)
John Levett receiving a Pheasant from his Retriever on his Estate
at Wychnor, his Keeper on a Pony beyond
signed and dated 'J. Ward R.A. 1812'
oil on canvas
26 × 36 in. (71 × 91.5 cm.)
London, 14 July 1994, £87,300 ($136,799)

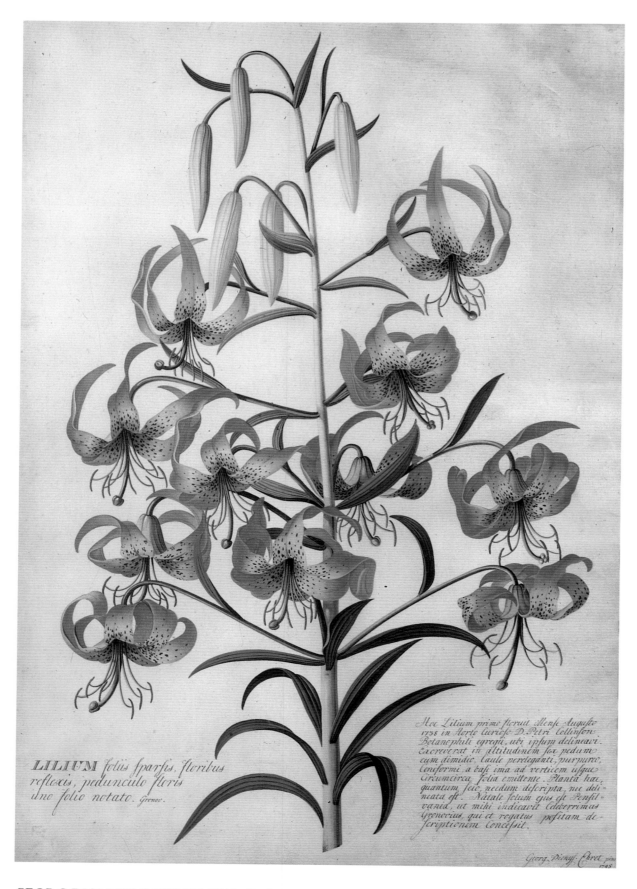

GEORG DIONYSIUS EHRET (1708-1770)
Lilium
signed, inscribed and dated 'LILIUM foliis sparsis floribus/
reflexis, pedunculo floris/uno folio notato. Gronov./Georg.
Dionys. Ehret pinx/1745'
pencil and watercolour heightened with white on vellum
$20\frac{1}{4} \times 14$ in. (51.4×35.6 cm.)
London, 12 July 1994, £67,500 ($105,975)

Right:
THOMAS
ROWLANDSON
(1756-1827)
Place Victoire à Paris
signed, inscribed as title
and dated
'1784-/T.Rowlandson'
and inscribed in a later
hand on the reverse of the
mount 'Nov. 1789 La
Place des Victoires. Paris'
pencil, pen and ink and
watercolour
$15 \times 21\frac{1}{4}$ in.
(38.2×54 cm.)
London, 12 July 1994,
£29,900 ($46,943)

PAUL SANDBY, R.A.
(1730/1-1809)
View of Eton College
from the Thames
signed and dated
'P Sandby. 1779'
pencil, pen and grey ink
and watercolour on
Whatman paper
$12\frac{1}{4} \times 19\frac{1}{8}$ in.
(31.2×48.5 cm.)
London, 9 November
1993, £32,200 ($47,592)

Right:
BENJAMIN ROBERT HAYDON
(1786–1846)
Study of William Wordsworth
inscribed and dated 'Wordsworth/For
Entry into Jerusalem/1815–'
pencil with touches of white
heightening on brown paper
$17\frac{1}{2} \times 12\frac{1}{4}$ in. (44.5 × 31.1 cm.)
London, 9 November 1993, £34,500
($50,991)
Now at Dove Cottage, Grasmere

JOHN FREDERICK LEWIS, R.A.,
P.O.W.S. (1805–1876)
Study of an Arab Sheikh
signed with intials 'J F L./ ARA'
pencil and watercolour heightened
with bodycolour
$8\frac{1}{2} \times 7$ in. (21.5 × 17.8 cm.)
London, 12 July 1994, £31,050
($48,749)

SIR DAVID WILKIE, R.A. (1785–1841)
A Study for 'Sir David Baird discovering the Body of Tipu
Sahib'
pencil, black chalk and watercolour
$16 \times 10\frac{3}{4}$ in. (40.6 × 27.2 cm.)
London, 12 April 1994, £34,500 ($50,646)

This hitherto unrecorded drawing seems to represent a late stage
in the evolution of the composition of Wilkie's picture of the
subject, completed in 1838 and now in the National Gallery of
Scotland. This was commissioned by Lady Baird, widow of
General Sir David Baird, in 1834 and exhibited at the Royal
Academy in 1839.

Right:
ARCHIBALD THORBURN
(1860–1935)
Ptarmigan in the Snow
signed and dated 'Archibald Thorburn
1898'
pencil and watercolour heightened
with bodycolour
$23\frac{1}{4} \times 37$ in. (59 × 94 cm.)
London, 3 June 1994, £32,000
($48,224)

VICTORIAN PICTURES

LANDSEER'S SCENE IN BRAEMAR: *THE APOTHEOSIS OF THE HIGHLAND STAG*

by John Christian

With superb, almost insolent, assurance, Landseer's *Scene in Braemar* dominated the saleroom in March as completely as it once dominated the dining room at Preston Hall. Exhibited at the Royal Academy in 1857, the picture was commissioned by Edward Ladd Betts, who had made a fortune constructing railways in partnership with the famous contractor Sir Morton Peto. In 1844 Peto had built himself a neo-Jacobean mansion at Somerleyton in Suffolk, employing as his architect the sculptor and draughtsman John Thomas, whom he would have known through their joint involvement with the new Palace of Westminster, Peto being the principal contractor, Thomas superintending the stonecarving. When, in 1850, Betts followed his partner's example by rebuilding Preston Hall at Aylesford in Kent, he too employed the versatile Thomas. Shortly before the catalogue of our sale went to press, a member of the Betts family, having seen an article on the Landseer in *Christie's International Magazine*, kindly produced photographs showing how it was hung in the dining-room. The effect was dramatic. The picture was placed at one end, high above a mirror and flanked by panels elaborately carved by Thomas with emblems of the chase. The walls to either side were hung with family portraits and other paintings specially commissioned by Betts, but neither these, the massive stone chimney-piece, nor the colossal chandelier, diminished the overwhelming impact of Landseer's picture. In his *Autobiography* William Powell Frith recalled being one of a party of artists who accompanied Landseer to see it and gave 'a unanimous chorus of applause'. Betts was so pleased that he insisted on paying the artist £800 instead of the £600 originally agreed.

In creating his grandiose scheme Betts was probably inspired by the engineer Isambard Kingdom Brunel, who commissioned a series of Shakespearean subjects for his dining room in the late 1840s. No fewer than five of the artists who painted pictures for Betts - Cope, Creswick, Stanfield, Maclise and Landseer himself - had also worked for Brunel. But Betts's main source of inspiration was the new Palace of Westminster. His employment of John Thomas was only one link among many. He owned books on the Palace and borrowed motifs from its decorative iconography. Two artists who painted literary subjects for his dining room, Cope and Maclise, were deeply involved with the murals at Westminster, while *Scene in Braemar* was a sequel to *The Monarch of the Glen* (John Dewar & Sons), which was designed for the refreshment room in the House of Lords though never actually installed.

Braemar is often compared to the *Monarch*, which was exhibited at the Royal Academy in 1851 and is probably Landseer's single most famous picture. *Braemar*, however, is much larger, while in spirit they are very different. The 'monarch' reigns in solitary splendour, his herd implied in his alert attitude but not physically present; the stag in *Braemar* has his hinds about him and bellows a challenge to the world, a magnificent image of pride and sexual aggression. His setting, too, is bleaker, the gleams of morning sunshine in the *Monarch* giving way to the swirling mists of autumn, the time of year when stags roar, hinds are in season, and the mountain hare assumes, as here, its white winter pelage. In fact the picture has a narrative and psychological dimension which is almost entirely lacking in the earlier work. The effect is achieved partly by the tension of the deer and the sublimity of their setting, but it is the presence of the hare (not a rabbit, as Ruskin pointed out) which adds the final touch of complexity. Landseer's art has a strong element of fable, and at least one early reviewer assumed that *Braemar* was an illustration to Aesop. This is not the case, but the hare, looking up so quizzically at the proud and noisy stag, certainly introduces a touch of humour and satire which subtly subverts the otherwise heroic conception. One is reminded of Landseer's most popular work as a humorist, *Dignity and Impudence* (1839, Tate Gallery).

Braemar is a late fruit of the passion for Scotland which Landseer had conceived in 1824 when he visited the country for the first time, staying with Sir Walter Scott and falling in love with the Highlands. Every autumn he would return to paint and shoot, and the legendary fame he enjoyed in his lifetime owed much to his ability to express the romance of Scotland which appealed so powerfully to all strata of Victorian society. If many of his Highland subjects were acquired by Queen Victoria and Prince Albert, or the great Whig magnates with whom he was on such good terms, the engravings after them were bought in vast numbers by the middle classes, and became much-loved household gods. *Scene in Braemar*, which takes its title from the town in the Western Highlands where he often stayed with the Marquess of Breadalbane, was engraved by his brother Thomas in 1859, making the picture, as F.G. Stephens noted, 'widely known'.

The financial crash of 1866 left Peto and Betts bankrupt, and in May 1868 Betts sold all his pictures, furniture, library and wine in a three-day sale at Christie's. *Braemar* was bought by Agnew's on commission for Henry William Ferdinand Bolckow, a German who had emigrated to England as a young man, set up as an ironmaster and become the presiding genius of Middlesborough, which he now represented in Parliament. He was a passionate collector of modern pictures, with a special fondness for animal subjects. Bolckow died in 1878, and for ten years the pictures remained in the possession of his son and widow, who lent many, including *Braemar*, to the Royal Jubilee Exhibition at Manchester in 1887; but in May the following year the cream of the collection was consigned for sale at Christie's. It was, in Redford's words, 'the great sale of the season', realising a total of £71,387, which at that time set a record. Among those who viewed it was the young Beatrix Potter, who recorded her admiration for *Braemar* in her journal.

The picture was again bought by Agnew's, this time on commission for Sir Edward Cecil Guinness, later first Earl of Iveagh, and it remained in the Guinness family until its sale this year. At each of its previous saleroom appearances it had fetched a remarkable price: 4,000 guineas at the Betts sale, by far the highest figure achieved; 4,950 guineas at the Bolckow sale, when it was only beaten by an outstanding Rosa Bonheur, itself outstripping Millais' masterpiece *The North-West Passage* (Tate Gallery). This fine tradition was maintained in March, when it was knocked down for £720,000, thus establishing a world record for the artist.

SIR EDWIN HENRY LANDSEER, R.A. (1802–1873)
Scene in Braemar – Highland Deer
oil on canvas
$106\frac{1}{2} \times 106\frac{1}{2}$ in. (270.4 × 270.4 cm.)
London, 25 March 1994, £793,500 ($1,186,283)
Record auction price for a work by the artist

FREDERIC, LORD LEIGHTON, P.R.A. (1830-1896)
Odalisque
oil on canvas
$35\frac{3}{4} \times 18$ in. (90.8 × 45.7 cm.)
London, 3 June 1994, £243,500 ($366,955)

This picture dates from the years when Leighton was establishing his reputation, having finally settled in London after an exhaustive continental training in 1859. It was exhibited at the Royal Academy in 1862 and warmly received by the critics; *The Times* described it as 'a consummate illustration of the *dolce far niente*', and Leighton himself considered it one of 'the best things I have done'. It belonged to the Tottenham coach-builder B.G. Windus, well known for his patronage of Turner and the Pre-Raphaelites, and is an interesting early essay in 'aesthetic' values, anticipating comparable figures painted by Albert Moore, Whistler and Burne-Jones in the later 1860s.

JAMES JACQUES JOSEPH TISSOT (1836-1902)
Quiet
signed and inscribed 'No.3 "Quiet"/oil painting/James Tissot/
17 Grove End Road/St John's Wood/London/NW' on an old
label on the reverse
oil on panel
12½ × 8½ in. (31.7 × 21.6 cm.)
London, 5 November 1993, £309,500 ($458,679)

This charming picture shows Kathleen Newton, Tissot's mistress
and muse during his later London years (1876-82), in the garden
of the house which she shared with the artist, 17 Grove End
Road, St John's Wood; the restive child on the right is her niece
Lilian Hervey. The picture is a recent rediscovery, although the
composition was known from Tissot's photographic record of his
work, which survives. There is another version (private
collection), differing in format and detail, and one of the two may
be the picture called *The Tale* which Tissot exhibited at
Birmingham in 1880 and at Liverpool two years later. He often
changed the titles of his pictures, making identification difficult.

HOLMAN HUNT'S 'MASTER HILARY – THE TRACER': A VISION OF THE 'AESTHETIC' CHILD

by John Christian

This attractive but slightly disturbing picture, the *clou* of our sale on 3 June, was the last of a trilogy of portraits that Hunt painted of his children. His position as the leading religious painter of his day did not preclude a strong attraction to the opposite sex, as his granddaughter Diana Holman-Hunt entertainingly recorded in her book *My Grandfather, His Wives and Loves* (1969). However, in 1865, at the age of thirty-eight, he finally settled for matrimony, marrying Fanny Waugh, the daughter of a prosperous London chemist. In August the following year, when Fanny was seven months pregnant, they set out for what would have been Hunt's second visit to the East, where he was committed to painting religious subjects on the spot where they had occurred; and on 20 December 1866 Fanny died at Florence after giving birth to a son. He was named Cyril Benoni (Hebrew for 'child of sorrow'). Nine years later Hunt married Fanny's younger sister Edith, flouting the Table of Affinities, outraging her family, and causing a permanent rift with his fellow Pre-Raphaelite Brother Thomas Woolner, who had married another Waugh daughter. Of this second marriage there were two children, Gladys, born in 1876, and Hilary Lushington, born on 6 May 1879.

Cyril was immortalised in a portrait sub-titled *The Fisherman* (1880, Fitzwilliam Museum, Cambridge), Gladys as a character from *The Vicar of Wakefield, Miss Flamborough* (1882, private collection), and Hilary in the present work. All three portraits were exhibited at the Grosvenor Gallery, *Master Hilary* appearing there in 1887. The Grosvenor had been launched ten years earlier as a liberal alternative to the Royal Academy, and had quickly established itself as a forum of artistic innovation and the flagship of the Aesthetic Movement. Hunt, by nature an outsider, supported it from the outset, and transferred to its successor, the New Gallery, in 1888.

Hilary had already appeared in his father's work as the Christ Child in *The Triumph of the Innocents* (1876-87, Walker Art Gallery, Liverpool). Our picture, which was being planned in December 1885 and is dated 1886, shows him at the age of seven, and, appropriately for a Grosvenor exhibit, presents a very 'aesthetic' image. It is painted in the 'greenery, yallery' tones that W.S. Gilbert had mocked in *Patience* in 1881. Hilary wears 'aesthetic' dress - blouse, knickerbockers and stockings, and is tracing a page from that quintessential attribute of the 'aesthetic' child, one of Walter Crane's picture books.

We see him through one of the French windows of the ground-floor drawing-room at Draycott Lodge, Fulham, a Regency villa to which the artist and his family had moved in 1881. He has stuck Crane's design - an illustration to the song 'Over the Hills and Far Away' from *The Baby's Opera* (1877) - to the window with sealing-wax, intending to trace it against the light with the pencil in his right hand. Behind him lie the shadowed recesses of the room - a spacious apartment filled with antiquities collected by Hunt on his travels, which Alice Meynell was to describe in an account of the house published in the *Art Annual* for 1893; while at his feet are a box of paints, his brushes in a glass of water, and an upturned plate which he evidently uses as a palette. The picture's strange sense of dislocation is due to the fact that we do not immediately realise that we are looking at the child through glass. His image is so clear that this only becomes apparent when we 'read' the composition closely, noting the relation of the glazing-bars to the foreground details and curtain; the swirls of green refracted light below the sitter's right elbow; the blanching of the palm and fingertips of his left hand as he presses them against the window; and the reflections in the glass of the jasmine, the Japanese anemones and the butterfly outside. (The house was covered with creepers, and Mrs Meynell described how the light of the drawing-room was 'coloured' by 'the green that move(d) in the breeze close to the windows'). This delight in spacial ambiguity was typical of Hunt, who explored comparable effects in such subject pictures as *The Awakening Conscience* (1853, Tate Gallery) and *The Lady of Shalott* (versions 1850-1905 at Melbourne, Manchester and Hartford, Connecticut).

When the picture was exhibited in 1887 the following quotation appeared in the catalogue: '"Be sure before painting to make a correct outline" - *Old-fashioned Manual of Art*'. While this was obviously appropriate to the subject, it was also relevant to Hunt himself, whose whole philosophy of art was based on the painstaking and accurate recording of objective reality. The picture was badly hung and received mixed notices. Despite a recent quarrel, Hunt's old friend F.G. Stephens spoke up loyally in his capacity as art critic of the *Athenaeum*, but *The Times* was deeply unhappy, claiming that in this 'extraordinary' picture 'Mr Hunt has allowed his learning to run into pedantry, and his devotion to what he calls nature to make him entirely oblivious of art.' Unlike his fellow P.R.B. John Everett Millais, Hunt had never been an 'easy' artist, and even in a portrait of a child was capable of arousing those feelings of disturbance and shock so often evoked by his religious masterpieces.

The picture was twice retouched at an early date. When it returned from the Grosvenor, Hunt himself revised the position of the figure before showing it again at the Autumn Exhibition of the Royal Birmingham Society of Artists. A more obvious alteration is revealed by the reproduction in Hunt's autobiography *Pre-Raphaelitism and the Pre-Raphaelite Brotherhood* (1905), which shows the knickerbockers plain, not striped, and the cap protruding from the boy's pocket instead of being thrust through his belt. These changes, according to Hunt family tradition, were made by E.R. Hughes, who assisted Hunt in later years when Hunt's eyesight was failing, notably by completing the large version of *The Light of the World* in St Paul's Cathedral. This certainly seems likely, the handling of the knickerbockers and cap differing from that of the rest of the picture, and being characteristic of Hughes.

It is also said that the cap was added at the suggestion of Millais, who was often consulted by Hunt on such matters. Whether or not this is true (and it should be noted that Millais had died nine years before the cap-less reproduction appeared in *Pre-Raphaelitism*), the addition is a stroke of genius, contributing enormously to the composition and providing a dramatic climax to the other touches of red (sealing-wax, stool-cover, paint-box, rose-hips) that enliven the subtle but distinctive colour scheme.

The picture remained in the artist's family until its sale in June. Hunt gave it to the sitter in May 1900 on the boy's twenty-first birthday; Hilary kept it until his death in 1949; and it was then inherited by his daughter, Diana Holman-Hunt, who died last year. It was last seen in public when it was lent to the Hunt Exhibition of 1969 (Walker Art Gallery, Liverpool, and Victoria and Albert Museum, London), an early milestone in the rehabilitation of Pre-Raphaelite painting which has been such a notable feature of taste since the 1960s.

WILLIAM HOLMAN HUNT, O.M. (1827-1910)
Master Hilary - The Tracer
signed with monogram and dated '8 Whh 6'
inscribed on the backboard 'For Hilary on his 21st Birthday / W.H.H.' and 'Given May 6th 1900 / W.H.H.'
oil on canvas
48⅛ × 26 in. (122.2 × 66 cm.)
London, 3 June 1994, £969,500 ($1,436,799)
Record auction price for a work by the artist

SIDNEY HAROLD METEYARD (1868-1947)
Love in Idleness
oil on canvas
$34\frac{1}{2} \times 41\frac{3}{4}$ in. (87.6 × 106 cm.)
London, 25 March 1994, £56,500 ($84,468)

Meteyard was a leading member of the Birmingham School, the group of young artists who emerged in the 1890s as a late local offshoot of the Pre-Raphaelite movement. Although they owed much to the earlier Pre-Raphaelites in general, the principal influence on them was Burne-Jones, a native of Birmingham who accepted the presidency of the Royal Birmingham Society of Artists in 1885 and took a keen interest in the Municipal School of Art, where so many of these painters trained. Meteyard would have met Burne-Jones when the master visited the School during a week's stay in Birmingham in October 1885, and was enormously impressed by the great set-pieces of his work to be seen in Birmingham, the *Star of Bethlehem* watercolour in the Art Gallery and the four colossal stained-glass windows in the Cathedral.

Like his hero, Meteyard was both a painter of easel pictures and a decorative artist. His pictures were never numerous, and perhaps fewer than ten survive. The present example is characteristic in its linear treatment of form and the refulgent, slightly acid, colours, both of which no doubt reflect his experience of working in stained-glass and enamel. The picture was exhibited in 1908, first at the Royal Academy and then at the Autumn Exhibition of the R.B.S.A. It is sometimes described as a pendant to *Love in Bondage*, his R.A. exhibit of 1901 which now represents him in the Birmingham Art Gallery, but as well as being smaller and seven years later, it is very different in mood, *Love in Bondage* expressing anxiety, tribulation and care, while *Love in Idleness* strikes a note of hedonism, luxury and playful irresponsibility. It would be fascinating to know if the two works bear any relationship to his private life. Little is known about this apart from the fact that he married his pupil Kate Eadie, who sometimes collaborated with him on decorative projects.

JOHN WILLIAM GODWARD (1861-1922)
The Delphic Oracle
signed and dated 'J.W. Godward 99'
oil on canvas
90 × 45 in. (228.6 × 114.2 cm.)
London, 3 June 1994, £111,500 ($165,243)

HORACE VERNET (French, 1789-1863)
At the Tomb of Colonel Monginot
inscribed 'Frc de Monginot/Cl de Dragons/ Mort à XXVII Ans/
Le VIII 7bxe MLCCCXIII', on the reverse 'blessé à Pirna le 22
Aoust (sic.) 1813' and 'Portes du temple de Mémoire/ouvrez
vous il l'a mérité/il vecut assez pour la gloire/trop peu pour ma
Félicité'
oil on canvas
20 × 24 in. (50.8 × 61.1 cm.)
London, 19 November 1993, £298,500 ($439,989)

This recently discovered work, dating from circa 1817, employs
romantic themes not used in Vernet's monumental battle scenes,
such as the *Death of Poniatowski* (1817) and *The Battle of Montmirail*
(1822).

Colonel Monginot died of wounds received at Pirna five days
before Napoleon's victory at Dresden in September 1813. A
French dragoon shows Monginot's tomb to his widow and

daughter. The moonlit city of Dresden dominates the
background and, appropriately, the picture reflects the influence
of German romanticism and, in particular, Caspar David
Friedrich. While symbols such as the tomb and willow, which
derive from popular seventeenth and eighteenth-century French
prints, emphasize the air of recent death, other themes display
Vernet's knowledge of German art. The moonlit setting, the
river, and, the over-sized boat, soon to carry away the parting
soul, were all images employed by Friedrich, whose *Chasseur in
the Forest* 1813-14 Vernet may have known.

After the Emperor's defeat and subsequent retreat to France,
French nationals could no longer openly visit Saxony. The
French dragoon thus leads Monginot's family to the tomb by
moonlight, at great risk in the political circumstances. The
picture's underlying tension is masked by the serenity and
mystical atmosphere of the scene, which establishes it as an
extraordinarily romantic statement for its date.

JEAN-BAPTISTE-CAMILLE COROT (French, 1796-1875)
Campagne de Naples
signed 'Corot'
oil on canvas
$16\frac{1}{2} \times 25$ in. (41.9 × 63.5 cm.)
New York, 25 May 1994, $409,500 (£272,093)

'Barbizon – it's wherever you may find it', wrote the art historian, Alexandra Murphy in 1991. Barbizon is a place in France, southeast of Paris in the countryside. With its forest and fields, it provided the subject matter for a group of artists that became known as the Barbizon School. Led by the great landscape painter, Theodore Rousseau and the champion of the peasant, Jean-François Millet, these artists were to define a new school of painting which would pave the way for the Impressionists. 1994 was the sixth year that a theme sale was devoted to Barbizon painting and its sister school, Realism at Christie's New York. Held each May, this special auction has become one of the highlights of the year. The catalogue for this innovative sale is unique in its format and includes scholarly, museum-quality texts, extensive biographies on the artists and an introductory essay written by a well-known scholar in the field. This sale has resulted in record prices for many of the artists, including Millet, Rousseau, Dupré and Courbet, but perhaps more important has served to re-introduce these important schools to a public eager to collect in this area. Barbizon has come to mean a clearing in the forest at Bas-Breau by Rousseau or Diaz, or a peasant returning home from work in the fields by Millet – it is a place, a subject, a mood.

JEAN-FRANÇOIS MILLET (French, 1814–1875)
The Road Mender (Le Cantonnier)
signed 'J.F. Millet'
black and white chalk on blue paper
$16\frac{1}{4} \times 12$ in. (41.3 × 30.5 cm.)
New York, 12 October 1993, $277,500 (£181,848)
Record auction price for a Millet grisaille drawing

JEAN-LOUIS-ANDRÉ-THÉODORE GÉRICAULT
(French, 1791–1824)
Un Cavalier Cabrant son Cheval
watercolour and black chalk
$8\frac{7}{8} \times 10\frac{7}{8}$ in. (22.3 × 27.3 cm.)
Monaco, 20 June 1994, Fr.1,443,000 (£171,235)

JEAN-FRANÇOIS MILLET (French, 1814–1875)
Animals Grazing at the Edge of a Pine Forest, Vosges
signed 'J.F. Millet'
pastel on brown–gray paper
$26\frac{3}{4} \times 36\frac{5}{8}$ in. (68 × 93 cm.)
New York, 25 May 1994, $530,500 (£351,557)

WILLIAM-ADOLPHE BOUGUEREAU (French, 1825-1905)
La Bouillie (Petite Fille Manageant sa Soupe)
signed and dated 'W-Bouguereau-1872'
oil on canvas
$31\frac{7}{8} \times 19\frac{3}{4}$ in. (80.9 × 50.2 cm.)
New York, 25 May 1994, $244,500 (£162,028)

ALEKSEI ALEKSEEVICH HARLAMOV (Russian, b. 1842)
The Arrangement
signed 'Harlamoff'
oil on canvas
29 × 40¾ in. (73.6 × 103.5 cm.)
London, 19 November 1993, £100,500 ($148,137)

JEAN-JOSEPH-BENJAMIN CONSTANT
(French, 1845–1902)
The Odalisque
signed and dated 'Benj. Constant. 1882'
oil on canvas
43 × 83 in. (109.2 × 210.8 cm.)
London, 17 June 1994, £166,500 ($252,913)

JOAQUIN SOROLLA Y BASTIDA (Spanish, 1863–1932)
Playa da Biarritz
signed 'J Sorolla B'
oil on board
6¼ × 8¾ in. (16 × 22 cm.)
London, 18 March 1994, £89,500 ($133,176)

CESARE TIRATELLI (Italian, b. 1864)
Market Day, near Rome
signed and inscribed 'Tiratelli. C/-Roma-'
oil on canvas
24½ × 53 in. (62 × 135 cm.)
London, 19 November 1993, £128,000 ($188,672)

FILIPPO PALIZZI (Italian, 1818-1899)
Il Capolavoro
signed and dated 'Filip. Palizzi/Napoli 1865'
oil on canvas
15½ × 23⅞ in. (39 × 59.5 cm.)
Rome, 31 May 1994, L.141,420,000 (£58,900)

CHARLES LEICKERT (Dutch, 1816-1907)
Summer: a river Landscape with Peasants conversing
and Washerwomen on a Landing Stage, a Ferry nearby,
a Town in the Distance
signed 'Ch. Leickert'
oil on canvas
33 × 51½ in. (84 × 131 cm.)
Amsterdam, 21 April 1994, Fl.184,000 (£65,248)

ALBERTO PASINI (Italian, 1826-1899)
A Market, Constantinople
signed and dated 'A. Pasini 1873'
oil on canvas
$31\frac{1}{2} \times 19$ in. (80.2 × 48.3 cm.)
London, 19 November 1993, £93,900 ($138,409)

Right:
NICHOLAOS GYSIS
(Greek, 1842-1901)
The Secret School
signed 'N.Gysis'
oil on panel
$22\frac{3}{4} \times 29\frac{1}{8}$ in. (58 × 74 cm.)
Athens, 13 December 1993,
Drachma 187,500,000 (£535,714)

This was the highlight of our first Greek
sale in Athens and fetched a record
auction price for any work by a
nineteenth-century Greek artist.

HERMANN DAVID SALOMON
CORRODI (Italian, 1844-1905)
An Arab Encampment at Sunset
signed and inscribed 'H. Corrodi. Roma'
oil on canvas
$34\frac{1}{4} \times 65$ in. (87 × 165.1 cm.)
New York, 14 October 1993, $233,500
(£153,417)
Record auction price for a work by the
artist

The sale of the Forbes Magazine
Collection of Orientalist Paintings,
Drawings, Watercolours and Sculpture
was 99% sold and realised $1,000,000
more than estimated.

EDGAR DEGAS (French, 1834–1917)
Danseuses se baissant (Les Ballerines)
signed 'Degas'
pastel on prepared board
14 × 19 in. (35.5 × 48.2 cm.)
Sold from the Estate of Joseph Gruss
New York, 2 November 1993, $7,042,500 (£4,748,820)

Ironically, although Degas was the greatest painter to attempt to interpret ballet, he worked at a time when the great Romantic epoch of the French ballet had long passed its zenith, and he was blind by the time Diaghilev re-invented it for our century. Thus, Degas recorded not specific great artists or great performances but rather the working efforts of the flesh and blood 'rats' (as the dancers were called) seen for what they were rather than a metaphor or myth.

This picture of 1885 is a striking cropped 'close-up'. Degas not only weaves a frieze of arms across the top, but anchors the foreground with nothing more than light, the harsh glare of the unseen gas footlights blanching the bowed dancers' profiles. These are not perfect beings but hard-working girls that Degas uses to express the sublime, both essence and surface. The serial symmetry of this daring composition is not found anywhere else in Degas' *oeuvre*.

CAMILLE PISSARRO (French, 1830–1903)
Le Marché autour de l'Eglise Saint-Jacques, Dieppe
signed and dated 'C. Pissarro 1901'
oil on canvas
$35\frac{3}{4} \times 28\frac{3}{4}$ in. (91 × 73 cm.)
New York, 2 November 1993, $3,962,500 (£2,671,949)

ALFRED SISLEY (French, 1839–1899)
La Manufacture de Sèvres
signed 'Sisley'
oil on canvas
$23\frac{5}{8} \times 28\frac{7}{8}$ in. (60 × 73.4 cm.)
London, 29 November 1993, £771,500 ($1,141,049)

This picture was painted in 1879

Right:
ALFRED SISLEY (French, 1839–1899)
Moret, vue du Loing, après-midi de mai
signed 'Sisley'
oil on canvas
$19\frac{3}{4} \times 25\frac{1}{2}$ in. (50 × 65 cm.)
New York, 10 May 1994, $1,652,500 (£1,106,832)

This picture was painted in 1888

PAUL CÉZANNE (French, 1839–1906)
Fruits
watercolour over pencil on paper
$9\frac{3}{8} \times 13\frac{5}{8}$ in. (23.8 × 34.6 cm.)
New York, 2 November 1993, $662,500 (£446,730)

CLAUDE MONET (French, 1840–1926)
Le Palais da Mula, Venise
signed and dated 'Claude Monet 1908'
oil on canvas
25 × 35½ in. (63.5 × 90 cm.)
Sold from the Estate of Neil A. McConnell
New York, 10 May 1994, $4,182,500 (£2,801,407)

Right:
HENRI ROUSSEAU, called LE DOUANIER
(French, 1844–1910)
Portrait de Joseph Brummer (Portrait-paysage)
signed and dated 'H Rousseau 1909'
oil on canvas
45⅝ × 34¾ in. (116 × 88.5 cm.)
London, 29 November 1993, £2,971,500 ($4,394,849)

Joseph Brummer (1883–1947) moved to Paris from his native
Hungary in the early years of this century. He studied in Matisse's
atelier and had many short-term jobs including working as a
stonemason for Rodin, but supported himself mainly by selling
Japanese prints. This was so profitable that in 1908 he opened his
first shop and sold 'primitive' sculpture. Between the wars he
established a gallery in New York. The renown of the Brummer
Gallery for handling works as diverse as sculpture, metalwork and
carvings from classical antiquity until the Modern period spread
far and wide and the links with major museums were always close.

Having the appearance of a theatrical backdrop, the background
foliage in this portrait is a creation of Rousseau's imagination
designed to complement the character of the sitter and to suit the
compositional structure of the picture. The mask-like hieratic
features of Brummer's face, rendered with tremendous finesse,
resemble to some extent the African sculptures in which he dealt.
The insouciant manner in which Brummer holds his cigarette in
his right hand adds a bohemian element to the general air of
shrewd respectability. This device recalls Rousseau's earlier
portrait of Pierre Loti in which the elements seem more
anecdotally disparate than in this more harmoniously
monumental picture.

MAURICE DE VLAMINCK (French, 1876–1958)
Paysage de Banlieue
oil on canvas
$25\frac{1}{2} \times 32$ in. (65 × 81 cm.)
New York, 10 May 1994, $6,822,500 (£4,569,658)

In this picture of 1905–6, we look down on a rural landscape
from above, and are shown a field of trees and flowers behind a
cluster of houses. It boasts a great sense of energy and its tonality
is brilliant. Vlaminck has created an image that does something
van Gogh never quite achieved: it is simultaneously restful and
agitating. Only the best works of the *Fauves* could achieve such a
seemingly impossible feat.

JAN TOOROP (Dutch, 1858–1928)
An Alley in Autumn, Herfslaan
signed 'J.Th. Toorop'
pencil and oil on board
24 × 22⅝ in. (61 × 57.5 cm.)
Amsterdam, 31 May 1994, Fl.287,500 (£100,180)

This characteristic work dates from 1908.

WASSILY KANDINSKY (Russian, 1866–1944)
Ohne Titel
watercolour on paper
$14 \times 15\frac{5}{8}$ in. (35.7 × 39.7 cm.)
London, 29 November 1993, £881,500 ($1,303,739)

This picture of 1912–13 expresses Kandinsky's interest in music and painting and his close friendship with the composer Arnold Schönberg. The dark blue, which for Kandinsky is a celestial colour reminiscent of a deep organ note giving rise to a desire for purity, is contrasted here with a sharp, bright yellow; the latter creating an 'intense trumpet blast' in Kandinsky's words. The drooping lines are a pictorial expression for melancholic sentiments, suggestive of sombre low notes, contrasted on the opposite side of the work by quick red brushstrokes and earthy brown and green spots. These, together with the sharp aggressive blue brushstrokes, correspond with the dissonant musical elements which characterise Schönberg's music. In addition to this, though, is the comparatively harmonious area where the red circle has around it a ring of orange, which is itself surrounded by a sweeping yellow band. These related colours are a small oasis of coherence in a mass of incoherence, just as passages of harmonious music are to be found in Schönberg's compositions.

PAUL KLEE (Swiss, 1879–1940)
Bühnenlandschaft
signed, dated and numbered 'Klee 1922/178'
oil on board
18¾ × 20⅞ in. (47.5 × 53 cm.)
London, 29 November 1993, £991,500 ($1,466,429)

Theatre pictures were a major feature of Klee's Bauhaus years in Weimar and Dessau. *Bühnenlandschaft* is the most important picture on this theme which combines two of Klee's great passions – music and the theatre. *Bühnenlandschaft* fits into the constructive theories of the Bauhaus years as Klee sought for a pictorial synthesis to give form to his vivid artistic imagination.

PIET MONDRIAN (Dutch, 1872–1944)
Composition avec blue, rouge et jaune
signed and dated 'PM '30'
oil on canvas
$28\frac{1}{2} \times 21\frac{1}{4}$ in. (72 × 54 cm.)
New York, 2 November 1993, $3,522,500 (£2,375,253)

PABLO PICASSO (Spanish, 1881–1973)
Violon, Bouteille et Verre
signed on the reverse 'Picasso'
oil, collage and charcoal on canvas
$25\frac{1}{2} \times 19\frac{3}{4}$ in. (65 × 50 cm.)
New York, 10 May 1994, $6,272,500 (£4,201,273)

Picasso spent the spring of 1913 in Céret and in Paris, where he
actively pursued the possibilities of collage, the most radical
component of Cubism which incorporated fragments of the
actual world into the hitherto exclusive domain of art. Picasso
enriched his increasingly complicated compositions by using bits
of wallpaper, passages of *faux bois*, scraps of newsprint, elements of
illusionistic painting, contradictory depth cues and various signs
which stood for similar objects as well as highly abstracted non-
referential shapes which nonetheless had punning visual analogies
to recognisable imagery. This remarkable painting of 1913
typifies the work of the period, which, for lack of a better term
has come to be known as Synthetic Cubism.

FRANTISEK KUPKA (Czech, 1871–1957)
La Gamme jaune
signed 'Kupka' and inscribed 'IIe étude pour "La Gamme jaune"'
oil on canvas
$30\frac{7}{8} \times 29\frac{1}{4}$ in. (78.5 × 74 cm.)
London, 28 June 1994, £139,000 ($214,894)

This picture was painted circa 1907

Right:
AMEDEO MODIGLIANI (Italian, 1884–1920)
Hanka Zborowska au Bougeoir
signed 'Modigliani'
oil on canvas
$18\frac{1}{4} \times 11\frac{5}{8}$ in. (46.3 × 29.5 cm.)
London, 27 June 1994, £1,486,500 ($2,308,535)

Hanka Zborowska, the sitter for this tender and intimate portrait of 1919, had come to Paris with her husband, Modigliani's friend and dealer, the poet Leopold Zborowski. Zborowski had taken over the management of Modigliani's affairs from Paul Guillaume during 1917, and devoted his energies to furthering the artist's career by searching for suitable models and studios as well as portrait commissions and rich patrons.

Hanka became, in the end, one of Modigliani's most frequent sitters, although the relationship between them always remained reserved and cautious. This emotional distance is evident in all the portraits of Hanka that Modigliani painted. Hanka stares out from the present work at the spectator, unflinching in her cold detached manner, whilst Modigliani attempts to give her warmth through the soft tones of the skin and the surrounding background, her poise, however, erect and withdrawn, remains uncompromising. The painter has striven to give form to Hanka's face with the characteristically pure lines, depicting the shape familiar from so many of his portraits; a perfect oval forming her face with small dark blue eyes, balanced delicately on an elegant long neck.

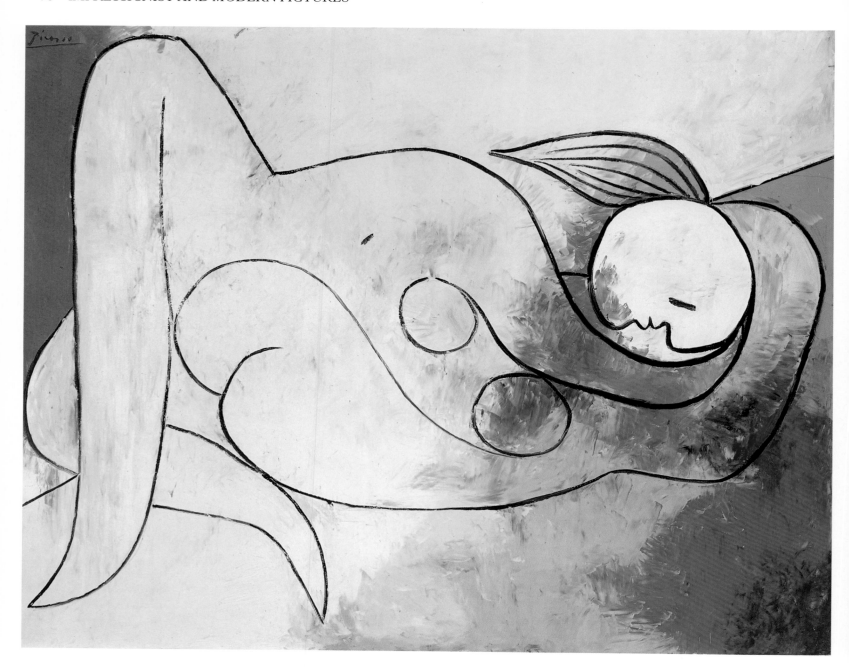

PABLO PICASSO (Spanish, 1881–1973)
Femme couchée à la mèche blonde
signed 'Picasso' and dated on stretcher '21 Décembre
M.CM.XXX.II'
oil on canvas
50⅞ × 63 in. (129.2 × 160 cm.)
Sold from the collection of Meshulam Riklis
New York, 10 May 1994, $4,622,500 (£3,096,115)

This present picture is an exceptional example of Picasso's extraordinary drawing skills. With a few curved black lines the artist outlines the nude body of Marie-Thérèse Walter asleep and is able to capture the sensuality, serenity and passive beauty of his love simultaneously. The artist's lush brushwork seems to caress Marie-Thérèse's sleeping body and especially her golden hair. The feeling of calm and comfort exuding from this portrait is reinforced by Picasso's deliberate choice of colours. *Femme couchée à la mèche blonde* may be seen as an allegory of beauty and pleasure.

TAMARA DE LEMPICKA (Polish, 1898–1980)
Adam et Eve
signed 'DE LEMPICKA'
oil on panel
$45\frac{3}{4} \times 28\frac{3}{4}$ in. (116 × 73 cm.)
Sold from the collection of Barbra Streisand
New York, 3 March 1994, $1,982,500 (£1,326,087)
Record auction price for a work by the artist

This major work by the artist is considered in the context of the
Barbra Streisand collection on p208

JOAN MIRÓ (Spanish, 1893–1983)
Personnages, Oiseaux, Etoiles
signed, inscribed and dated on the reverse 'Miró 1–3–1946
Personnages, oiseaux "étoiles"'
oil on canvas
$28\frac{3}{4} \times 36\frac{1}{4}$ in. (73 × 92 cm.)
London, 27 June 1994, £1,871,500 ($2,906,440)

SALVADOR DALÍ (Spanish, 1904–1989)
L'Ascension de Christ (Pietà)
signed and dated 'S. Dalí 1958'
oil on canvas
$45\frac{1}{4} \times 48\frac{3}{8}$ in. (115 × 123 cm.)
New York, 2 November 1993, $2,422,500 (£1,633,513)

In a letter written at Neuilly at 3 a.m. on 15 April 1951, the artist comments on his own divine inspiration:

> I want my next Christ to be the painting containing the most beauty and joy that has ever been painted up to today. I want to paint a Christ who will be absolutely the contrary in everything from the materialist and savagely antimystic Christ of *Grünewald*!

Absolute monarchy, perfect aesthetic cupola of the soul, homogeneity, unity and biological, hereditary, supreme continuity. All of the above will be suspended near the cupola of the sky. Below, crawling and supergelatinous anarchy, viscuous heterogeneity, ornamental diversity of the ignominious soft structures compressed and rendering the last piece of their ultimate forms of reactions 'Anarchical Monarchy.' This is the '(almost divine) harmony of opposites' proclaimed Heraclitus, which only the incorruptible mould of ecstasy will one day form using new stones from the Escorial.

WILLI BAUMEISTER (German, 1889–1955)
Monturi, Diskus III (mit Schwarzwald)
signed and dated 'Baumeister 3.54'
oil and sand on hardboard
$72\frac{3}{4} \times 51\frac{1}{8}$ in. (185 × 130 cm.)
London, 29 November 1993, £485,500 ($328,262)
A record auction price for the artist

ALBERTO GIACOMETTI (Swiss, 1901–1966)
Trois Hommes qui marchent I
bronze
signed and numbered 'A. Giacometti 2/6'
cast in 1948; number two in an edition of 6
28½ in. (72 cm.) high
New York, 10 May 1994, $1,872,500 (£1,254,186)

This work reflects Giacometti's fascination with people in the street. He wrote: 'They increasingly form and re-form living compositions in unbelievable complexity ... the men walk past each other without looking.' The three men are walking in different directions apparently with no relationship to one another except in the coherence of the composition. This creates an enormous sense of individual isolation.

MODERN BRITISH AND IRISH PICTURES

JACK BUTLER YEATS, R.H.A. (1871–1957)
The Haute Ecole Act
signed 'Jack B Yeats'
oil on canvas
24 × 36 in. (61 × 91.5 cm.)
Dublin, 29 June 1994, I.E.P.223,500 (£221,068)

We held our eighth and most successful sale of Irish Paintings in Dublin in conjunction with Hamilton Osborne King at The Royal Hibernian Academy of Arts Gallagher Gallery: this totalled I.E.P.737,000 (£725,393).

The highlight of the sale was *The Haute Ecole Act*. Considered to be one of the finest works by Yeats from the 1920s still in private ownership, the picture was bought by an Irish private collector who also purchased the other Yeats from the same source, *The Banquet Hall, Deserted*, which realised I.E.P.66,000 (£64,960).

In *The Haute Ecole Act* as in other circus paintings Yeats uses the big top as a structure of imagery for life, for its tragedy and comedy. The tragedy in this picture is the unhappy face of the clown portraying the loneliness of the artist in love with a beautiful but disdainful equestrian who looks down remotely at the row of spectators in the foreground.

RODERIC O'CONOR, R.H.A. (1860–1940)
Village, Brittany
signed and dated 'R. O'Conor 1897
Pont-Aven at Lezaven
oil on canvas
$36\frac{1}{2} \times 29$ in. (92.5 × 73 cm.)
London, 11 March 1994, £60,000 ($90,060)

A previously unseen date and inscription on the stretcher of *Village, Brittany* confirmed that this work was painted at Pont Aven at Lezaven Farm, the studio that O'Conor had shared with Gauguin, during 1898. Previously there had been speculation among scholars that this work had been painted at Rochefort-en-Terre in 1896 during a period of ill-health, but the colour range had eluded explanation. The discovery of the location and date have resulted in a new title *Houses at Lezaven*, and accounts for the radical new development in the artist's work.

WALTER RICHARD SICKERT, A.R.A. (1860–1942)
Chopin
signed 'Sickert'
oil on canvas
$20\frac{3}{4} \times 16\frac{1}{2}$ in. (52.8 × 42 cm.)
London, 23 November 1993, £44,000 ($64,900)

DAVID BOMBERG (1890–1957)
Meditation
signed and dated 'Bomberg 1913'
oil on panel
16 × 13 in. (41 × 33 cm.)
London, 23 November 1993, £38,000 ($56,050)

SIR WILLIAM RUSSELL FLINT, R.A. (1880–1969)
The Judgement of Paris
signed and dated 'W. Russell Flint 1935'
oil on canvas
47 × 69¼ in. (119.5 × 176 cm.)
London, 23 November 1993, £58,000 ($85,550)

DAVID SHEPHERD (b. 1931)
African Children
signed and dated 'David Shepherd – 67'
oil on canvas
27 × 49¼ in. (68.6 × 125 cm.)
South Kensington, 3 June 1994, £110,000
($165,770)
Record auction price for a work by the artist

HAROLD GILMAN (1876–1919)
Interior (Mrs. Mounter)
signed 'H. Gilman'
oil on canvas
15 × 13 in. (38 × 33 cm.)
Sold from the Estate of the late Rhoda Samuel
London, 11 March 1994, £100,000 ($150,100)

Originally in Sir Louis Fergusson's fine group of
Camden Town paintings, this work was illustrated in
Lewis and Fergusson's *Appreciation* published after
Gilman's untimely death from influenza in 1919. It is
one of only six portraits of the artist's landlady Mrs.
Mounter which are considered to be the finest works of
the artist's maturity. The Walker Art Gallery, Liverpool,
the Ashmolean, Oxford, the Tate Gallery, London and
Leeds City Art Gallery each house one of the portraits
painted in 1916–17 at 47, Maple Street.

GRAHAM SUTHERLAND, O.M. (1903–1980)
Lane Opening
signed and dated 'Sutherland 44–45'
oil on board
$36\frac{3}{4} \times 28\frac{1}{2}$ in. (93.5 × 72.5 cm.)
London, 25 November 1993, £62,000 ($92,132)

Lane Opening was originally in the collection of Sir
Michael Balcon who purchased it from the Lefevre
Gallery's exhibition of *Recent Paintings by Francis Bacon,
Frances Hodgkins and Graham Sutherland* in 1945 for
£105. Sutherland had first explored this theme in a
number of works which culminated in the Tate
Gallery's masterpiece, *Entrance to a Lane* from 1939. *Lane
Opening* is a return to the subject after the period spent
as an official War Artist during the Second World War.

TOPOGRAPHICAL PICTURES

WILLIAM HODGES, R.A. (British, 1744–1797)
View of Calcutta taken from Fort William
oil on canvas
$35\frac{3}{4} \times 60\frac{1}{2}$ in. (90.7 × 153 cm.)
London, 15 July 1994, £210,000 ($328,169)

THOMAS HEARNE (British, 1744–1817)
View of Antigua: English Harbour, Freeman's Bay, and Falmouth
Harbour, Monk's Hill etc. from the Hill near the Park
pen and brown ink, watercolour and bodycolour
$20\frac{3}{4} \times 60$ in. (52.7 × 152.4 cm.)
London, 15 July 1994, £62,000 ($96,658)

Right:
EDMUND PINK (British, active 1821–5)
The City and Province of Rio de Janeiro, Brazil – a folio of
forty-four watercolours from the artist's *Sketches in Brazil taken
during a Residence there, in the Years 1821, 22, 23, 24 & 25*
London, 15 July 1994, £45,500 ($70,934)

The City and Province of Sâo Paolo, Brazil – a folio of twenty-
four watercolours from the artist's *Sketches in Brazil taken during a
Residence there, in the Years 1821, 22, 23, 24 & 25*
London, 15 July 1994, £41,100 ($64,116)

J. ALPHONSE PELLION (French, active 1817–1820)
Coupang; Ile Timor – Occupation domestique
signed with monogram 'AP'
pen and brown ink, watercolour
$11\frac{1}{4} \times 14\frac{1}{2}$ in. (28.6 × 36.8 cm.)
London, 15 July 1994, £13,800 ($21,528)

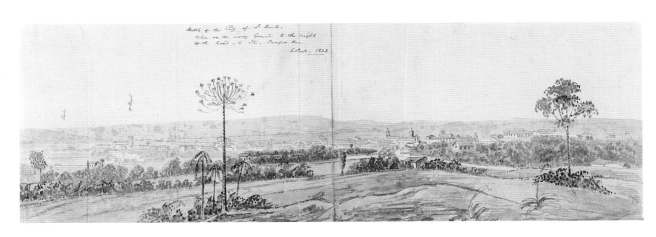

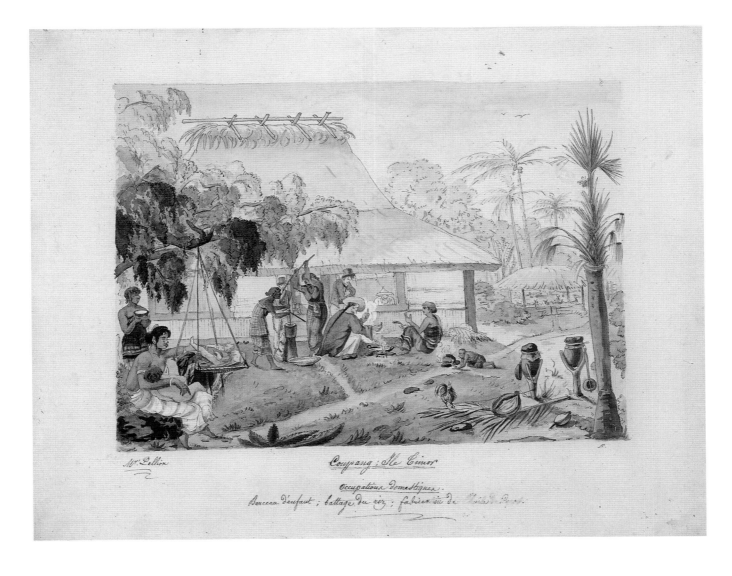

Left:
EUGENE VON GUERARD (1811–1901)
North View from Daylesford
signed and dated 'Eug: von Guérard 1864'
oil on canvas
$25\frac{5}{8} \times 49\frac{5}{8}$ in. (65 × 126 cm.)
Melbourne, 18 April 1994, A.$345,000 (£169,783)

SIR HANS HEYSEN (1877–1968)
Morning Light
signed and dated 'Hans Heysen 1909'
watercolour
$21\frac{5}{8} \times 29\frac{7}{8}$ in. (55 × 76 cm.)
Melbourne, 18 April 1994, A.$172,500 (£84,892)

SIR GEORGE RUSSELL DRYSDALE (1912–1981)
The Bore Keeper's Camp
signed 'Russell Drysdale'
oil on canvas
$23\frac{5}{8} \times 29\frac{3}{4}$ in. (60 × 75.5 cm.)
Brisbane, 5 June 1994, A.$180,000 (£87,192)

Russell Drysdale's interior paintings show the interrelationship of
man and his environment. They gave Australians a new way of
looking at their landscape which had previously focused upon the
lush grazing country of the coastal areas. Drysdale depicted the
harsh life on the fringes of settlement in the red desert of Central
Australia. Critics frequently dwelt upon the aspects of isolation
and loneliness which they found compelling in these paintings;
however, Drysdale's focus was the timeless enduring quality of
the terrain and its inhabitants. His monumental figures are
intended as archetypes of the strong, resilient and self-sufficient
characters of the Australian outback.

AMERICAN PICTURES

CHARLES DEAS (1818–1867)
Indian Warrior on the Edge of a Precipice
signed and dated 'C Deas 1847'
oil on canvas
$36\frac{1}{2} \times 27\frac{1}{2}$ in. (92.8 × 67 cm.)
New York, 22 September 1993, $310,500 (£204,815)

Above:
EDWARD MORAN (1829–1901)
The *Madeleine's* Victory Over the *Countess of Dufferin*,
Third America's Cup Challenger, 11 August, 1876
signed and dated 'Edward Moran 1876'
oil on canvas
24 × 42 in. (61 × 106.7 cm.)
New York, 3 December 1993, $156,500 (£105,529)

Right:
MARTIN JOHNSON HEADE (1819–1904)
Apple Blossoms
signed and dated 'MJH 1878'
oil on board
8 × 10 in. (20.3 × 25.4 cm.)
New York, 22 September 1993, $50,600 (£33,377)

WINSLOW HOMER (1836–1910)
The Whittling Boy
signed and dated 'Homer 1873'
oil on canvas
$15\frac{1}{2} \times 22\frac{5}{8}$ in. (39.4 × 57.4 cm.)
Sold from The Malden Public Library
New York, 26 May 1994, $1,102,500 (£730,616)

This picture illustrates Homer's fascination with colour and
natural light. He creates the warm afternoon summer light with
sweeps and jolts of varying greens and the keenly chosen tones of
yellow and brown which highlight the boy and his broad
brimmed hat.

The *Whittling Boy* reflects the state of the country's mind during
the years following the Civil War. This period was considered to
be the most turbulent and confusing in American history, as the
devastating impact of the Civil War, coupled with burgeoning
technology and a rapidly growing industrialised environment
generated a strong sense of disorientation. As a much more
complex and progressive way of life emerged, there developed an
aspiration to recapture a lost innocence which was manifested in
a preoccupation with children and youth. In this picture of a
single figure in a simple environment, Homer, with his
sophisticated use of colour and incredible command of light,
created an icon representing harmony, innocence and hope.

JOHN SINGER SARGENT (1856–1925)
Mrs. Archibald Douglas Dick
signed and dated 'John S. Sargent 1886'
oil on canvas
$63\frac{1}{2} \times 36\frac{5}{8}$ in. (161.2 × 93 cm.)
New York, 3 December 1993, $772,500 (£520,904)

In 1885, after a discouraging winter in Paris, Sargent longed to return to England. Shortly thereafter he moved to the Cotswold village of Broadway, which became a retreat for artists and writers including Henry James, Alfred Parsons, Francis Millet and Edmund Gosse. His new surroundings inspired Sargent, and he began to experiment with the reflection of light and colour associated with the Impressionists.

Mrs Archibald Douglas Dick was born in 1863, Isabelle Parrott, daughter of John Parrot, a Virginian banker and merchant. She married Brigadier Archibald Dick in 1883 and bore one son and six daughters. This and the untraced companion portrait of Brigadier Dick were commissioned by Mrs Dick's mother and are both of 1886.

Above:
WILLIAM MERRITT CHASE (1849–1916)
Dorothy
signed 'Chase'
oil on canvas
20 × 16 in. (51 × 40.7 cm.)
New York, 3 December 1993, $134,500 (£90,695)

STANTON MACDONALD-WRIGHT (1890–1973)
Conception Synchromy
signed with initials
oil on canvas mounted on board
30 × 12 in. (76.2 × 30.5 cm.)
New York, 26 May 1994, $360,000 (£238,569)

Right:
GEORGIA O'KEEFFE (1887–1986)
East River, New York, No. II
pastel on paper
$10\frac{3}{4} \times 28$ in. (27.5 × 71 cm.)
Sold from the Estate of Flora Stieglitz Strauss
New York, 26 May 1994, $288,500 (£191,186)

OTIS KAYE (1885–1974)
Easy Come, Easy Go
signed 'O. Kaye' and 'O.K.' twice
oil on panel
$21 \times 25\frac{5}{8}$ in. (53.1 × 65.1 cm.)
New York, 22 September 1993, $107,000 (£70,580)

MARSDEN HARTLEY (1877–1943)
Madawaska – Acadian Light-Heavy
signed and dated 'Marsden Hartley 1940'
oil on masonite
40 × 30 in. (101.6 × 76.2 cm.)
New York, 26 May 1994, $662,500 (£439,032)

An uncompromising masculinity and strength looms out of this
picture. Barbara Haskell notes that in this series, Hartley
'abandoned his habit of painting from memory to work directly
from his subject, a French-Canadian light-heavyweight boxer he

had met while living in Bangor ... As with his 'Archaic Portraits,'
Hartley simplified form into large shapes delineated by discrete
areas of colour ... the design is less mannered with a rich scale of
intermediate shades of bonded colour.'

In Hartley's Katahdin series, he struggled to 'do the mountain's
portrait,' to explain for himself the metaphor of man as mountain,
mountain as man, and the two achieved in his mind a fluid
interchangeability. The Madawaska, potent with physical energy,
was as statuesque and iconic as Katahdin itself, looming like a
giant, and no less indomitable.

MILTON AVERY (1885–1965)
Artist's Family by the Sea
signed and dated 'Milton Avery 1944'
gouache and pencil on paper
$22\frac{1}{2} \times 30\frac{3}{4}$ in. (57 × 78.2 cm.)
New York, 3 December 1993, $134,500 (£90,695)

HENRY F. FARNY (1847–1916)
A Lucky Shot
signed and dated 'H.F. Farny 1903'
gouache on paper laid down on board
$11\frac{1}{8} \times 17\frac{1}{2}$ in. (28.2 × 44.5 cm.)
New York, 16 March 1994, $74,000 (£49,664)

LATIN AMERICAN PICTURES

JOAQUIN TORRES-GARCIA (Uruguayan, 1874–1949)
Grafismo
signed and dated 'JTG 1936'
oil on canvas
20 × 16¼ in. (51 × 41 cm.)
New York, 24 November 1993, $178,500 (£119,879)

Born in Uruguay, Torres-Garcia left for Spain as a young artist.
There his early development of style tended toward neo-classic
Greek-inspired figures and landscapes. In 1926, he found himself
in Paris and a profound transformation of his art took place. In
the late 1920s his discovery of Pre-Colombian art led the artist

more and more toward the development of his *universalismo
constructivo* which included a growing repertoire of signs derived
from indo-American sources. While Uruguay itself did not
possess a large heritage of pre-Colombian cultures, Torres-Garcia
embraced all of South America in his search for pre-Hispanic
cultural references.

In *Grafismo*, Torres-Garcia presents us with a perfect example of
his philosophy of *universalismo constructivo*. Arcaic symbols and
signs are carefully arranged throughout the composition, which is
executed in his typical monochromatic tones.

RUFINO TAMAYO (Mexican, 1899–1991)
Niños Jugando Con Fuego
signed and dated 'Tamayo 0–47'
oil on canvas
50 × 67⅞ in. (127 × 172.5 cm.)
New York, 18 May 1994, $2,202,500 (£1,460,737)
Record auction price for an easel work by the artist

Rufino Tamayo spent most of the 1940s in New York, where he had the opportunity to study the North American and European *avant garde*, an exposure which clearly marked his future artistic production. Nothing impressed him more than seeing Picasso's *Guernica* at the Museum of Modern Art and his work thereafter demonstrates clearly the strong impression this made on him. While Tamayo's style remained very much his own, the emotional context of *Guernica* is reflected in many of his paintings of that time.

Niños Jugando Con Fuego can be considered a metaphor of mankind. It is of universal nature, expressing the love of dangerous games, deeply inherent in everyone. Mexico's pre-Hispanic culture, and colours derived from popular art, are employed to render the work powerfully expressive and full of vitality. It is a picture which inspires both awe and apprehension, while at the same time serving as a tribute to the artist's extraordinary Mexican spirit.

FERNANDO BOTERO (Columbian, b. 1932)
Frutas
signed and dated 'Botero 68'
oil on canvas
$61\frac{1}{2} \times 74\frac{3}{4}$ in. (156.2 × 190 cm.)
New York, 24 November 1993, $552,500 (£371,054)

The world of Latin America breathes through Botero's paintings.
His grand forms convey a sense of voluptuousness and languid
enjoyment of life's pleasures.

The larger than life figures of his compositions are mostly
engaged in such activities as eating and drinking, playing cards or
relaxing in wondrous landscapes, sleeping in tiny beds or riding
on inflated horses. Still-lifes are among Botero's favourite
subjects, bursting with richly coloured tropical fruits, and often
surrounded by slightly sinister details such as flies, ants, or open
drawers.

But like all serious painters, Botero is first and foremost interested
in the eternal problem of putting paint on canvas and discussing
his paintings formally rather than in terms of their vocabulary.
Frutas is precisely such a painting, showing a neat, white
tablecloth topped by an almost bath-tub like fruitbowl laden with
succulent fruit. The lines are clearly defined, elegant and
straightforward. The half-peeled orange is poised at the edge of
the table, inviting the viewer to taste its juicy flesh, knife and fork
at the ready. Everything speaks of contained formality, allowing
us to enjoy and participate in a tranquil scene.

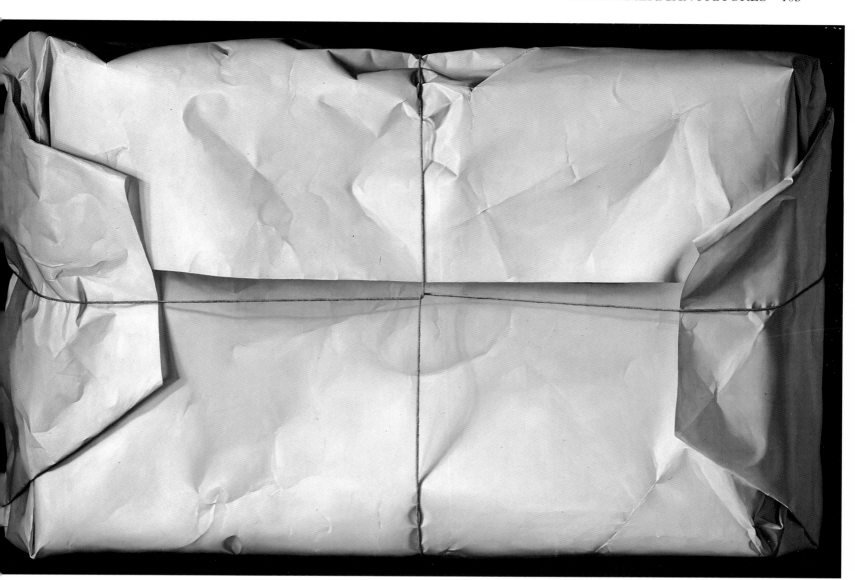

CLAUDIO BRAVO (Chilean, b. 1936)
White Package
signed and dated 'MCMLXVII'
oil on panel
$39\frac{3}{8} \times 59$ in. (100 × 150 cm.)
New York, 18 May 1994, $365,500 (£242,406)

When Claudio Bravo moved to Spain from his native Chile in the 1960s, he supported himself primarily through painting portraits. Colour, volume and texture would be an integral part of his approach to portrait painting. During the same period Bravo embarked upon a series of wrapped packages: 'I think I was originally inspired by Tapis and Rothko's work was also instrumental but in a more indirect way.' In 1970, he had his first exhibition of wrapped package pictures at the Staempfei Gallery in New York, his first major departure from portraiture. In a certain sense these represent a balance between representation and abstraction and there is a notable play between colour and texture, which gives the paintings both depth and bulk.

White Package is a perfect example of this fusion of the classical, and especially Spanish, still-life tradition whereby the monumental size of the object holds the viewers attention, while at the same time there is an implied mystery and eeriness that links it to Surrealism.

CONTEMPORARY ART

RICHARD DIEBENKORN (American, 1922–1993)
Berkeley #37
initialled and dated 'RD 55'
oil on canvas
$69\frac{3}{4} \times 69\frac{3}{4}$ in. (177.2 × 177.2 cm.)
Sold from the Carnegie Museum of Art
New York, 3 May 1994, $662,500 (£441,667)

Right:
JEAN FAUTRIER (French, 1898–1964)
Les Seins Nus
signed and dated ''45'
oil and pigment on paper mounted on canvas
$18\frac{1}{8} \times 21\frac{5}{8}$ in. (46 × 55 cm.)
London, 30 June 1994, £298,500 ($460,884)

JEAN DUBUFFET (French, 1901–1985)
Deux Figures dans un Paysage
signed and dated ''49'
oil on hessian
35 × 45 in. (89 × 116 cm.)
London, 2 December 1993, £518,500 ($771,010)

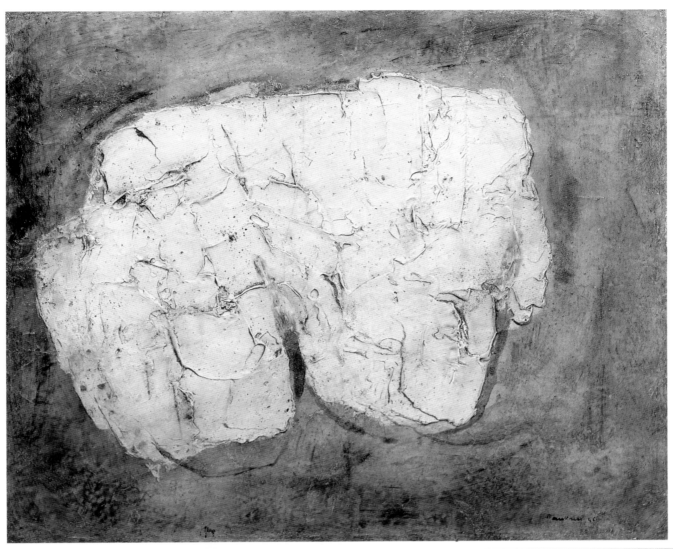

JACKSON POLLOCK (American, 1912–1956)
Number 22, 1949
signed and dated 'Jackson Pollock 49'
oil and enamel on paper mounted on masonite
$27\frac{7}{8} \times 22\frac{7}{8}$ in. (70.8 × 58.1 cm.)
Sold from the Collection of Meshulam Riklis
New York, 3 May 1994, $1,762,500 (£1,179,000)

Number 22, 1949 was created during Pollock's most
important period, 1947–50, when he fully mastered the
technique that enabled him to extend the limits of painting
as it had previously been perceived. He had been
struggling since the early 1940s to find the means to release
onto the canvas the powerful subject matter that haunted
him, subjects derived from the unconscious.

Brushwork had somehow inhibited him and he turned
increasingly to the liberating techniques of dripping and
pouring fluid paint – oil, aluminium, and enamel – from
sticks and brushes onto unprimed canvas that was tacked to
the floor of his studio in Springs, Long Island.

Number 22, 1949 is exceedingly rich, its surface extremely
varied. The patterns and webs of the dripped and poured
paint create great depth over the majority of the painting's
surface, while still pulling back from the edges, reflecting
Pollock's most characteristic compositional technique. His
palette is vibrant and varied, with bold yellow, red, green,
blue-grey, aluminium, and white. This richness of colour
is emphasised by the calligraphic black strokes, which call
to mind Pollock's totemic paintings from the early and
mid-1940s.

ARSHILE GORKY (American, 1904–1948)
Year After Year
signed and dated 'A. Gorky 47'
oil on canvas
$34\frac{5}{8} \times 40\frac{7}{8}$ in. (86.5 × 104 cm.)
New York, 9 November 1993, $3,852,500 (£2,620,748)

Gorky lived in New York during the 1930s and was deeply involved in the American vanguard movements of that time. In fact, many look to Gorky's works as a barometer of the major trends. During and after World War II, the American art scene was driven primarily by European artistic movements, beginning with Cubism. As early as 1926, Gorky had identified Picasso and Matisse as the artistic 'masters' of the twentieth century, soon adding Miró and Léger to their ranks. Like his American peers, he modelled many of his early works on their masterpieces.

Soon the Surrealist movement began to flourish in Europe, spreading quickly to America. During the war a number of Surrealist artists emigrated to New York. Young New York artists, including Pollock, de Kooning, Rothko, Newman, Gottlieb, and Still, welcomed the new and exciting atmosphere created by Surrealists such as Max Ernst, Yves Tanguy, Matta Echaurran and André Breton, the spokesman for the movement.

The young Americans embraced the new freedom of 'automatism', or painting from the subconscious. Accordingly, their works from the 1940s are replete with surrealistic imagery, primarily painted in blacks, greys, and browns, and mostly executed on small canvases.

But it was Gorky who created the most beautiful and celebrated works of the 1940s, taking Surrealism and making it his own. While the works of his contemporaries were small, his were oversized; while their works were monochromatic, his were vibrant. Gorky was the first American to move beyond mere adaptation of European styles, creating a bold personal style of his own.

For Gorky, the philosophy of Surrealism was a release from the powerful influences of the past, particularly Picasso. Not content with painting imagery of the mind, Gorky painted the world around him, abstracting what he saw into scarcely readable images. He painted still lifes, interiors and landscapes of Virginia, where he summered, and Connecticut, where he lived. One of Gorky's best paintings from the 1940s is *Year after Year*, a boldly-coloured, classic image executed in 1947. The iconography suggests a view of the Housatonic River near Gorky's house in Sherman, Connecticut.

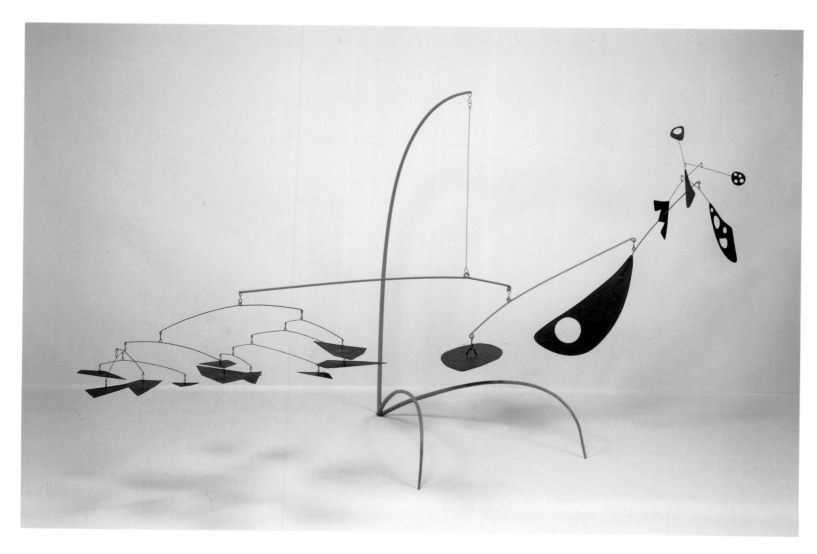

WILLEM DE KOONING (American, b. 1904)
Untitled XIV
signed twice 'de Kooning' on the stretcher
oil on canvas
80 × 70 in. (203.2 × 177.8 cm.)
New York, 3 May 1994, $882,500 (£588,333)

Untitled XIV, painted in 1982, is a joyously lyrical work. The large canvas is filled with buoyant drawing, its abstract calligraphy is utterly sensual, although freed from any specific references to the human or landscape subjects that dominated de Kooning's work of the previous five decades. As Peter Schjeldahl remarked with reference to de Kooning's paintings of the 1980s: 'The author of the paintings appears to harbour no particular concerns or intentions, driven by an organic inclination, an instinct, for unhurried, endless, and all-forgetful joy.'

Describing de Kooning's technique in his late paintings, Carter Ratcliff observed:

> Something extraordinary happens in the 1980s. Dragging a wide metal edge through heavy masses of paint, de Kooning turns scraping into a king of drawing. A process of subtraction makes an addition, a stately flurry of draftsmanly gestures. De Kooning has always layered and elided his forms. Now he reminds us that he does the same with his methods.

In many respects, *Untitled XIV* recapitulates in a grandly lyrical manner de Kooning's Cubist and black and white abstractions of the 1940s, but filtered through the experiences and paintings of the intervening decades, most notably the sun and light-filled East Hampton landscapes.

HENRI MATISSE (French, 1869–1954)
Grande Odalisque à la culotte bayadère
lithograph
$21\frac{3}{8} \times 17\frac{1}{4}$ in. (54.3 × 43.8 cm.)
New York, 19 November 1993, $244,500 (£165,875)
Record auction price for a print by the artist

HENRI DE TOULOUSE-LAUTREC (French, 1864–1901)
Elles
set of twelve lithographs printed in colours
$20\frac{3}{4} \times 16$ in. (52.6 × 40.7 cm.)
London, 1 December 1993, £441,500 ($653,862)

EDWARD HOPPER (American, 1882–1967)
Night on the El Train
etching
$7\frac{1}{2} \times 8$ in. (19.1 × 20.4 cm.)
New York, 9 May 1994, $48,300 (£32,329)

Right:
DAVID HOCKNEY (British, b. 1937)
An Image of Celia
lithograph and screenprint in colours, with collage
$67 \times 48\frac{3}{4}$ in. (170 × 124 cm.)
London, 1 December 1993, £38,900 ($57,611)

ROY LICHTENSTEIN (American, b. 1923)
Peace through Chemistry II
lithograph
$37\frac{1}{4} \times 63$ in. (94.6 × 160 cm.)
New York, 20 November 1993, $26,450 (£17,944)

SCULPTURE

AN EARLY ENGLISH IVORY

by David Ekserdjian

The unicorn has always been considered not only the most sacred but also the most appealing of all mythological beasts. From ancient times it was recorded that its horn had magical powers: anyone who drank from the horn was protected from illness, while a contaminated pool of water into which the unicorn dipped its horn would instantly be made pure. The unicorn also came to be seen as a symbol of Christ, and the third-century theologian Tertullian recorded that 'Christ is meant by it and the horn denotes Christ's cross'. It was believed that the only way to capture a unicorn was by using a virgin as bait, since the creature, unable to resist her, would invariably come and rest its head in her lap. Two of the most admired series of medieval tapestries, the *Dame à la Licorne* in the Musée de Cluny in Paris and the *Chasse à la Licorne* in the Cloisters Museum in New York, take these legendary beliefs as their theme. By the later sixteenth century, some commentators explained the unicorn's elusiveness by its proud refusal to join the other animals on Noah's ark and consequent extinction.

If unicorns were hard to find, their horns were not completely unknown. A small Arctic whale, the narwhal (*Monodon monoceros*), has a single horn which was assumed to be that of the fabled unicorn. Such horns were arguably as highly prized as any of the wonders of nature, and were among the principal adornments of secular and especially ecclesiastical treasuries. As late as the renaissance, the horns were still tremendously sought after, and Isabella d'Este, the Marchioness of Mantua, who was referred to as *La prima donna del mondo*, had one in her *Studiolo* alongside paintings by Mantegna and Correggio. Leonardo da Vinci drew the unicorn dipping its horn and resting its head in a virgin's lap, and when François I of France's son, Henri de Valois, married Caterina de'Medici in 1533, Pope Clement VII gave them a decorated unicorn horn. Benvenuto Cellini was involved in the commission, but in the event it was awarded to one of his rivals. In his *Autobiography*, he records that the horn was 'the most beautiful one ever seen', and that it alone cost seventeen thousand ducats. Although Michelangelo may in the end have received twice as much, he recorded in a letter that he had agreed to paint the Sistine Chapel ceiling for three thousand ducats.

Because of the inherent value of narwhal horns, they were only carved under exceptional circumstances. The present example is one of a mere two surviving horns of extremely closely comparable design and execution, which appear to have been carved in England in the mid-twelfth century. The other, which is less well preserved, is in the Victoria and Albert Museum, and was included in the exhibition of English Romanesque Art at the Hayward Gallery in London in 1984 and subsequently in the 1992 exhibition at the National Gallery of Art in Washington.

The style of both pieces has been associated with the decorative vocabulary of one of the columns to the right of the central portal of the west end of Lincoln Cathedral, which is datable to around 1145, but that in its turn depends upon the lateral portals of the façade of St. Denis, and there is no compelling need to believe that the horns were carved in Lincoln or nearby. Other elements in their decoration find parallels in manuscript illuminations produced in St. Alban's and Bury St. Edmund's in the second quarter of the twelfth century.

It seems clear that the two horns are products of the same workshop, although not necessarily of the same carver, since the Victoria and Albert piece is markedly more deeply cut. In both, the lower section is carved in the form of an octagon, with bands of decoration alternating with plain surfaces, which were presumably originally covered with strips of copper, probably gilded. Pin-holes and some surviving copper pins, as well as areas of green staining on the Victoria and Albert example, support this suggestion. In the upper section of both horns the decoration follows the spiral form of the horn itself, again alternating with plain bands. Between the two sections is another unadorned area, which may well have been the place where the horn was meant to be held. In each case, the decoration consists of figures and foliage below, winged dragons and fantastical beasts with foliage above. The horn in the Victoria and Albert Museum has lost part of its top, but was carved all the way up, whereas the last few inches of the present example are left blank. This suggests that the horn was originally crowned with a metal fitting of some sort. Both horns have been slightly rubbed at their bases, perhaps as a result of the subsequent addition of metal cladding at their feet.

The narwhal horn in the Victoria and Albert Museum has come to be described as a 'ceremonial staff', but it has to be admitted that such a form of words does little to explain its original function, and fails even to clarify whether it is to be imagined in a sacred or a secular context. However, in view of the association of the unicorn with Christ, it seems more likely that these most precious of objects were reserved for religious ceremonies, and one can easily imagine them being carried in some great cathedral procession. One possibility is that they were used for carrying candles, in which case they would have been surmounted by metal drip pans. Both the British Museum and Jesus College, Cambridge, own fourteenth-century English wax candlesticks which were topped by some sort of collar into which a smaller candle was set. They too are tapered and decorated with a spiral design, and it may well be that those naturally occurring properties of narwhal horns suggested their employment in such a context. There is no shortage of written references to processional candles, or indeed of visual representations of them from the period. There remains the question of how the same workshop should have come to produce two of these remarkable staffs at much the same date. It is tempting to wonder whether the evident correspondence between the two horns is not to be explained by the simple fact that they were originally made as a pair.

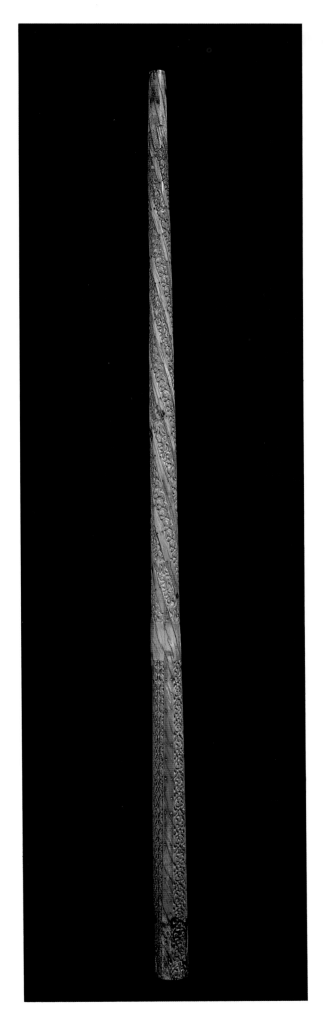

A carved Narwhal Horn
English, mid-12th Century
$44\frac{7}{8}$ in. (114 cm.) long
London, 5 July 1994, £441,500 ($679,910)

Left:
A fragmentary Tapestry depicting two Scenes from the Life of the
Abbess Sabina
Alsace, 14th Century
33 × 33 in. (83.8 × 83.8 cm.)
London, 5 July 1994, £166,500 ($256,410)

A carved Mirror-case Cover
ivory
Paris, second quarter 14th Century
$5\frac{3}{8}$ in. (13.7 cm.) high
London, 7 December 1993, £128,000 ($192,000)

GIOVANNI ANTONIO BIANCHINI (Italian, active circa
1556–70)
A rectangular Micromosaic of Saint Jerome in the Wilderness
Third quarter 16th Century
24 × $20\frac{3}{8}$ in. (61 × 51.8 cm.)
London, 5 July 1994, £67,500 ($103,950)

Cast by ANTONIO SUSINI (Italian, active 1580–1624) from
models by GIAMBOLOGNA (Flemish, 1529–1608)
A Pair of Groups of a Lion attacking a Horse and a Lion attacking
a Bull (the former illustrated)
bronze
9½ and 8⅛ in. (24.2 and 20.7 cm.) high
Sold from the collection of the Earl of Radnor
London, 7 December 1993, £441,500 ($662,250)

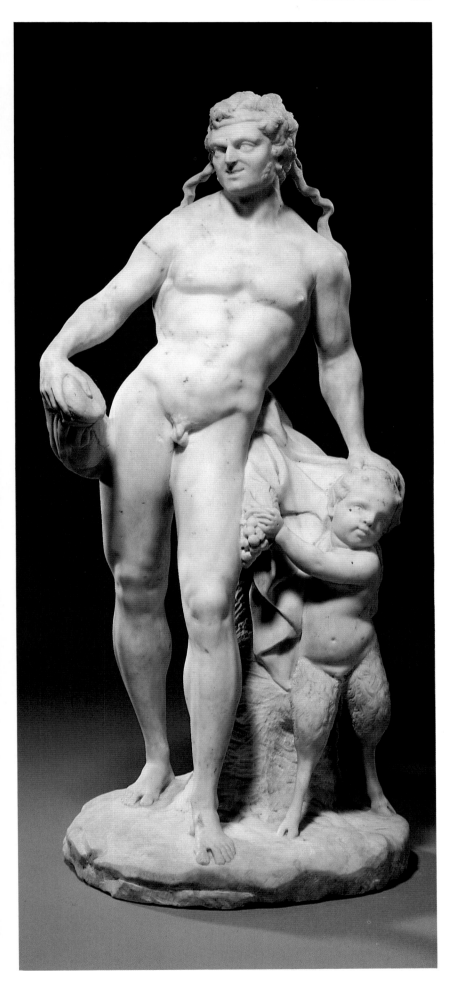

MICHAEL RYSBRACK (British, 1694–1770)
A carved Figure of the Goddess Friga
Portland stone
circa 1728–30
70 in. (177.7 cm.) high approx.
London, 5 July 1994, £54,300 ($83,622)

FRANCESCO BERTOS (Italian, active circa 1693–1735)
A carved Group of Bacchus and a young Satyr
marble
early 18th Century
23½ in. (59.7 cm.) high
London, 5 July 1994, £67,500 ($103,950)

Left:
A Sundial Figure of Chronos
signed 'COADE LONDON 1792'
Coade stone
51 in. (129.5 cm.) high overall; the disc 19 in. (48.2 cm)
diameter
Wrotham Park, 21 June 1994, £57,600 ($88,416)

A George III Chimney-piece (detail illustrated)
signed 'COADE 1796 LONDON'
Coade stone
74 in. (188 cm.) high; 102 in. (259.6 cm.) wide; 9 in.
(22.9 cm.) deep
Clifton Little Venice, 6 June 1994, £38,900 ($58,545)

FRANCESCO FABI-ALTINI (Italian, 1830–1906)
An Italian Figure of David returning from Battle
signed and dated 'F. FABI-ALTINI ROMA 1882'
white marble
the figure 58¾ in. (149 cm.) high; the pedestal 39 in. (99 cm.) high
London, 17 March 1994, £96,100 ($143,189)

Cast from models by JEAN BAPTISTE CARPEAUX (French, 1827–1875)
A Pair of Figures of a Neapolitan fisher Boy and Girl entitled *'Jeune pecheur a la coquille'* and *'Jeune fille a la coquille'* (the latter illustrated)
bronze
the girl: 39 in. (99 cm.) high; 19½ in. (49.5 cm.) wide; 16¼ in. (41 cm.) deep
the boy: 35½ in. (90 cm.) high; 19½ in. (49.5 cm.) wide; 16¼ in. (41 cm.) deep
Sold from the collection of the late Sir Robert Abdy, Bt.
London, 17 March 1994, £63,100 ($94,019)

Left:
ANTOINE-LOUIS BARYE (French, 1796–1875)
La Force; and L'Ordre
inscribed 'BARYE' and 'F. BARBEDIENNE, Fondeur. Paris.'
bronze
19 in. (48.2 cm.) and 18¾ (47.6 cm.) high
New York, 12 October 1993, $63,000 (£96,138)

FREDERICK SACKRIDER REMINGTON (American, 1861–1909)
The Cheyenne
inscribed 'Frederic Remington 1901', 'COPYRIGHTED BY.' and 'Roman Bronze
Works. N.Y.' and on the underside stamped '8'
bronze, 20 in. (50.7 cm.) high
New York, 3 December 1993, $552,500 (£372,556)

LYNN CHADWICK (British, b. 1914)
Teddy Boy and Girl II
signed, dated and numbered 'Chadwick 57
227 2/4'
bronze
82 in. (208 cm.) high
London, 25 May 1994, £62,000 ($93,558)

FRENCH FURNITURE

The Sale of the M. Hubert de Givenchy Collection

by Bertrand du Vignaud

The end of 1993 saw one of the most memorable episodes in the recent history of the saleroom: the auction of the collection of M. Hubert de Givenchy, the famous French couturier who, following the example of his well-known predecessor Jacques Doucet at the beginning of the twentieth century, brought together a collection which will stay in the memory of connoisseurs throughout the world.

However, even if with the benefit of hindsight the success of the sale seems inevitable, it was far from being predicted by the cassandras of the art market who, in the months preceding the sale, spread rumours that were more or less alarmist and foretold a semi-success because of the morose climate of day. Thus the auction was a triumph: the *International Herald Tribune* even spoke of it as an 'historic sale'. There were several reasons for this.

In the first place, the name itself and the personality of M. Hubert de Givenchy counted for much. Assembled over the last thirty years, his collection of furniture and works of art attested to a profound knowledge of the French *ébenistes* and *bronziers* of the seventeenth and eighteenth centuries, complemented by an extreme refinement of taste and an exceptional sense of decor. The collection was housed in the Parisian home of M. de Givenchy, the Hôtel d'Orrouer, a large seventeenth-century house in the heart of the most elegant *quartier* of Paris, the Faubourg Saint Germain.

The quality of the furniture and works of art, and the glamour of their provenance, also played an important role. The collection included masterpieces once owned by the royal families of France, Britain and Russia as well as from many of the most prestigious collections (Talleyrand, Crozat de Tugny, Buckingham, Ashburnham, Hillingdon, Rothschild, Comte de Cobenzle, Tournon-Simiane, David-Weill among others), cumulatively offering a microcosm of the taste of the last three centuries.

Equally remarkable was the distinction of the outstanding *ébenistes*, *bronziers*, clockmakers and silversmiths represented in the collection: André-Charles Boulle, Contant d'Ivry, Etienne Levasseur, Joseph Baumhauer, Adam Weisweiler, Jean-Baptiste Tilliard, Jean-Baptiste Séné, Georges Jacob, Charles Cressent, François Rémond, Jean-Baptiste Odiot, Martin-Guillaume Biennais, Paul Storr, Gottlieb Menzel, Johannes Lencker and Balthasar Friedrich Behrens to name but the most famous.

The love and respect M. de Givenchy had for his objects all his life was expressed to the last minute before these were dispersed, and drew admiration from all Christie's specialists. At every stage of the preparation of the sale, their attitude was inspired by his.

The auction was preceded by an exceptional international promotion campaign. A sumptuous catalogue was published in both French and English. This notable production, prepared under the supervision of Charles Cator, the Director of the European Furniture Department, recorded the research undertaken by Christie's experts and the discoveries they made. These included numerous previously unknown provenances, notably that of the Régence chimney appliqués created for the Place Vendôme hôtel of the financier Crozat de Tugny to a design by

Contant d'Ivry: when these had been sold publicly a few years earlier, their original provenance was not recognised. In other instances in the catalogue, works of art were considered for the first time in the context of their original setting, or associated with preparatory drawings or specific patrons.

The worldwide publicity campaign launched for the Givenchy sale was on an exceptional scale, and journalists were briefed in Paris, London and New York. Both during the months leading up to the auction and those following it, the world's press gave it a star billing. Christie's exhibited the collection in New York where more than a thousand visitors a day came to Park Avenue to admire it. In Paris the collection found an ideal site in the salons of the 'Foundation Mona Bismarck', beautifully redecorated for the occasion and, finally in Monaco, a marquee was specially erected and hung with the dark green which was M. de Givenchy's favourite colour.

On the evening of 4 December in the presence of a crowd which had come from all over the world and with thirty telephone lines installed for the occasion, Christie's established a new world record for a single owner furniture sale with a total of Fr.155,500,000 (£17,670,455).

Prices achieved were remarkable and a number of records were set. The ebony, marquetry and gilt-bronze bureau-plat by André Charles Boulle reached Fr.18,800,000, a record price for the artist, to become the second most expensive piece of French furniture ever sold on the auction market. The other Boulle pieces also made exceptional prices; the pair of Louis XIV *guéridons* which had belonged to the duchesse de Talleyrand reached Fr.6,800,000, more than double their pre-sale estimate, while the Louis XVI bibliothèque basse by Etienne Levasseur for Monsieur Lebrun husband of Marie-Antoinette's favourite painter, Madame Vigée-Lebrun, went for over Fr.11,000,000. In all, five pieces of furniture were sold for over Fr.5,000,000 which demonstrated the strength of the interest in French furniture of high quality in fine condition.

Outstanding among the works of art, were the *appliques de cheminée* more than a metre high and executed in 1745–7 for Joseph-Antoine Crozat de Tugny which reached Fr.5,328,000, and an imposing pair of Louis XV porphyry vases which made nearly Fr.3,000,000. Even the less celebrated pieces of furniture made high prices, for example the Louis XVI giltwood chair stamped by Bauve which fetched Fr.577,200, nearly double its estimate.

A dozen important objects in silver or plate, of which the most celebrated was the chandelier made for King George II of England (see p. 160–1), completed this magnificent collection and with their quality and provenance testified to the *grand goût* of M. Hubert de Givenchy.

The sale of the collection of M. Hubert de Givenchy is part of a great tradition, over 200 years long, of historic sales organised by Christie's for the numerous French clients for whom it is an honour and a pleasure to work.

ANDRÉ-CHARLES BOULLE (1642–1732)
A Louis XIV ebony, brass and tortoiseshell *Bureau Plat*
32¼ in. (82 cm.) high; 74½ in. (189 cm.) wide; 36 in. (91.5 cm.)
deep
Sold from the collection of M. Hubert de Givenchy
Monaco, 4 December 1993, Fr.18,870,000 (£2,145,537)
Record auction price for a piece of furniture by Boulle

Attributed to JOSEPH BAUMHAUER (active circa
1749–1770)
A Louis XV tulipwood, amaranth and marquetry *Bureau Pupitre à
Ecrire Debout*
$46\frac{1}{4}$ in. (70.5 cm.) high; 41 in. (104 cm.) wide; $27\frac{3}{4}$ in. (70.5 cm.)
deep
Sold from the collection of M. Hubert de Givenchy
Monaco, 4 December 1993, Fr.10,545,000 (£1,198,977)

Right:
A Pair of Louis XV gilt-bronze three-light *Girandoles de Cheminée*
with the *C couronné poinçon*, 1745–9
53 in. (135 cm.) high; 16 in. (41.5 cm.) wide
Sold from the collection of M. Hubert de Givenchy
Monaco, 4 December 1993, Fr.5,328,000 (£605,799)

ORIENTAL PORCELAIN WITH FRENCH GILT-BRONZE MOUNTS

by Charles Cator

The romantic and poignant history of the pair of ewers from Luton Hoo remained undiscovered until the researches of Patrick Leperlier in the *Archives* in Paris revealed that they had belonged to Marie-Antoinette. They are clearly identifiable in the comprehensive list of the Queen's most precious objects which she arranged to be packed and taken into safe-keeping by the *marchand-bijoutier* Dominique Daguerre following the invasion of Versailles on 6 October 1789. It is highly probable that Louis XVI had acquired the vases – but with Louis XV gilt-bronze mounts – for her in 1782 from the celebrated collection of the duc d'Aumont, who had in turn acquired them from the sale in 1769 of the connoisseur Louis-Jean Gaignat. The distinctive profile of the ewers and their remarkable colour, varying from blue to violet depending on the light, would have appealed to the Queen's taste for the exotic and unusual. Pierre Gouthière was probably responsible for replacing the old-fashioned rococo mounts with neo-classical ornament of dazzling quality and elegance, creating the perfect expression of the Queen's refined patronage. Obviously always highly prized, they were not included in the revolutionary sales and were next recorded *circa* 1805 at the château de Saint-Cloud in the principal apartments refurbished for Napoleon's use.

The inventory numbers on their bases enabled them to be traced through the Saint-Cloud inventories and show that they remained there throughout the first half of the nineteenth century, surviving all the turbulent changes of regime. It is fascinating that the 1818 inventory lists them in the salon of Marie-Antoinette's daughter, the duchesse d'Angoulême. The last mention of them is at Saint-Cloud in 1855 in the *Grand Salon* of the Empress Eugènie, then on 28 June they were removed from the inventory. The precise circumstances of their removal is still unknown, as is their subsequent history until they were acquired early this century by Sir Julius Wernher, Bt. for his collection displayed at Bath House, Piccadilly. Their rediscovery is a thrilling and illuminating addition to our knowledge of Marie-Antoinette's most personal and treasured collection.

If Marie-Antoinette's ewers epitomise the late neo-classical style, the superb gilt-bronze and Chinese porcelain vase, also from Sir Julius' collection, celebrates the brilliance of the mid-eighteenth Parisian *bronziers*. The oriental vase, with its eye-catching mottled red and turquoise glaze, has been skillfully united with the sumptuous but controlled rococo mounts, lavishly gilded, to create a completely integrated and balanced work of art remarkable for its scale and boldness. The vases' mounts are struck with the C *couronné poinçon,* a tax mark indicating that they were made between 1745 and 1749.

Left:
Attributed to PIERRE GOUTHIÈRE (French 1732–1813)
A pair of ormolu-mounted Chinese aubergine porcelain Ewers
(see frontispiece) supplied to Marie-Antoinette for the Cabinet
Intérieur de la Reine at the Château de Versailles, circa 1783
(detail illustrated)
19 in. (48.5 cm.) high; 11 in. (28 cm.) wide
London, 9 June 1994, £1,046,500 ($1,579,169)

Above:
A Louis XV ormolu-mounted Chinese red and turquoise flambé-
glazed porcelain Vase and Cover
with the *C couronné poinçon*, 1745–9
$17\frac{1}{2}$ in. (44.5 cm.) high; 14 in. (35.5 cm.) wide
London, 9 June 1994, £298,500 ($450,437)

Above:
MARTIN CARLIN (active 1766–1785)
A Louis XVI ormolu-mounted Sèvres porcelain, *bois satiné,*
amaranth, tulipwood and parquetry *Table en Chiffonnière*
stamped once 'M. CARLIN' and 'JME'
the plaque marked with the Sèvres interlaced L's, with date letter
for 1782
$30\frac{3}{4}$ in. (78 cm.) high; 15 in. (38 cm.) diameter
Sold by the Trustees of the late Nicholas Meynell, Esq.
London, 9 June 1994, £419,500 ($633,026)

A Pair of Consulat ormolu six-light Candelabra (one illustrated)
$52\frac{1}{2}$ in. (133 cm.) high; 20 in. (51 cm.) wide
Monaco, 5 December 1993, Fr.1,554,000 (£176,913)

Right:
PIERRE GARNIER (circa 1720–1800)
A Louis XV ormolu-mounted and brass-inlaid amaranth
Bureau à Cylindre
stamped fifteen times 'P. GARNIER' and dated 1767
44.5 in. (113 cm.) high; $77\frac{1}{8}$ in. (196 cm.) wide; 39 in.
(99 cm.) deep
Monaco, 20 June 1994, Fr.6,216,000 (£737,629)

PIERRE ROUSSEL (1723–1782)
A Transitional ormolu-mounted tulipwood and marquetry
Table à la Bourgogne, the top inlaid with arms of the Princes of
Esterházy
stamped once 'P. ROUSSEL' and 'JME'
35 in. (85 cm.) high; 27 in. (68.5 cm.) wide; $27\frac{1}{2}$ in.
(70 cm.) deep, open
London, 9 December 1993, £150,000 ($223,950)

JEAN-HENRI RIESENER (1734–1806)
A Louis XVI ormolu-mounted mahogany *Armoire*
stamped twice 'J.H. REISENER' and once 'H. RIESENER'
95½ in. (242.5 cm.) high; 82 in. (208.5 cm.) wide; 26 in. (66 cm.)
deep
Monaco, 20 June 1994, Fr.2,220,000 (£263,439)

Attributed to DAVID ROENTGEN (German, 1743–1807)
A German ormolu-mounted and brass-inlaid mahogany and plum-pudding mahogany *Secrétaire à Abattant*
49 in. (124.5 cm.) high; 36½ in. (93 cm.) wide; 13 in. (33 cm.) deep
London, 9 December 1993, £111,500 ($166,470)

David Roentgen opened his Paris establishment and was appointed *Ebéniste Mécanicien* to Louis XVI and Marie-Antoinette in 1780.

This lady's fall-front *secrétaire/bonheur-du-jour*, with its galleried cornice and corner-shelves, derives from a French prototype of the 1770s. With its restrained *antique* ornament and superbly figured mahogany façade, comprising a single veneer panel, it typifies the style created by David Roentgen of Neuweid.

Left:
An Italian Renaissance walnut and parquetry Cassone
Florentine, basically late 15th Century
41 in. (102.4 cm.) high; 94 in. (235 cm.) wide;
35 in. (237.5 cm.) deep
New York, 1 June 1994, $96,000 (£63,450)

A Venetian polychrome-decorated and parcel-gilt
bombé Commode
mid-18th Century
$32\frac{3}{4}$ in. (83 cm.) high; $45\frac{1}{2}$ in. (115.5 cm.) wide;
$23\frac{1}{2}$ in. (60 cm.) deep
London, 9 December 1993, £128,000 ($191,104)

Attributed to LUIGI PRINOTTO (Italian, circa 1712–1780)
A Turin ivory-inlaid palisander and parcel-gilt serpentine
Commode
circa 1736
$40\frac{1}{8}$ in. (102 cm.) high; $53\frac{1}{2}$ in. (136 cm.) wide;
$23\frac{3}{4}$ in. (60.5 cm.) deep
Monaco, 20 June 1994; Fr.1,776,000 (£210,751)

ENGLISH FURNITURE

A Pair of George II mahogany Library Armchairs (one illustrated)
New York, 9 October 1993, $277,500 (£182,326)

These chairs are part of a distinguished set, of which one pair is in
the Irwin Untermyer Collection in the Metropolitan Museum of
Art. This particular pair was part of the collection formed by the
late H.J. Joel at Childwick Bury in Hertfordshire, from where
they were sold at Christie's in 1978.

Right:
A George II mahogany Bookcase
112 in. (284.5 cm.) high; 86 in. (218.5 cm.) wide;
18 in. (46 cm.) deep
Sold from the collection of the late Sir Philip Shelbourne
Myles Place, Salisbury, 25 October 1993, £221,500 ($328,263)
Record auction price for a piece of furniture in a house sale

This pedimented and richly carved mahogany bookcase,
designed in the George II 'Palladian' manner was part of the
library furnishings commissioned by Richard Jervoise (d.1762),
following his inheritance of Herriard Park, Hampshire, in 1743.

THOMAS CHIPPENDALE (1718–1779)
A Pair of George III giltwood Sofas (one illustrated)
43 in. (110.5 cm.) high; 93 in. (234 cm.) wide;
33 in. (84 cm.) deep
Sold by the Trustees of the Lord Brocket Will Trust, removed
from Brocket Hall, Hertfordshire
London, 7 July 1994, £254,500 ($392,948)
Record auction price for a pair of sofas by Chippendale

On 7 July 1994 Christie's sold part of the giltwood Saloon
furniture commissioned by Sir Penistone Lamb, 1st Viscount
Melbourne (d.1819) for Brocket Hall, Hertfordshire and supplied
in the early 1770s by Thomas Chippendale, cabinet-maker of St.
Martin's Lane. The furniture was designed in the 'antique'
manner, to harmonise with the architecture and richly painted
ceiling of the great room that had been created by the architect
James Paine (d.1789). The candelabrum-torchères and a damask-
upholstered sofa featured in his *Noblemen and Gentlemen's Houses*,
1783, pl. LVIII. The torchères' tripod-altar plinths, with their
festive ram-heads and laurel-festooned 'Apollo' medallions,
harmonised with the medallion-backed chairs, whose laurel-
wreathed seats were originally upholstered in crimson damask
'exceeding rich flowered'.

Right:
THOMAS CHIPPENDALE (1718–1779)
A Pair of George III giltwood open Armchairs (one illustrated)
Sold by Order of the Trustees of the Lord Brocket Will Trust,
removed from Brocket Hall, Hertfordshire
London, 7 July 1994, £166,500 ($257,076)

THOMAS CHIPPENDALE (1718–1779)
A Pair of George III giltwood Torchères (*one illustrated*)
60¾ in. (154 cm.) high; 13¼ in. (23.5 cm.) diameter
Sold by the Trustees of the Lord Brocket Will Trust, removed
from Brocket Hall, Hertfordshire
London, 7 July 1994, £177,500 ($274,060)
Record auction price for a pair of torchères (candlestands) by
Chippendale

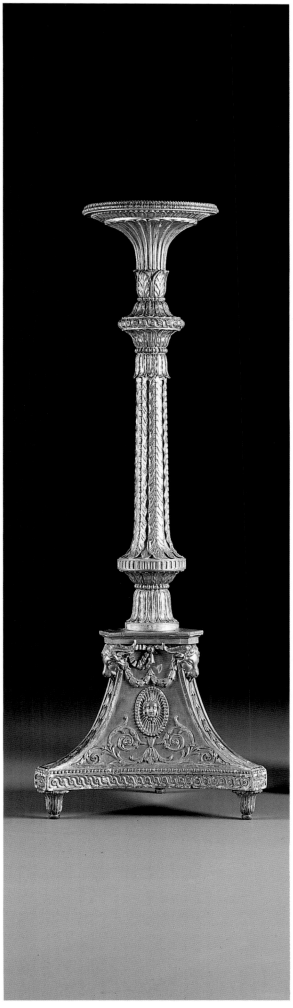

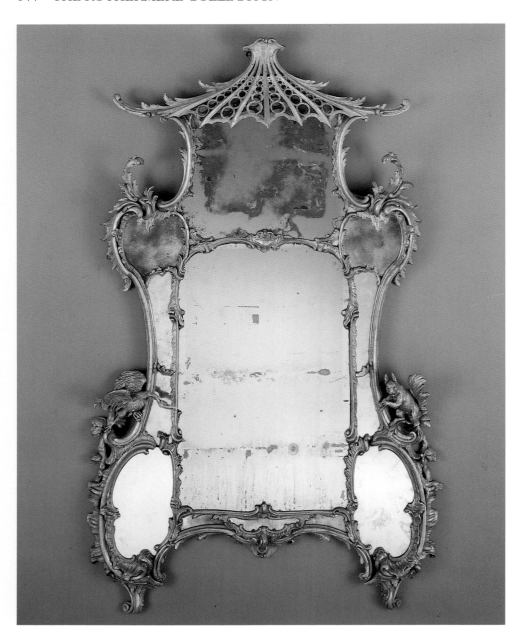

A George III giltwood Mirror
80 in. (208 cm.) high; 48 in. (122 cm.) wide
Sold from the Estate of Mary, Viscountess
Rothermere
New York, 16 April 1994, $85,000 (£57,666)

THOMAS CHIPPENDALE (1718–1779)
A Pair of George III grey and white-painted
Bergères from the David Garrick Suite of
Seat Furniture
circa 1768
Sold from the Estate of Mary, Viscountess
Rothermere
New York, 16 April 1994, $79,500 (£53,935)

This suite was commissioned by the actor
David Garrick (d.1779) for his villa at
Hampton, Middlesex and supplied by Thomas
Chippendale, cabinet-maker of St. Martin's
Lane. The '8 French Arm Chairs', sofa and
'2 large Tub chairs', painted blue and white
and upholstered in blue damask featured in his
1768 account.

Attributed to THOMAS CHIPPENDALE (1718–1779)
A George III mahogany four-poster Bed
124$\frac{3}{8}$ in. (316 cm.) high; 91 in. (231 cm.) wide;
82$\frac{5}{8}$ in. (210 cm.) deep
Monaco, 20 June 1994, Fr.777,000 (£92,204)

This mahogany-posted bed, with acanthus-scrolled and damask-upholstered cornice, was commissioned by William, 5th Baron Craven (d.1769) for Combe Abbey, Warwickshire and is very likely to have formed part of the furnishings supplied by Thomas Chippendale, cabinet-maker of St. Martin's Lane.

A Set of twelve Regency mahogany Dining-Chairs after a design
by Thomas Sheraton (two illustrated)
London, 7 July 1994, £463,500 ($715,644)
Record auction price for a set of dining-chairs

This set of finely carved mahogany dining-chairs is likely to have
been supplied to the 2nd Earl Talbot whose son also succeeded as
the 18th Earl of Shrewsbury. These robust chairs are designed in
the Roman or antique manner that was introduced around 1800
by the architect Charles Heathcote Tatham (d.1842). Their
reeded frames are enriched with the bacchic-lion ornament that is
appropriate for banqueting or dining-rooms. Their lion-
monopodiae derive from marble antiquities such as those from
Tatham's own collection that he assembled during his studies in
Rome in the mid-1790s. A closely related armchair pattern was
engraved in 1804 and published by Thomas Sheraton in his
Cabinet Encyclopaedia, 1805, pl. I.

Right:
A Pair of Regency ormolu-mounted and brass-inlaid Rosewood
Boulle Occasional Tables, inlaid in *premier* and *contre partie* (one
illustrated)
$29\frac{3}{4}$ in. (75.5 cm.) high; $22\frac{3}{4}$ in. (58 cm.) square
London, 18 November 1993, £84,000 ($123,984)

A Regency bronze-mounted and part-bronzed mahogany
Bookcase
101 in. (256 cm.) high; 122¼ in. (310 cm.) wide;
17½ in. (44.5 cm.) deep
London, 18 November 1993, £89,500 ($132,102)

This bookcase was designed in the early nineteenth-century
'antique' manner and includes many eloquent quotes from
antiquity; a scroll-pedimented cabinet and flanking cabinets with
'bust-plinth' pediments. Its reed-clustered pilasters support a
cornice that is carved with the poet's wreath between palm-
scrolled *thrysae*, and the doors' lozenged-compartments comprise
scroll-ended reeds bearing Egyptian lotus-buds. Those of the side
cabinets are centred by rosette-medallions binding crossed
thrysus-like reeds.

GILLOWS of Lancaster
A Set of twenty-four Regency mahogany open Armchairs
(one illustrated)
Sold on behalf of the Executors of the late Mrs. Helen Langford–
Brooke
Mere Hall, 23 May 1994, £210,500 ($317,855)
For an account of the Mere Hall sale see p.308

The Gilder Family Queen Anne carved walnut Desk-and–
Bookcase
Philadelphia, circa 1735
101 in. (256.5 cm.) high; $42\frac{1}{4}$ in. (107.3 cm.) wide;
24 in. (67 cm.) deep
New York, 22 January 1994, $345,500 (£230,949)

A Chippendale carved mahogany five-legged Card-Table
New York, 1760–80
27¾ in. (70.5 cm.) high; 34 in. (86.4 cm.) wide; 16¾ in. (42.5 cm.)
deep
New York, 23 October 1993, $123,500 (£83,446)

New York City craftsmen of the mid-eighteenth century produced regionally distinct five-legged card tables, such as this example, rather than the more standard four-legged tables made elsewhere in the Colonies. By 1771, New York was second only to Philadelphia in size and mercantile activity and the seaport community supported a wealthy clientele who wanted fashionable furnishings from local urban-trained craftsmen.

This is one of a small number of tables from an unidentified cabinet shop, which differs from related New York City tables in that the carving embodies characteristics associated with carving found on Philadelphia furniture. Indicative of the transient nature of craftsmen, the artisan who embellished this group may well have trained in Philadelphia and moved to New York where he began work with the cabinet-maker that produced this stylish table.

A William and Mary carved maple Armchair
New York, 1700–20
51½ in. (130.8 cm.) high; 27½ in. (69.8 cm.) wide;
18 in. (45.7 cm.) deep
New York, 22 June 1994, $79,500 (£51,961)

A Chippendale carved walnut high Chest of Drawers
Philadelphia, 1760–80
94 in. (238.8 cm.) high; 44 in. (111.2 cm.) wide;
23½ in. (59.7 cm.) deep
New York, 22 June 1994, $107,000 (£69,935)

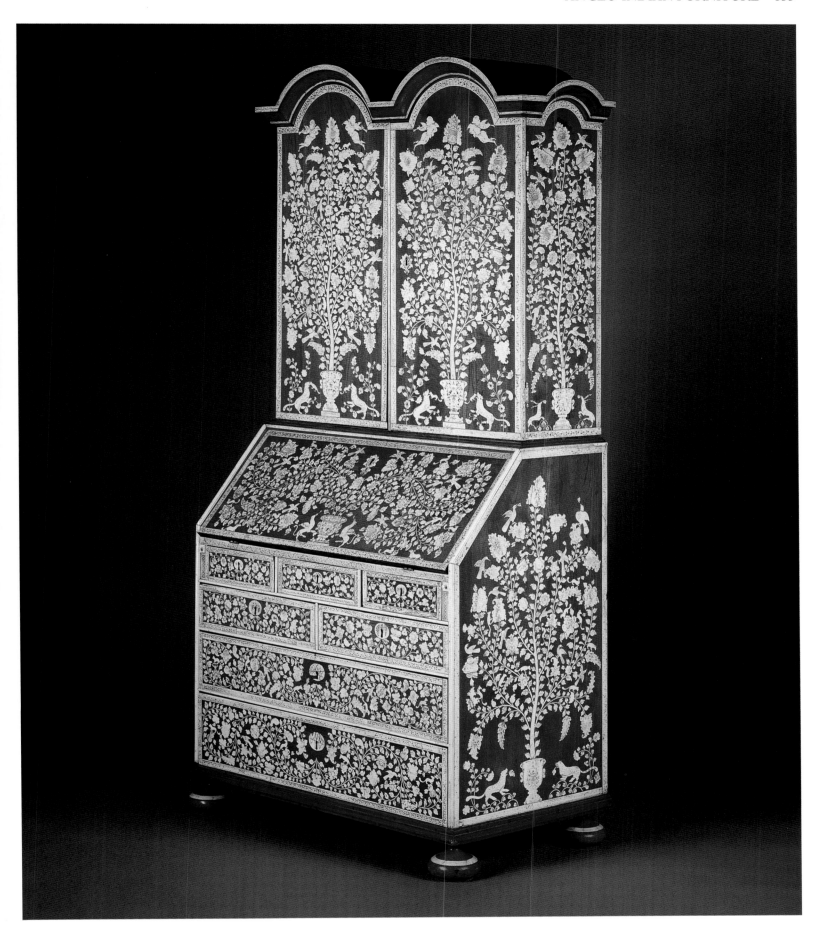

An Anglo-Indian mahogany Bureau-Cabinet
mid-18th Century
86 in. (218.5 cm.) high; 43 in. (109 cm.) wide;
24 in. (61 cm.) deep
London, 18 November 1993, £100,500 ($148,338)

The bureau-cabinet's design, with arched domes in the Louis
XIV manner, corresponds with early eighteenth-century English
examples in walnut or colourful japan. Its Dutch-style decoration
of flowering shrubs with birds, butterflies, exotic and mythical
animals and celebrating amorini with Fame's trumpet, derives
from seventeenth-century Indian Palampore cotton hangings.
Such exotic-veneered furniture, richly-inlaid with engraved
ivory, was commissioned through the East Indian Company
trading in Bengal and is particularly associated with Vizagapatam.

A Bruges Tapestry: a triumphal Procession
mid-16th Century
137 × 125 in. (345 × 316 cm.)
London, 19 May 1994, £54,300 ($81,830)

Right:
A Beauvais Tapestry, representing Sculpture and
Painting in the foreground, and Music and Poetry
beyond
late 17th/early 18th Century
$100\frac{1}{2}$ × 107 in. (251 × 267 cm.)
New York, 1 June 1994, $74,000 (£48,909)

RAPHAEL DE LA PLANCHE (French, active
circa 1625–70)
A Set of five Louis XIII Paris mythological
Tapestries from the Story of Diana, after Toussaint-
Dubrueil (Diana appealing to Jupiter for Vengeance
against Niobe illustrated)
(1561–1602)
circa 1633
136 × 198 in. (342 × 505 cm.)
New York, 11 January 1994, $230,000 (£154,155)

A LOUIS XV SAVONNERIE CARPET

by William Robinson

One look says it all: unabashed, bold, brilliant, powerful, regal. This carpet was not made for a court famed for its discretion or modesty. It embodies the supreme French confidence of the period. The intensity of colour, the power of the corner scrolls, and the abundance of the overflowing fruit and flowers are all made simply to serve as a background to the central dominance of the royal arms of the French king. The scale of the original, measuring nearly 6 metres square, further enhances the initial powerful impact of this outstanding carpet. It is not surprising that it easily outstripped any previous price paid at auction for a carpet.

In 1735, when the carpet was designed, France was at its height of power and influence within Europe. Louis XV had succeeded his great-grandfather, Louis XIV, 'Le Roi Soleil', at the age of five in 1715. In 1735 he was 25, in his prime, a young and powerful king who took a strong interest in the arts. Every design for a carpet produced at the Savonnerie had to go for royal approval before it could be woven and he was well-known for turning down compositions, the products of months of labour. Carpet designs that came through the royal veto were abundantly filled with the symbols of royalty, such as the French crown, the entwined mirrored letter 'L' for Louis, and the royal arms of three fleurs-de-lys on a blue ground that dominate the present composition. A slightly later design for four quarter carpets, worked to appear as a whole to present before the king, is in the French national archives. Before the royal presentation the Comte de Vandières had already noted two as being more suitable, yet only on one of these is noted the royal *bon, approuvé*. It was the one in which the fleur-de-lys was the most prominent. Furthermore, *bon* is noted against one that had not been selected by Vandières, but which was the only other one of the four to contain any direct symbol of royalty. If that was the criterion for royal approval, it is not surprising that the present design was very successful.

The design was prepared by Pierre-Josse Perrot. He is recorded as a designer for the royal *ateliers* in the fields of interior design, tapestry and in particular carpets. The earliest mention of his name is at the Gobelins Tapestry workshop in 1715, while the earliest carpet design by him, in conjunction with Blain de Fontenay the younger, is dated 1724. By the time the present carpet was designed, Perrot was undoubtedly the leading designer at the Savonnerie, producing cartoons many of which, like the present example, were re-woven a number of times due to their popularity with the king. The designs for most of the carpets woven at the Savonnerie between 1735 and 1750 can be attributed to him. Typical are the bold but controlled scrolling acanthus leaves executed in bright colours on a dark ground, which succeed similar but more subtly coloured motifs of the Louis XIV period. Also typical are the dense floral swags.

Once the design had achieved royal approval it was sent to the *Manufacture Royale de la Savonnerie*. This acquired its name having been established in 1630 in the premises of an old soap factory. The original foundation served the double purpose of producing highly prestigious carpets for the court, and providing employment at very cheap wages for orphans from the *Hôpital Général de Paris*. As part of the original foundation, the *Hôpital General* in its turn had control of the buildings at the Savonnerie. In 1673, after long battles between the *Hôpital* and the controller of the factory, Louis XIV assumed direct royal control, placing it in the charge of Colbert, the vigilant Minister of Finance. The twenty years after this were probably the most successful in the history of the factory. They were those in which the ninety-three massive carpets, each 354 in. (899 cm.) long, for the *Grand Galerie de la Palais du Louvre*, were woven. The production of these, more than anything else, ensured the lasting reputation of the Savonnerie.

For connoisseurs at the beginning of this century it was these Grand Galerie carpets, together with the thirteen carpets woven immediately before them for the *Galerie d'Apollon*, which were the greatest prizes to obtain for their collections. Today they are still equally respected. In the last year Christie's had sold two of the ninety-three examples, each lacking its end panels. The sixty-first or eighty-ninth of the series was sold in New York, 30 October 1993, for $660,000, while the ninety-first was sold in Monaco, 5 December 1993, for Fr.3,330,000. Enthusiasm for the more exuberantly coloured Louis XV carpets, not so great at the beginning of the century, was led by the Rothschilds during the furnishing of Waddesdon Manor, Buckinghamshire. In addition to the *Grand Galerie* carpets in their collection, they purchased no less than eight Louis XV carpets.

The first carpet woven from the Perrot cartoon which also served for the present example was delivered to the King's château of La Muette for use in the dining room in 1735. The second, delivered in 1740, was for use at the Château de Choisy. Further examples were made at later dates. Today, two examples are in French museums: one at the Château de Fontainbleau; a second, in poor condition, made with truncated corners, is now in the Nissim de Camondo Museum in Paris. A third was sold by the Earl of Roseberry through Christie's in 1939 and is now in the Cleveland, Ohio, Museum of Art. But it is the present example, due to its outstanding condition, which shows best the power of the original design and the intensity of colour. These are the factors which demonstrate why Perrot was the favourite designer for the king. Its drawing is slightly better controlled than that of the other three, indicating that it was one of the first to be delivered. In addition to this, it has spent generations in the owner's family folded in a cupboard under the stairs until discovered by Christie's. It has therefore survived with its original colours and with its full pile showing no trace of wear. Its record price for any carpet at auction was fully deserved.

A Louis XV Savonnerie Carpet
circa 1740–50
224 × 238 in. (567 × 603 cm.)
London, 9 June 1994, £1,321,500 ($1,994,144)
Record auction price for a carpet

A Louis XVI Carpet
Probably Aubusson or Beauvais
circa 1770–80
229 × 278 in. (581 × 706 cm.)
London, 9 June 1994, £573,500 ($865,412)

A Louis XIV Savonnerie Carpet
made for the Grand Gallerie du Louvre
circa 1682
$220\frac{1}{2} \times 133\frac{7}{8}$ in. (560×340 cm.)
Monaco, 5 December 1994, Fr. 3,330,000 (£378,624)

SILVER

THOMAS REHWENDT I (German, active 1670–1790)
A Pair of parcel-gilt silver Flasks
Berlin, circa 1690
engraved with the arms of Friedrich I as Elector of Brandenburg
$14\frac{1}{4}$ in. (36.2 cm.) high
(145 ozs.)
New York, 21 October 1993, $426,000 (£285,141)

GEORG KOBENHAUPT (German, active 1540–1586)
A Set of five parcel-gilt Beakers
with engraved scenes between silver-gilt bands engraved with
Latin and German inscriptions each relating to a sign of the
Zodiac
Strasbourg, circa 1570
3½ in. (9 cm.) high
(27 ozs.)
Geneva, 17 May 1994, SFr.377,500 (£176,319)

DIRK VAN DE GOORBERG (Dutch, 1747–1811)
A walnut and ebonised silver-mounted Tea-Casket
Delft, 1771
6½ in. (16.5 cm.) high; 9 in. (23 cm.) long
Amsterdam, 4 May 1994, Fl.66,700 (£23,907)

LORENZ BILLER II (German, 1649–1726)
A silver-gilt Ewer
Augsburg, 1708–10
overall height 14 in. (35.5 cm.)
(59 oz.)
Sold from the Estate of Mary, Viscountess Rothermere
New York, 14 April 1994, $63,000 (£42,712)

A silver-gilt Table Service
engraved with a coat-of-arms with coronet above with silver
blades
probably French or Portugese, second half 18th Century, with
later French control marks only
(323 ozs.)
Sold from the collection of M. Hubert de Givenchy
Monaco, 4 December 1993, Fr.4,440,000 (£504,832)

JEAN-BAPTISTE-CLAUDE ODIOT (French, 1763–1827)
A French Imperial silver-gilt Dish, Cover, Stand and Liner from
the Madame Mère Service
Paris, 1806
12¼ in. (31 cm.) high; the bowl 11 in. (28 cm.) diameter
(139 ozs.)
Geneva, 16 November 1993, SFr.421,500 (£189,694)

A Pair of James I Candlesticks
London, 1618, maker's mark CC tree between
8 in. (20.2 cm.) high
(26oz.)
Sold from the Estate of Mary, Viscountess Rothermere
New York, 14 April 1994, $211,500 (£143,390)

English silver candlesticks from before the Restoration are exceedingly rare although such simple utilitarian pieces must have been quite common at the time. The form is not, however, unique, for another example of virtually the same design, hallmarked for 1615 and with the maker's mark WC, is known which was formerly in the collection of Madame Gautret-Goldsmith and exhibited by Spink in 1975.

SILVER

THE HANOVER CHANDELIER

by Christopher Hartop

It was in Italy that Kent met Richard Boyle, 3rd Earl of Burlington who, recognising that his talents lay in architecture rather than painting, promoted his career. Burlington secured for him court commissions, such as that to decorate and furnish Kensington Palace for George I. It was through Burlington's influence that in 1726 Kent was appointed Master Carpenter of the King's Board of Works and in 1728 Inspector of Paintings. On 10 July 1735 he was promoted to the post of Master Mason and Deputy surveyor of the King's Works and in 1739 he became Portrait Painter to the King.

In view of Kent's standing at court, it is hardly surprising that he should have been commissioned to design chandeliers and other plate for the ruling Brunswick family's summer palace at Hanover. His festive decorations celebrating the marriage of the King's daughter Anne, the Princess Royal, in 1734 had been much admired for their 'very fine taste'.

Yet while Kent's genius in architecture, landscape gardening and ornamental design has been extensively explored, his designs for plate have received little attention. In 1744 John Vardy, Kent's clerk in the Office of Works, published *Some Designs of Mr. Inigo Jones and Mr. William Kent* which includes fourteen designs for silver articles, including the present chandelier. Doubtless Vardy's intention was for Kent to be seen as the worthy successor to Jones, whose work had been so lauded by Burlington.

Interestingly, the connection between Kent's 'Chandelier for the King' included in Vardy's book and the silver chandeliers made for George II was not pointed out until 1954, when Francis Johnson drew attention to it in a letter to *Country Life*.

Documents studied by Ellenor Alcorn in the Niedersächsisches Hauptstaatsarchiv include a contract dated 20 January 1737 directing Balthasar Friedrich Behrens, a Hanover silversmith, to make a pair of silver chandeliers after a wooden model which presumably, like Kent's design, was sent to Hanover from England.

The pair of chandeliers was delivered to the court on 3 September, 1736. The King, staying at Herrenhausen at the time, was sufficiently pleased with them to order a further three, for which Behrens was provided with an additional 364 pounds of silver. The additional chandeliers were delivered the following November.

The finished chandeliers differ very slightly from Kent's published designs and it is clear that either certain modifications had to be made to translate the design into silver or that the design was simplified by the engraver for the sake of clarity. For example, the central baluster standard has been extended to run the whole length of the chandelier to allow the addition of a strengthening iron rod. Similarly, the sphynx have been given more solid platforms on which to rest.

The chandeliers incorporate a number of key elements in Kent's Palladianism, most of which he absorbed during his sojourns in Italy. The ease with which he appears to handle plastic concepts such as silver design suggest that he may have been influenced by the work of Filippo Juvara, a member of the celebrated Sicilian family of goldsmiths and designers, whom he

may have met while in Rome. On the King's chandelier, the Hanoverian badge of a prancing horse is united with youthful genii amidst fruit garlands. Their commissioning came at a time when Hanover had suddenly acquired new prominence at the English court as the King was paying unusual attention to his German principality.

Whether the King had already commissioned Kent to design the chandeliers while he was still in Hanover, or whether he waited until he returned to England is uncertain. Kent worked extensively for Queen Caroline, designing architectural follies for her in the grounds of Kensington Palace and at Richmond, as well as designing the Queen's Library at St. James's Palace in 1736. 'A Silver Standish for the Late Queen in Merlin's Cave' was included in Vardy's book of plates and was evidently made for the Queen's garden retreat at Richmond.

No doubt pleased with the chandeliers, the King gave Behrens further orders for silver: following the delivery of the last chandelier in November 1737. Most of Behrens's surviving work is in the plain style, with emphasis on line rather than ornament, that was so popular in England during the first part of the eighteenth century and, like the chandeliers themselves, his work is always of the highest standard of execution. In 1739 Behrens was created Court Goldsmith, a post he held until his death in 1760 at the age of fifty-nine.

George II was succeeded in 1760 by his grandson as George III who never during the course of his sixty-year reign visited his German possessions, although in 1814 he assumed the title of King of Hanover. The Royal chandeliers were, however, brought to England in 1803 and hung at Windsor Castle. The archives at Hanover record their shipment by way of St. Petersburg, no doubt to avoid the Napoleonic threat on the Continent. Three of the chandeliers were hung in the Ballroom, or Queen's Gallery and the remaining two in the adjoining room, the Queen's Drawing Room. The chandeliers appear in W. Wild's watercolour view of Windsor which were published in W.H. Pynes's *Royal Residences* in 1816 and 1817. By then however the chandeliers had already been returned to Herrenhausen where the Duke of Cambridge, the youngest son of George III, was Governor-General.

In 1924 a significant portion of the Hanoverian plate was offered for sale privately. Much of the English silver was purchased by the Vienna dealer Gluckselig and subsequently sold by the London dealers Crichton Brothers. The chandeliers were purchased by the dealer Elkan Silverman on 25 September 1924. Their subsequent history is unknown; they were not exhibited with much of the rest of the silver at Crichton Brothers and appear to have been sold privately. Two of the set appeared on the London market in 1937 and were the subject of an article in *The Connoisseur* by W. W. Watts, former Keeper of Metalwork at the Victoria and Albert Museum. These appear to be the pair which were purchased by Lord Fairhaven to hang in the library at Anglesey Abbey, his house in Cambridge which is now the property of the National Trust. Another of the set was purchased by the Museum of Fine Arts, Boston, in 1985.

BALTHASAR FRIEDRICH BEHRENS (German, 1701–1760)
George II's silver Chandelier, designed by William Kent
Hanover, 1736–37
46 in. (117 cm.) high
Sold from the collection of M. Hubert de Givenchy
Monaco, 4 December 1993, Fr.19,980,000 (£2,271,745)
Record auction price for silver

GABRIEL FELLING, (British, active 1676–1714)
A William III provincial 'Whistle' Tankard
Bruton, circa 1695
marked on body, cover and handle with maker's mark
6¾ in. (17 cm.) high
(24 ozs.)
London, 13 July 1994, £54,300 ($85,088)

Right:
DAVID WILLAUME I (British, 1658–1741)
A George I two-handled octagonal Wine Cooler
London, 1718, Britannia Standard
7½ in. (18.5 cm.) high
(104 ozs.)
London, 10 November 1993, £133,500 ($196,379)

PETER ARCHAMBO (British, d.1767)
A George II silver-gilt Salver engraved with the cypher of
George, 2nd Earl of Warrington (1675–1758)
London, 1732
10½ in. (27 cm.) diameter
(41 ozs.)
London, 13 July 1994, £29,900 ($46,853)

Left:
WILLIAM CRIPPS, (British, d.1767)
A George II Epergne
London, 1754
marked on frame, bowl, dishes and two
branches
$11\frac{1}{4}$ in. (28.5 cm.) high
(188 ozs.)
London, 13 July 1994, £27,600
($43,249)

PAUL DE LAMERIE (British,
1688–1751)
A George II Salver
London, 1742
$19\frac{3}{4}$ in. (50 cm.) diameter
(105 ozs.)
New York, 14 April 1994, $145,000
(£98,305)

Above:
PAUL STORR (British, 1771–1844)
A George III circular 'Ragout' Dish,
Cover and Liner
London, 1801
15 in. (38 cm.) long
(71 ozs.)
London, 10 November 1993, £25,300
($37,216)

Right:
JOHN BRIDGE (British, 1755–1849)
A George IV silver-gilt presentation
Tankard
engraved on one side with the Royal
arms, Garter motto and crown and, on
the other side, with the Royal badge
within the Garter, the front engraved
'Royal Yacht Club Cowes 1827'
London, 1827
$13\frac{1}{2}$ in. (34 cm.) high
(99 oz.)
New York, 21 October 1993, $68,500
(£45,850)

ROBERT GARRARD II (British, 1793–1881)
The Howe Garniture comprising a large silver mounted mirror
plateau and pair of seven–light candelabra, 1839/40, bearing the
arms or cypher of Queen Adelaide, Consort of King William IV,
and a ten light candelabrum, 1852, applied with the arms of
Richard, 1st Earl Howe
London, 1839–40 and 1852
(total weighable silver 1,659 ozs.)
New York, 14 April 1994, $277,500 (£188,136)

This Victorian table garniture was presented by Queen Adelaide
to Earl Howe.

JOHN BRIDGE (British, 1755–1849)
and ROBERT GARRARD II (British, 1793–1881)
Two silver-gilt double decanter Trolleys
one with maker's mark of John Bridge, London, 1828, the other
with that of Robert Garrard, London, 1849
20¾ in. (52.5 cm.) long overall
(220 ozs.)
London, 11 May 1994, £72,000 ($107,208)

BENJAMIN SMITH III (British, 1793–1850)
A Pair of George IV silver-gilt Wine Coolers
London, 1826
10¾ in. (27.5 cm.) high
(302 ozs.)
London, 2 March 1994, £62,000 ($92,070)

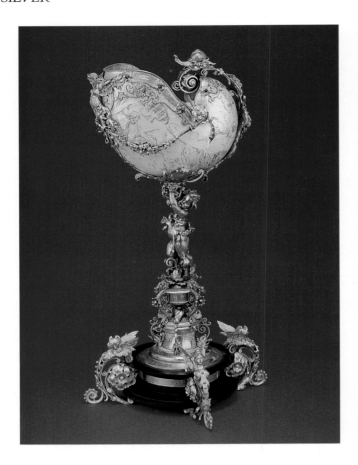

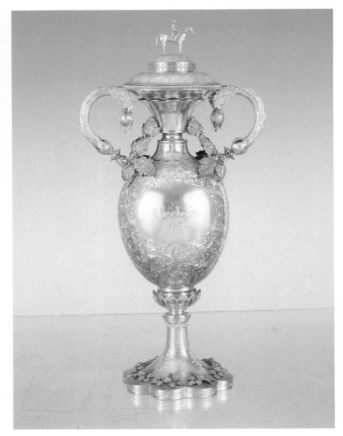

Top, from left:
A 17th Century-style parcel-gilt Nautilus Cup,
designed by Hermann Götz for E.D. Wollenweber,
Germany
late 19th Century
18¼ in. (46.5 cm.) high
Amsterdam, 1 December 1993, Fl.95,450 (£33,491)

EDWARD FRANCIS ANTONIUS FISCHER (Australian,
active 1855–1885)
The Geelong Cup, an Australian gold two-handled racing Cup
and Cover
1879, applied mark 'E.FISCHER/GEELONG'
13¾ in. (35 cm.) high
(21.4 ozs.)
Sydney, 19 August 1993, A.$143,000 (£69,269)

Left:
ROBERT GARRARD II (British, 1793–1881)
A set of four Victorian figural Salts
London, 1877
height of tallest 7 in. (17.8 cm.)
(67 ozs.)
London, 11 May 1994, £25,300 ($37,672)

Above:
GORHAM MANUFACTURING CO.
A Martele Flagon, designed by William C. Codman for the Paris
Exposition of 1900
maker's mark of Gorham Manufacturing Co., Providence, 1900
marked with Gorham sample mark 4294 in oval; cover and
handle also with French control marks
15⅝ in. (39.7 cm.) high
(77 ozs.)
New York, 21 January 1994, $96,000 (£64,171)

PORTRAIT MINIATURES

Left:
HEINRICH FRIEDRICH FÜGER (Austrian,1751–1818)
Tsarina Catherine the Great of Russia (1729–1796)
signed and dated 1796
$3\frac{5}{8}$ in. (8.9 cm) diameter
Geneva, 18 May 1994, Sfr.74,750 (£34,913)

IGNAZIO PIO VITTORIANO CAMPANA
(Italian, 1744–1786)
Queen Marie-Antoinette of France (1755–1793)
$2\frac{3}{4}$ in. (6.6 cm) diameter
Geneva, 16 November 1993, Sfr.57,500 (£25,877)

LUC SICARDI (French, 1746–1825)
A young Lady
signed and dated 1789
$2\frac{7}{8}$ in. (6.9 cm) diameter
Geneva, 18 May 1993, Sfr.69,000 (£32,227)

Right:
SAMUEL COOPER (British, 1609–1672)
A Lady
on vellum
signed with monogram
oval, 3in. (7.5cm.) high
London, 10 November 1993, £23,000 ($33,833)

OZIAS HUMPHRY, R.A. (British, 1742–1810)
Sir Elijah Impey (1732–1809)
gold frame with plaited hair surround, diamond set bandings
and ribbon cresting, the reverse with plaited hair and diamond
set initials 'E.I.'
oval, $1\frac{1}{2}$ in. (3.8cm.) high
London, 10 November 1993, £10,925 ($16,071)
Sir Elijah Impey was Chief Justice of India in 1773–1789.

RICHARD COSWAY, R.A. (British, 1742–1821)
A young Girl
The gold frame with plaited hair on the reverse
oval, $2\frac{7}{8}$in. (7.3cm.) high
London, 10 November 1993, £12,650 ($18,608)

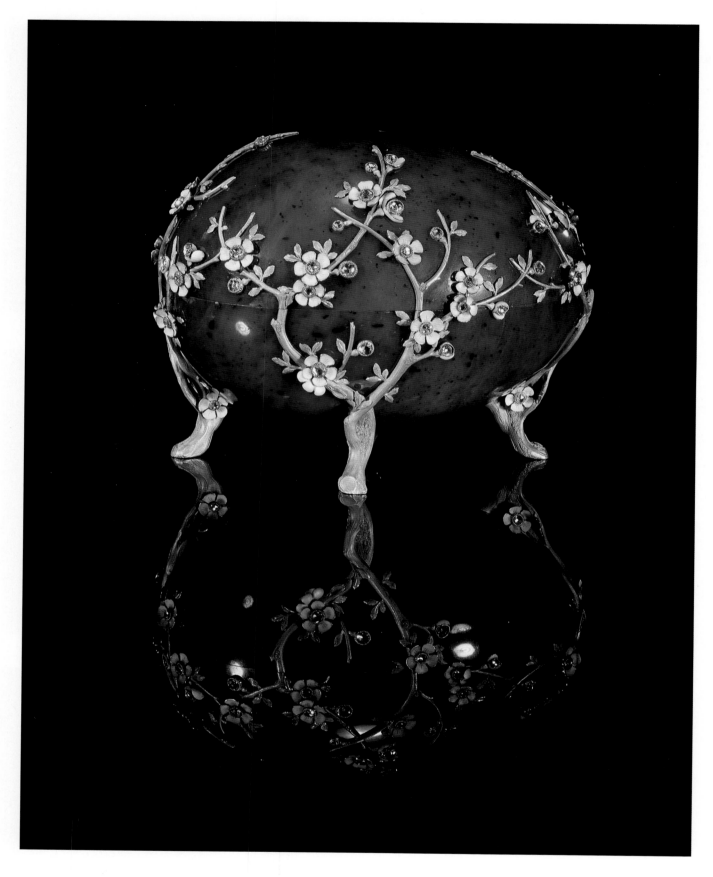

FABERGÉ
workmaster Michael Perchin (1860–1903)
An 'Apple Blossom' enamel, four colour gold-mounted nephrite
Easter Egg
St. Petersburg, 1901
$5\frac{1}{2}$ in. (14 cm.) long
Geneva, 17 May 1994, S.Fr.1,213,500 (£566,791)

FABERGÉ
A 'Noble Ice' jewelled enamel, platinum and silver mounted
Easter Egg and Surprise Watch
unmarked, St. Petersburg, circa 1910
the egg $3\frac{7}{8}$ in. (9.9 cm.) long; the watch $2\frac{3}{8}$ in. (6 cm.) high
Geneva, 17 May 1994, S.Fr.311,500 (£145,493)

FABERGÉ
workmaster Henrik Wigström (1862–1923)
A jewelled, guilloche enamel, nephrite gold-mounted Parasol
Handle
St. Petersburg, 1908–17
$3\frac{5}{8}$ in. (9.3 cm.) high
Geneva, 17 November 1993, S.Fr.201,500 (£90,684)

FABERGÉ
workmaster Michael Perchin (1860–1903)
A large jewelled, enamel and silver-gilt mounted carved
bowenite Model of an Elephant with a Howdah
St. Petersburg, circa 1890
the fitted case $8\frac{7}{8}$ in. (22.5 cm.) high; $8\frac{7}{8}$ in. (22.5 cm.) long
Geneva, 17 May 1994, S.Fr.157,500 (£73,564)

JEWELLERY

THE ARCHDUKE JOSEPH DIAMOND

by Raymond Sancroft-Baker

The sale last May in Geneva of the Archduke Joseph Diamond was a special occasion for several reasons. It is rare to find so large a diamond, 78.54 carats, being offered for sale and especially so when it is D colour, the highest possible grade. It had a few minor blemishes and was therefore given a clarity grading of SI1 (slight inclusion 1) but sold with a drawing which indicated that, if re-cut, it could be made flawless. What also made this an exceptional diamond was that it almost certainly came for the Golconda mines which were in the Indian state of Hyderabad. It is very difficult to put into words what separates a Golconda diamond from any other; only when one compares one stone with another can one fully appreciate the subtle differences that make these Indian stones so desirable. They seem to have a transparency and an innate purity that is lacking in other diamonds and were found in the alluvial gravels of river banks or areas that once contained rivers that flowed thousands of years ago. Diamonds were known in India as early as 600 B.C. and tended to be exported through the port of Alexandria. The Alexandrian astronomer Ptolemy, circa 150 B.C., wrote of the 'diamond rivers in India'.

Tavernier, the great seventeenth-century traveller, visited a number of these mines in the 1650s and most of what we know today is due to his accounts. The best known mines were at Kollur in the southern part of the kingdom of Golconda. It was in this region that some of the most famous diamonds have been found, including the Koh-i-Noor, the Regent, and the Tavernier Blue. It is said that over fifty thousand people of all ages and sexes were at work on the south bank looking for the chance to discover their fortune, or more likely someone else's fortune!

This wonderful stone, so full of character and life, derives its name from its first recorded owner, Joseph August Victor Clemence Maria, Archduke of Austria and Palatinate of Hungary, the great grandson of Emperor Leopold II of the House of Habsburg. Archduke Joseph August (1872–1962), had a distinguished military career becoming a Field Marshal during the First World War. He was subsequently named first Regent of Hungary, a position he held until he was forced to abdicate by the Allies. When Hungary was occupied by the Soviet Union at the end of the Second World War he emigrated to America.

It is believed that the Archduke gave the diamond to his son Joseph Francis (1895–1957), and records show that it was deposited in the vault of the Hungarian General Credit Bank in 1933 and sold in 1936. This was, therefore, the first time for nearly sixty years that this exceptional stone had been offered for sale.

Needless to say it attracted widespread interest and was sold for S.Fr.9,683,500 (£4,357,575), to be re-cut once again, re-set and enjoyed by a new, very privileged owner.

The Archduke Joseph Diamond
78·54 carats
D colour and SI1
Geneva, 18 November 1993, S.Fr.9,683,500 (£4,357,575)

Archduke Joseph August

Clockwise, from top left:

A Pair of fancy coloured diamond Ear
Pendants
Geneva, 18 November 1993,
S.Fr.2,687,500 (£1,209,375)

An unmounted cushion-shaped fancy
light green Diamond
5.30 carats
London, 22 June 1994, £287,500
($442,750)

An unmounted rectangular-cut fancy
intense yellow Diamond
11.93 carats
Geneva, 19 May 1994, S.Fr.971,500
(£456,605)

A fancy light pink and light pink
diamond two stone Brooch
12.76 carats in total
London, 22 June 1994, £419,500
($646,030)

A Pair of diamond cluster Ear Pendants
Geneva, 18 November 1993, S.Fr.
207,000 (£93,150)

A rectangular-cut fancy intense yellow
diamond Ring
3.66 carats
New York, 8 December 1993, $145,500
(£97,485)

An unmounted pear-shaped fancy
purplish pink Diamond
10.83 carats
Geneva, 18 November 1993,
S.Fr.6,163,500 (£2,773,575)

An unmounted pear-shaped fancy pink
Diamond
6.32 carats
New York, 19 October 1993, $1,047,500
(£701,825)

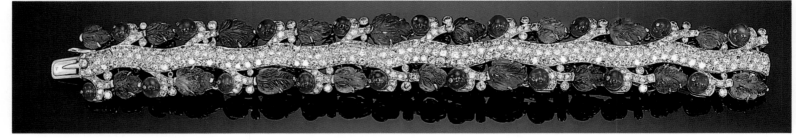

Inset, Left:
A Victorian emerald and
diamond Brooch
the emerald 5.81 carats
London, 8 December 1993,
£91,700 ($142,135)

A Pair of emerald and diamond Earclips
Geneva, 19 May 1994, S.Fr.289,500 (£136,065)

VAN CLEEF & ARPELS
An emerald and diamond pendant Necklace
Geneva, 19 May 1994, S.Fr.421,500 (£198,105)

An Art Deco emerald, ruby, diamond and enamel Bracelet
circa 1925
Geneva, 19 May 1994, S.Fr.201,500 ($94,705)

Inset, Right:
CARTIER
An emerald single stone Ring
Geneva, 18 November 1993,
S.Fr.190,500 (£85,725)

Top, from left:
An emerald and diamond Jabot Pin
circa 1920
London, 8 December 1993, £36,700 ($56,885)

A rectangular-cut emerald and diamond Ring
the emerald 33.97 carats
New York, 19 October 1993, $145,500 (£97,485)

BULGARI
A Pair of emerald and diamond Ear Pendants
Geneva, 19 May 1994, S.Fr.36,800 (£17,296)

Centre, from left:
VAN CLEEF & ARPELS
A Pair of emerald and diamond Ear Pendants
Geneva, 19 May 1994, S.Fr.190,500 (£89,535)

VAN CLEEF & ARPELS
An emerald and diamond sunflower Brooch
New York, 19 October 1993, $74,000 (£49,580)

VAN CLEEF & ARPELS
A ruby, sapphire, emerald and diamond Bracelet
circa 1930
London, 8 December 1993, £69,700 ($108,035)

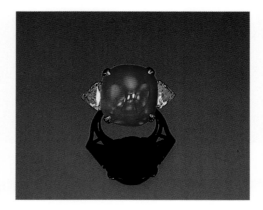

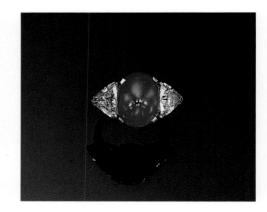

Top, from left:
A Pair of ruby and diamond Earclips
New York, 12 April 1994, $464,500 (£315,860)

VAN CLEEF & ARPELS
A Pair of invisibly-set ruby and diamond Earclips
New York, 8 December 1993, $77,300 (£51,791)

Centre:
An Art Deco ruby and diamond Bracelet
circa 1935
Geneva, 18 November 1993, S.Fr.74,750 (£33,637)

Above, from left:
CHAUMET
A Burmese ruby single-stone Ring
12.05 carats
Geneva, 19 May 1994, S.Fr.377,500 (£177,425)

VAN CLEEF & ARPELS
A Burmese ruby and diamond Ring
24.26 carats
Geneva, 19 May 1994, S.Fr.333,500 (£156,745)

A Burmese ruby and diamond Ring
9.95 carats
Geneva, 19 May 1994, S.Fr.108,000 (£50,760)

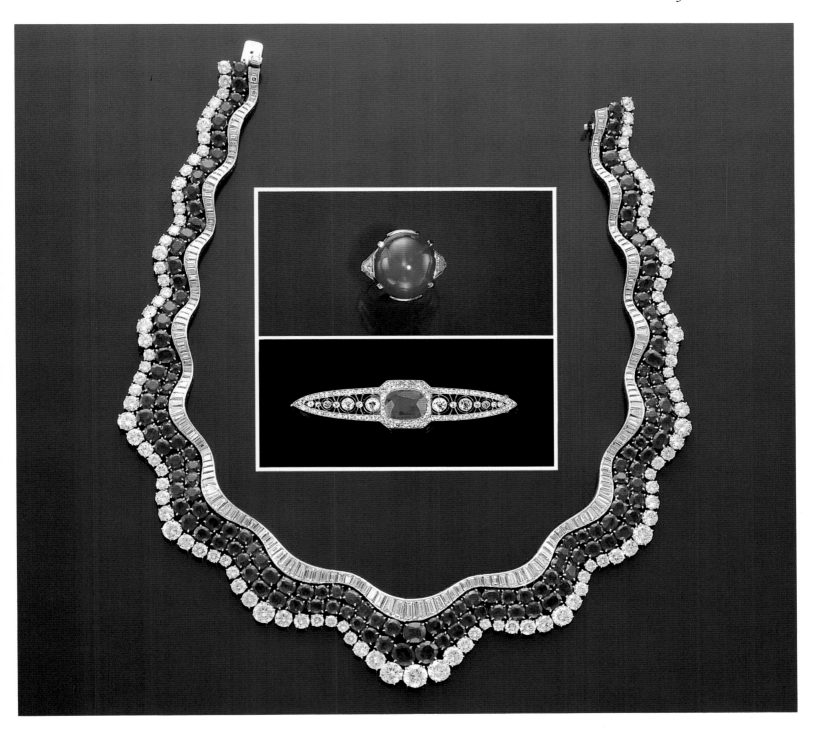

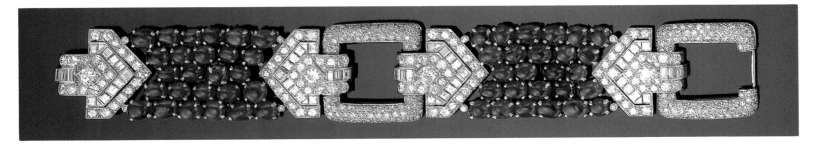

WINSTON
A Burmese ruby and diamond Necklace
New York, 12 April 1994, $244,500 (£166,260)

An Art Deco cabochon ruby and diamond Bracelet
circa 1935
New York, 8 December 1993, $46,000 (£30,820)

Inset from top:
WINSTON
A Burmese star ruby and diamond Ring
the ruby 26.40 carats
New York, 12 April 1994, $1,080,500 (£734,740)

A Burmese ruby and diamond Brooch
circa 1920
London, 22 June 1994, £26,450 ($40,733)

A diamond Necklace
New York, 12 April 1994, $162,000
(£110,160)

WINSTON
A Pair of diamond Ear Pendants
the pear-shaped drops weighing 15.24
and 16.80 carats, both D colour
St. Moritz, 17 February 1994,
S.Fr.1,983,500 (£932,245)

Above:
VAN CLEEF & ARPELS
A Pair of diamond Ear Pendants
the pear-shaped drops weighing 19.43
and 19.16 carats, both D colour
Geneva, 18 November 1993,
S.Fr.3,413,500 (£1,536,075)

Left:
BULGARI
A sapphire and diamond clip Brooch
St. Moritz, 17 February 1994,
S.Fr.102,500 (£48,175)

A rectangular-cut diamond Ring
19.43 carats, D colour and VVS2
Geneva, 19 May 1994, S.Fr.1,213,500
(£570,345)

A rectangular-cut diamond Ring
20.54 carats, D colour and flawless
New York, 19 October 1993, $1,267,500
(£849,225)

A rectangular-cut diamond Ring
20.11 carats, E colour and VS1
New York, 12 April 1994, $662,500
(£450,500)

WINSTON
A pear-shaped diamond Ring
12.03 carats, D colour and VVS2
Geneva, 19 May 1994, S.Fr.531,500
(£249,805)

A marquise-cut diamond Ring
17.11 carats, D colour and VS1
New York, 12 April 1994, $431,500
(£293,420)

A pear-shaped diamond Ring
30.33 carats, D colour and VVS1
New York, 12 April 1994, $1,058,500
(£719,780)

A cushion-shaped diamond Ring
23.48 carats
St. Moritz, 17 February 1994, S.Fr.509,500
(£239,465)

An unmounted oval-cut Diamond
20.32 carats, D colour and flawless
Geneva, 18 November 1993, S.Fr.1,323,500
(£595,575)

Top:
The Wellington Koo Necklace
An Imperial jadeite bead Sautoir
Hong Kong, 2 May 1994,
H.K.$6,950,000 (£593,408)

A Pair of jadeite and diamond Earrings
Hong Kong, 2 May 1994,
H.K.$2,220,000 (£189,549)

Above, from left:
A carved jadeite Plaque
Hong Kong, 2 May 1994, H.K.$1,890,000
(£161,372)

A Pair of jadeite Earrings
Hong Kong, 2 May 1994, H.K.$570,000
(£48,668)

A jadeite and diamond Buddha Pendant
Hong Kong, 2 May 1994, H.K.$592,000
(£50,546)

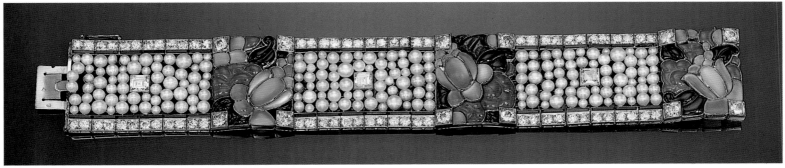

Top, from left:
CARTIER
An Art Deco diamond, white and grey pearl Sautoir
circa 1925
Geneva, 19 May 1994, S.Fr.245,500 (£115,385)

CARTIER
A pearl Ring, circa 1920
Geneva, 19 May 1994, S.Fr.34,500 (£16,215)

CARTIER
A Pair of diamond and pearl Ear Pendants
Geneva, 19 May 1994, S.Fr.179,500 (£84,365)

Centre:
VAN CLEEF & ARPELS
A Pair of sapphire and diamond Earclips
Geneva, 19 May 1994, S.Fr.174,000 (£81,780)

WINSTON
A cabochon sapphire and diamond Ring
42.98 carats
New York, 12 April 1994, $107,000 (£72,760)

LINZELER & MARCHAK
An Art Deco gem set, pearl and diamond Bracelet
circa 1925
Geneva, 19 May 1994, S.Fr.74,750 (£35,132)

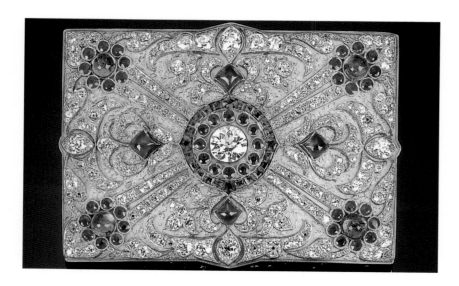

Clockwise, from top left:
BOUCHERON
A gem set belt Buckle
circa 1920
London, 22 June 1994, £24,150 ($37,191)

CARTIER
An Art Deco coral and gem set Vanity Case
circa 1927
New York, 19 October 1993, $189,500 (£126,965)

CARTIER
An Art Deco lacquer, enamel and gem set Vanity Case
circa 1927
Geneva, 19 May 1994, S.Fr.74,750 (£35,132)

LACLOCHE
An Art Deco coral and diamond Bracelet
circa 1925
London, 22 June 1994, £8,625 ($13,282)

CARTIER
A coral and diamond chimera Bangle
London, 22 June 1994, £38,900 ($59,906)

BOURDIER
An Art Deco coral, jade and enamel Vanity Case
circa 1930
Geneva, 18 November 1993, S.Fr.74,750 (£33,637)

Right:
CARTIER
An Art Deco coral, enamel and gem set Desk Clock
circa 1925
Geneva, 19 May 1994, S.Fr.113,500 (£53,345)

CARTIER
A rock crystal, mother of pearl, diamond and onyx "model A"
Mystery Clock
circa 1930
Geneva, 19 May 1994, S.Fr.322,500 (£151,575)

Top:
An Edwardian diamond Necklace
circa 1910
London, 22 June 1994, £144,500 ($222,530)

Above, from left:
TIFFANY
A diamond and enamel daffodil Brooch
New York, 8 December 1993, $13,800 (£9,246)

TIFFANY
A diamond, enamel and ruby orchid Brooch
circa 1889
New York, 12 April 1994, $101,500 (£69,020)

An antique diamond flower Brooch
circa 1860
New York, 19 October 1993, $34,500 (£23,115)

Top:
A Kashmir sapphire and diamond pendant Necklace
the sapphire 107.28 carats
Geneva, 18 November 1993, S.Fr.707,500 (£318,375)

Top, Inset:
BULGARI
A sapphire and diamond cluster Brooch
From the collection of the late Audrey Hepburn
Geneva, 18 November 1993, S.Fr.91,500 (£41,175)

Inset, centre, from left:
SCHLUMBERGER
A sapphire and diamond Ring
London, 22 June 1994, £32,200 ($49,588)

VAN CLEEF & ARPELS
An invisibly-set sapphire and diamond flower Brooch
New York, 19 October 1993, $79,500 (£53,265)

A sapphire and diamond line Bracelet
Geneva, 19 May 1994, S.Fr.421,500 (£198,105)

EUROPEAN CERAMICS

MAIOLICA FROM THE COLLECTION OF ARTHUR M. SACKLER

by Jody Wilkie

In the seventeen years that I have been at Christie's, I have had the privilege of handling the sale of some superb objects, several of which are now in museum collections. But if asked to name the single most exciting moment of my career to date, it would have to be the moment my colleague Alice Duncan and I were first let into 'The Enclave' to evaluate the Sackler maiolica for sale at auction. There – spread out on every available flat surface – were what seemed like hundreds of pieces of pottery painted with crushed gem stones, so rich were the colours vibrating under the florescent glow of the warehouse lights.

In fact, there were just under one hundred and fifty pieces of Renaissance pottery – everything from small salts to enormous chargers and wine cisterns – all decorated in the same limited palette of blue, green, yellow, ochre and manganese and all shimmering under the lustred or highly glazed surfaces for which the potters of the sixteenth, seventeenth and eighteenth centuries are justly renowned.

Arthur M. Sackler, a research scientist, entrepreneur, and one of America's premier art collectors and patrons, assembled his collection between 1979 and 1982, with pristine condition as a primary concern. He viewed it as the missing link between his formidable collections of European terracottas and those of ceramics from Ancient Greece, Rome, the Middle East and the Far East. Taken as a whole, these collections form a record of the potter's art throughout history – one of Dr. Sackler's goals in forming his collections.

The whimsy and freshness of maiolica painting – especially on wares produced in and around the Duchy of Urbino, the Veneto, the Marches and Tuscany in the sixteenth century and at Castelli in the seventeenth and eighteenth centuries – is readily apparent in the Sackler Collection. Many dated examples serve as anchors in attributing and documenting whole classes of wares. The superior quality of the maiolica in the Arthur M. Sackler Collection, the fineness of its painting, the variety of the shapes included and the large number of workshops whose production is represented enable the collection to serve as an invaluable teaching aid for the student of European ceramics.

In the early 1430s, Italian pottery was revolutionised. Almost overnight, the useful pottery widely produced in Tuscany evolved from the simple to the grandiose. In the process, maiolica (as it was coming to be called) lost its overly useful function while retaining its traditional shapes. Pharmacy drug-jars and dishes in a variety of sizes remained the staple products, but were soon used for display, lined along the walls of the grander pharmacies and amassed on the richly carved chests or *cassoni* found in the houses of the prosperous Tuscans of the day.

Colour was a key element in all Italian Renaissance art. Painters of maiolica, however, worked under conditions very different from the conventional masters. Their colours, limited in range to begin with, changed dramatically with the firing process. But once fired, the colours of maiolica do not change; the painted image remains exactly as it left the kiln, giving this artform a unique vitality.

With the development of richly pigmented glazes and metallic lustres, the maiolica workshops of artists such as Giogio Andreoli, Nicola da Urbino, Francesco Zanto Avelli da Rovigo, Orazio Fontana, Domenico da Venezia, the Patanazzi family and the Grue family were able to produce wares of a brilliance and intensity previously unknown on European ceramics. Their work can be broadly divided into two categories: *istoriato* wares painted with mythological, biblical and historic subjects, and wares painted with the decorative vocabulary of the sixteenth century such as grotesque beasts, military and musical trophies and stylized arabesques.

Selections from the maiolica collection were exhibited at the National Gallery of Art, Washington D.C. (September 1982–January 1983) and at the Museums of Fine Art, Palace of the Legion of Honour, San Francisco, California (July 1986–8). Unlike the other collections formed by Dr. Sackler, with the exception of a small pamphlet published in conjunction with the Washington, D.C. show, no comprehensive catalogue of the maiolica collection was ever published. It is my hope that the identification in the sale catalogues of each red Sackler registration number will help to track these pieces over the coming years as having been part of this wonderful assemblage of Renaissance ceramics put together by an extraordinary man.

An Urbino allegorical Istoriato Tondo
painted with an allegory of The Sack of Rome by Francesco
Xanto Avelli da Rovigo
circa 1527–30
$10\frac{3}{8}$ in. (26.3 cm.) diameter
Sold from the collection of Arthur M. Sackler
New York, 6 October 1993, $140,000 (£92,400)

An Urbino *Istoriato* Charger
painted with the Rape of Helen by Nicola da Urbino
circa 1535
$20\frac{3}{8}$ in. (51.8 cm.) diameter
Sold from the collection of Arthur M. Sackler
New York, 6 October 1993, $134,000 (£88,779)

Right:
An Urbino *Istoriato* Vasque
painted with the Contest between the Muses and the
Pierides in the workshop of Orazio Fontana
circa 1550
$9\frac{1}{2}$ in. (24 cm.) high; $19\frac{1}{4}$ in. (48.9 cm.) wide
Sold from the collection of Arthur M. Sackler
New York, 6 October 1993, $178,500 (£117,812)

A Pair of Pedestal Salts
16th Century
School of Fontainebleau, from the circle of
Bernard Palissy
6 in. (15.2 cm.) high
Sold from the collection of Arthur M. Sackler
New York, 1 June 1994, $36,800 (£24,323)

A Meissen White Ewer (*Untierkrug*) for the Japanese Palace, Dresden
blue crossed swords mark, circa 1732
23½ in. (58 cm.) high
Sold from the collection of the late Siegfried and Lola Kramarsky
New York, 30 October 1993, $277,500 (£186,242)

Right:
A Böttger polished red stoneware octagonal Teapot and Cover
Meissen, impressed former's mark of Peter Geithner, circa 1715
6½ in. (16.5 cm.) wide
Sold from the collection of the late Siegfried and Lola Kramarsky
New York, 30 October 1993, $123,500 (£82,886)

A Böttger porcelain Jug with Hausmalerei decoration
Meissen, circa 1720
10 in. (25.5 cm.) high
Sold from the collection of the late Siegfried and Lola Kramarsky
New York, 30 October 1993, $112,500 (£75,503)

A Meissen Coffee-Pot and Cover
blue crossed swords mark, circa 1735
10 in. (25.5 cm) high
Sold from the collection of the late Siegfried and Lola Kramarsky
New York, 30 October 1993, $96,000 (£64,430)

An Ansbach faience hexagonal Vase
manganese L mark to base, circa 1730
11 in. (28 cm.) high
Sold from the collection of the late Siegfried and Lola Kramarsky
New York, 30 October 1993, $72,900 (£48,926)

Left:
A Berlin Garniture of five blue-ground
'Munich' Vases
blue sceptre marks, incised lines, 1834
one $30\frac{3}{4}$ in. (78 cm.) high, one pair 24 in.
(61 cm.) high and one pair 20 in. (51 cm.) high
London, 11 October 1993, £243,500
($374,016)

A Meissen Pair of Parrots modelled by
J. J. Kändler
Pressnummern 26, circa 1745
$7\frac{1}{2}$ in. (19 cm.) high
London, 11 October 1993, £29,900 ($45,926)

A Sèvres Plate, the centre painted with
Papiers peints/Impression et Satinage
printed blue interlaced C mark enclosing
fleurs-de-lys above Sèvres/28, 1820–35
$9\frac{1}{4}$ in. (23.5 cm.) diameter
London, 14 June 1994, £33,350 ($50,692)

A Staffordshire slipware Royal armorial deep
Charger by William Talor
circa 1685
$13\frac{3}{8}$ in. (44 cm.) diameter
London, 7 June 1994, £20,700 ($31,132)

A Chelsea Group of *La Nourrice* modelled by
Joseph Willems
red anchor mark on base, circa 1755
$7\frac{11}{16}$ in. (19.5 cm.) high
London, 7 June 1994, £12,075 ($18,160)

GLASS

A ceremonial Goblet and Cover
late 17th Century
17⅞ in. (45.5 cm.) high
London, 23 November 1993, £67,500 ($99,292)

Right:
An enamelled large deep Bowl
Venetian, circa 1500
12⅞ in. (32.5 cm.) diameter
London, 15 June 1994, £21,850 ($33,124)

A canary-yellow and mixed-twist Wine-Glass
English, circa 1765
5¾ in. (14.5 cm.) high
London, 23 November 1993, £8,050 ($11,841)

A Bakhmet'ev double-walled Tumbler, decorated by
Aleksandr Petrovich Vershinin
Nikolsko, near St. Petersburg, circa 1800
5⅛ in. (13 cm.) high
London, 23 November 1993, £23,000 ($33,833)

A two-colour opaque-twist Wine-Glass
English, circa 1765
6½ in. (16.3 cm.) high
London, 15 June 1994, £11,500 ($17,434)

MODERN DECORATIVE ARTS

THE DR. THOMAS HOWARTH COLLECTION OF CHARLES RENNIE MACKINTOSH AND HIS CIRCLE

by Roger Billcliffe

The largest private collection of the work by the Glasgow architect Charles Rennie Mackintosh was sold at King Street, on 16 February 1994. The property of Dr. Thomas Howarth, of Toronto, the collection had been assembled while Dr. Howarth was living in Glasgow in the 1940s, working on his Ph.D. thesis on Mackintosh. This work was published in 1952 and remains the most comprehensive biography of a remarkable architect and artist, whose work has, over the last twenty years, finally received the international acclaim it had always deserved.

A number of collectors now specialise in the work of Mackintosh and, although some of their collections contain superb individual pieces, these could never match the Howarth Collection in breadth or scale. As a collector, I doubt whether Howarth set out to plot the specific direction his collection might take, or search for particular drawings or pieces which might fill gaps, in the way many collectors might, who are working at greater chronological distances from their subjects. In some ways, Howarth may well have been spoilt for choice, but as an academic, teaching architecture and working on his thesis, he had a limited budget for acquisitions. It is, however, a collection directed by a discerning eye and, in its variety and its depth of material, one which echoes the two major public collections of Mackintosh's work at Glasgow University and the Glasgow School of Art. This is hardly surprising, perhaps, when one remembers that Thomas Howarth was instrumental in the establishment and development of both those collections in the 1940s.

It had been known for some time that Dr. Howarth was seeking a home for his collection and, after much deliberation and negotiation, it was sent to Christie's for sale. There is no doubt that the news of the dispersal of the Howarth Collection at auction caught the imagination of collectors, both public and private, across the world. Mackintosh's furniture has appeared regularly in the saleroom since the early 1970s, achieving higher and higher prices; occasionally his flower drawings and late watercolours painted in France in the 1920s, have also come up for sale, and these too have attracted eager bidding. There was, and still is, however, very little of Mackintosh's work in museums outside Britain, with the exceptions of good groups in the Musée d'Orsay, Paris, and the Richmond Museum of Fine Art, Virginia and isolated, but key examples in New York and Chicago. In recent years Mackintosh's reputation has been rising in Japan – one of his sources of inspiration – fostered by a number of touring exhibitions and publications. It is not surprising therefore, that Amercian and Japanese buyers were so excited by news of the auction and proved enthusiastic competitors. The publication of a detailed and scholarly sale catalogue together with pre-sale exhibitions in America and at Glasgow, prior to the view in London, presented a unique opportunity to Mackintosh's many students and admirers, who would otherwise have never been priviledged to study this seminal collection. Rarely has a sale of twentieth-century material attracted such extraordinary crowds as those who came to King Street to participate in the viewing, the seminar and the record-breaking auction.

The strength of the Howarth Collection lay not only in the individual pieces of furniture, but also in the range of graphic work and incunabula of Mackintosh's life that Howarth was able to acquire from so many primary sources in the 1940s, less than twenty years after Mackintosh's death. The first seventy lots consisted of drawings from one of two sketchbooks executed by Mackintosh during his tour of Italy in 1891: the second of these is in the Hunterian Art Gallery, University of Glasgow. Such early drawings had never been on the market before and almost all similar works are now in public collections; many bidders hoped to acquire at least one of these elegant drawings. The most expensive item in this section of the sale was a very fine watercolour of the Arch of Titus, Rome (£14,950), but other fine studies, such as those of the Campanile at Pistoia Cathedral (£2,990) and the church of S. Abondio at Como (£2,760) were less expensive. An exceptionally fine drawing of Montacute House, Somerset, executed in 1895, brought £8,625 and a rare early watercolour of Wareham, Dorset, of the same year, made £23,000.

Dr. Howarth, as Professor Emeritus of Architecture at the University of Toronto, was particularly interested in the drawings and sketches which Mackintosh made for his own architectural and design projects. Very few of these survive outside museum collections and interest in this part of the sale was intense, as exemplified in the £18,400 price for a study of the studios which Mackintosh designed at Cheyne Walk, London, in 1920. Some drawings for furniture, never seen at auction before, also achieved very strong prices, including a drawing of the benches in the Argyle Street Tea Rooms, Glasgow (£13,800), a design for an exhibition stand (£14,375) and more remarkably, the working drawing for one of the most famous of all Mackintosh's designs, the Order Desk chair at the Willow Tea Rooms, Glasgow (£31,050).

The work of Mackintosh's friends and colleagues in the so-called 'Glasgow Four', Herbert and Frances MacNair, and his wife, Margaret Macdonald, was also well represented in the collection, providing a rare opportunity to see Mackintosh's work in the context of the aesthetic spirit in Glasgow at the time that was inspired, developed and propelled by these four artists. A precise and delicate pencil drawing for a book-plate by Margaret fetched £5,750, while her watercolour study for perhaps her most important work, a large gesso panel, *The May Queen*, realised £36,700. Mackintosh's companion design, *The Wassail*, at £80,700, set one of the many records at the auction.

It was the furniture and associated designs, however, which, not unexpectedly, proved to be the high point of the sale. Mackintosh's furniture is recognised internationally as being among the

st innovative of the past two centuries and there was strong
rnational competition to acquire the seventeen lots in the
tion. Furniture from the Argyle Street Tea Rooms was well
resented and six chairs, from the Billiards and Smoking
oms, fetched between £19,550 and £69,700, breaking auc-
records for similar pieces several times over. One of the icons
Mackintosh's career was the high-backed chair with oval back-
, made for the same tea rooms, around 1898. Dr. Howarth
ned two variants of this design and a third was sent by
ckintosh to the Eighth Vienna Secession Exhibition of 1900,
ere it was bought by the artist Koloman Moser. A single chair
offered here and intense competition from Britain, Germany,
erica and Japan, both in the saleroom and on the telephone,
k the price to £309,000, almost ten times the previous auction
ord for a chair of similar design and over six times the top
mate. This was also to prove a world record price for any
ntieth-century chair.

ong the several items of furnishings offered, a lamp shade made
Mackintosh's own house and a grille from the Willow Tea
oms brought record prices for his metalwork of £19,550 and
4,500 respectively.

CHARLES RENNIE MACKINTOSH, F.R.I.B.A.
(Scottish, 1868–1928)
An ebonised mahogany Writing Cabinet, designed for
Walter W. Blackie Esq., Hill House, Helensburgh
1904
$44\frac{1}{4}$ in. (112.6 cm.) high; 37 in. (94 cm.) wide ($71\frac{1}{4}$ in.
[181.2 cm.] open); $18\frac{3}{8}$ in. (46.7 cm.) deep
Sold from the collection of Dr. Thomas Howarth
London, 17 February 1994, £793,500 ($1,168,882)
Record auction price for a piece of twentieth-century furniture

The most important single pieces of furniture in the Howarth
Collection were the writing cabinet and washstand designed for
Hill House, Helensburgh, as part of the commission for his major
patron, Walter Blackie, and a settle, designed in 1917 for
Mackintosh's last tea room, The Dug Out, in Glasgow.

Interest in the writing cabinet, one of Mackintosh's best known
creations and perhaps his most successful, had intensified in the
days leading up to the sale and the bidding between a representative of a British collector and a Japanese collector was fierce and
quickly broke all records previously set at auction, or elsewhere,
for Mackintosh's furniture. The cabinet was finally sold for
£793,500, the auction record for any piece of twentieth-century

furniture, and most gratifyingly, the piece will remain in Britain. The washstand sold for £95,000 and was bought by an American collector, and the Dug-Out settle fell to the buyer of the desk for £54,300.

Such prices, no doubt in part reflect the prestige attached to the provenance of the Howarth Collection, but they also serve to confirm, once and for all, the importance of Mackintosh's work, not only in relation to twentieth-century design, but also in the broader context of the history of design.

CHARLES RENNIE MACKINTOSH, F.R.I.B.A. (Scottish, 1868–1928)
A high-back oak Chair
circa 1898–99
Sold from the collection of Dr. Thomas Howarth
London, 17 February 1994, £309,500 ($455,893)
Record auction price for a twentieth-century chair

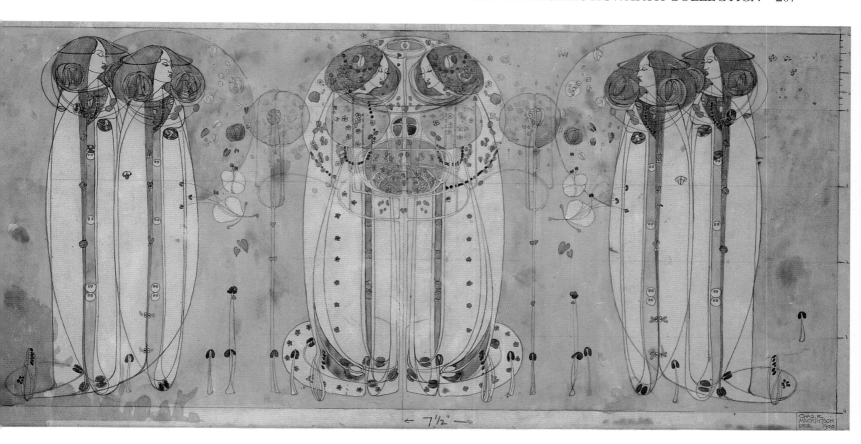

CHARLES RENNIE MACKINTOSH, F.R.I.B.A. (Scottish, 1868–1928)
The Wassail
signed and dated 'CHAS.R/MACKINTOSH DES.1900'
pencil, watercolour, bodycolour, on oiled tracing paper
$13\frac{1}{6}$ in. (32.9 cm.) high; $27\frac{3}{4}$ in. (69.3 cm.) wide
Sold from the collection of Dr. Thomas Howarth
London, 17 February 1994, £80,700 ($118,871)

CHARLES RENNIE MACKINTOSH, F.R.I.B.A. (Scottish, 1868–1928)
A painted Settle
1917
$31\frac{1}{2}$ in. (80 cm.) high; 54 in. (137.1 cm.) wide; $26\frac{3}{4}$ in. (68 cm.) deep
Sold from the collection of Dr. Thomas Howarth
London, 17 February 1994, £54,000 ($79,983)

THE BARBRA STREISAND COLLECTION

by Nancy A. McClelland

In a stellar career spanning more than three decades, Barbra Streisand had dedicated her life and art to the pursuit of excellence in all forms. Whether recording a first album that became the nation's top-selling record by a female vocalist, garnering an Academy Award for Best Actress in her film debut, or creating and starring in the first film ever produced, written, and directed by a woman, she has consistently pursued and maintained only the highest standards of excellence. It is therefore not surprising that, in the more private realm of collecting art, Ms. Streisand had achieved the same well-deserved attention.

Throughout her career, Ms. Streisand had been a dedicated collector of works produced during the Art Nouveau and Art Deco periods. She had committed herself to acquiring and displaying the best of what each movement had to offer. The sale of these collections marks an effort by Ms. Streisand not only to simplify her life, but to focus her efforts toward creative, professional projects as well as humanitarian causes, particularly through the recently created Streisand Foundation.

After seven years of intermittent discussions with Ms. Streisand concerning the sale of her collection, events coalesced to bring 'The Sale' to the forefront, following the release of her highly acclaimed film *The Prince of Tides*. In 1992 the collection of American Arts and Crafts furniture featuring the work of Frank Lloyd Wright and Gustav Stickely was installed in the dining room, living room, and foyer of her Beverly Hills home, thereby displacing her Art Nouveau collection, which went into storage. The 1992 installation of her collection of fine eighteenth-century and early nineteenth-century furniture, which she began collecting in 1990, completed the cycle of transition from European decorative arts to American decorative arts. Finally, the donation of her $15,000,000 Malibu compound in 1993 to the Santa Monica Mountains Conservancy further determined the time of the auction. One of five houses on her Malibu compound, the Art Deco house was decorated in the 1970s, replete with a Rolls Royce and a 1933 Dodge Roadster in the garage to complement the comprehensive decorative scheme.

Ms. Streisand's wish to simplify her life included the decision to be more public than she had been heretofore. In 1993, her first live concert in 27 years was planned for New Year's Eve and New Year's Day in Las Vegas. A live concert tour of America and England followed the stunning success of those two concerts, all of which generated unprecedented acclaim. In keeping with her new public life, Ms. Streisand remained an integral participant in the promotion and sale of her property, particularly throughout the four-city international tour of her collection. Prior to Christie's auction in March, Ms. Streisand appeared at a joint benefit sponsored by Christie's and the Streisand Foundation in Los Angeles which benefited the UCLA Breast Center.

The sale of Ms. Streisand's collection of twentieth-century decorative and fine arts collection on 3 and 4 March 1994 paid an extraordinary tribute to her 30 years of collecting through the overwhelming response from buyers. Many factors contributed to the success of the sale, perhaps most notably Ms. Streisand's celebrity and the attention brought by the international tour. At the close of the entire sale, which was 100% sold, the results totalled $6,200,000, surpassing the total high end of the pre-sale estimates by $1,700,000. Frank Stella's *The Pearls* circa 1962 (estimated at $80,000–100,000), which she purchased from Leo Castelli, sold in the May Contemporary Paintings sale, where it doubled the pre-sale estimate and fetched $178,500.

Arguably the most sought-after lot in the March sale was the Tamara de Lempicka *Adam and Eve* of 1932, which sold for a world record price for the artist of $1,980,000, against an estimate of $600,000–800,000(p.79). Ms. Streisand paid only $135,000 for this painting in 1984. Lempicka, a Polish artist who went to Paris during one of the most significant periods of heightened interest in the fine and particularly the decorative arts, became the leading female exponent of the Art Deco style in painting during the 1920s and 1930s. Clearly one of the great icons of this artists *oeuvre*, the offering of *Adam and Eve* was well-timed, considering that a retrospective of Lempicka, organised by the Academie of France, ran concurrently in Rome and created additional excitement for this exceptional work.

Another object that precipitated great excitement was Ms. Streisand's Cartier Portico Pendule à Gravité clock. Created in 1927 by Maurice Couet, the master who first created these 'mystery clocks' for the House of Cartier, this example was one of three gravity clocks to have been created. The mechanism of the beautiful Shinto temple-gate-designed clock is operated by lifting the clock face to its highest position between two jade columns. As the clock face falls, the gears inside are wound by its descent on tracks located on the facing sides of the columns. Bought by Ms. Streisand in 1984 for approximately $33,000, the clock sold for $316,000 against an estimate of $100,000–150,000 to the museum established by Cartier that exhibits masterpieces from the firm's earlier era.

Examples of the leading exponents of the Art Nouveau movement were well represented in Ms. Streisand's collection. Particularly appealing to her were the flora and fauna of the Ecole de Nancy exemplified in her furniture by Louis Majorelle and Emile Galle. Perhaps the most widely known aspect of her collection, however, were those works by the American master lampmaker, Louis Comfort Tiffany. The greatest piece in Ms. Streisand's collection was her 'Cobweb' lamp circa 1906, a rare lamp of which perhaps only a dozen are known. This lamp was purchased by Ms. Streisand from Lillian Nassau in 1979 for $70,000 and sold for $717,500 in Christie's sale. The lamp was a stunning composition of a leaded glass cobweb canopy with apple blossom sprigs interspersed and joined to a tesserae mosaic base, displaying a springtime vision of paper-white narcissi. A Tiffany 'Peony' lamp on a mosaic base, around which Ms. Streisand decorated her living room in Beverly Hills, was an exceptionally rare combination of shade and base; the colours of the favrile glass shade, which range from red and green to gold, are precisely reflected in the mosaic colours and the turtleback tiles of the base. As with the Tiffany 'Cobweb' lamp, the mosaic-clad bases are very highly prized by collectors, which contributed in part to the 'Peony' lamp achieving a new record price for that model of $332,500.

At the close of the stunning two-day auction, Ms. Streisand, who listened in from her home in Beverly Hills, said that she was 'thrilled with the results of the sale. The highlights for me were the Lempicka and the Cartier clock. The sale meant a lot to me, as it represented more than 30 years of collecting, beginning with my first purchase at age 18.' She also noted that 'all those wonderful things had been saved from being damaged in the recent earthquake, which broke many things in my home.' Christie's too was pleased to have had the good fortune to offer this extraordinary collection.

TIFFANY STUDIOS
A 'Cobweb' leaded glass, mosaic and bronze Table Lamp
circa 1909
stamped 'TIFFANY STUDIOS NEW YORK D658'
29 in. (73.8 cm.) high; 20 in. (51.5 cm.) diameter of shade
Sold from the collection of Barbra Streisand
New York, 3 March 1994, $717,500 (£479,933)

TIFFANY STUDIOS
A 'Peony' leaded glass, turtleback tile and bronze Table Lamp
circa 1910
stamped 'TIFFANY STUDIOS NEW YORK 5169'
29 in. (73.8 cm.) high; 22 in. (555 cm.) diameter of shade
Sold from the collection of Barbra Streisand
New York, 3 March 1994, $332,500 (£222,408)

MAURICE COÜET (French, 1885–1963) for CARTIER
A jade portico 'Pendule à Gravité' Clock
circa 1927
$9\frac{1}{2}$ in. (21.4 cm.) high
Sold from the collection of Barbra Streisand
New York, 3 March 1994, $316,000 (£211,371)

FRANK LLOYD WRIGHT (American, 1869–1950)
A leaded glass Window, designed for the Avery Coonley
Playhouse, Riverside, Illinois
circa 1912
24 in. (61 cm.) high; $38\frac{3}{8}$ in. (97.5 cm.) wide
New York, 11 December 1993, $154,000 (£103,148)

CHARLES ROHLFS (American 1853–1936)
A carved oak Hall Chair
1900
New York, 11 June 1994, $32,200 (£21,611)

Almeria, a cold-painted bronze and ivory Figure, cast and carved
from a model by Demêtre Chiparus (French, 1888–1950)
circa 1930
stamped 'BRONZE' and '11'
26 in. (66 cm.) high including base
New York, 11 June 1994, $134,500 (£89,191)

ANTIQUITIES

THE CANFORD ASSYRIAN RELIEF

by Christine Insley Green

It took just three minutes for the most expensive sculpture ever sold at auction to achieve £7,701,500 in London on 6 July 1994. That it was an antiquity, an Assyrian bas-relief measuring 72 × 46 in. (183 × 117 cm.) took many people by surprise. The relief came from the great palace of King Ashurnasirpal (883–859 B.C.) at Kalhu (biblical Calah) known by its modern name of Nimrud. It depicted a winged, bearded, protective deity (*apkalle*), carrying two daggers and a whetstone in his belt, anointing or purifying with a cone the beardless, powerful, figure of the eunuch and royal arm's bearer, who carries the king's bow, quiver, and sceptre into the royal presence. Although the exact nature of this ritual is uncertain, it appears that the king's spiritual potency is being maintained magically by purifying anyone who comes into royal contact. Other guardian spirits also appear in front of the Sacred Tree or in doorways, places which needed protection. Ashurnasirpal, unknown until Layard's discoveries, built his new capital on the banks of the Tigris, and from his own accounts built his splendid palace out of stone and wood. This gypsum (or 'Mosul marble') relief would have come from what the excavator termed Room C of the palace. From comparison with other reliefs it is likely the hair, beard and eyes and certain details would have been painted. The main royal buildings and palaces were built on a raised mound overlooking the river. Temples, museums exhibiting the spoils of war (the Black Obelisk of Shalmaneser was found here), piazzas, administrative buildings, gardens and waterways reflected the wealth of his empire. The reliefs in his palace depicted him as the spiritual and victorious leader of his people. The cuneiform inscriptions confirmed these claims.

It was the brilliant young archaeologist Henry Layard who brought the Assyrians to life. In his early twenties he came under the patronage of Sir Stratford Canning, Ambassador at Constantinople, who sent him on reconnaissance missions throughout the Ottoman Empire. While travelling in Mesopotamia he witnessed the early French excavations by Paul Botta at Khorsabad, the city of King Sargon II. Inspired, he applied for and received a firman from the Grand Vizier to excavate at Nimrud and Nineveh and export to England whatever stones he found desirable. Between 1846 and 1851 he undertook the excavations and meticulous recording of these two sites, and arranged for the transport of the sculptures by river to Basra, in spite of the local tribal wars and the hostility of the Turkish governor.

Although supported by the Trustees of the British Museum, who received the bulk of excavated material, he turned to Sir John Guest, the wealthy husband of his cousin Lady Charlotte, for help in meeting some of the transport costs. In recognition of Sir John's generosity, some of the winged, human-headed bulls, and sculptural reliefs arrived at the Guest home, Canford Manor, where they were installed in Nineveh Court, a building specially designed by Sir Charles Barry to house the new treasures. The arrival of the Assyrian antiquities caused a sensation especially since they confirmed many of the biblical accounts. Layard was dubbed 'Mr. Bull' and eventually entered politics as a disciple of

the Tory Disraeli, advocating the Turkish viewpoint in the complex Eastern Question. He married the daughter of Sir John and Lady Guest and embarked on a successful political career for which he received a knighthood.

In 1919 the Guest's grandson Lord Wimborne disposed of the bulk of the collection to Kelekian, an Armenian dealer living in New York, who eventually sold this to John D. Rockefeller, who later donated it to the Metropolitan Museum, New York. In 1923 Canford Manor became an independent school. Nineveh Court was converted into the school tuck-shop known as 'The Grubber'. The relief of Ashurnasirpal, whitewashed, and inset between two casts from the British Museum, was used as a dartboard, until an American Professor John Russell, visiting the school to research his book on the history of Nineveh Court queried its antiquity. Dr. Julian Reade of the Western Asiatic department of the British Museum confirmed not only its antiquity but that it was the missing slab six from Room C of Ashurnasirpal's palace, thought to have been lost in the Tigris.

The spectacular power and quality of this relief and the importance of its provenance combined to attract worldwide interest. The applause at the end of the sale was not just for the price but an echo of the excitement that such pieces had aroused 150 years before on their arrival in England.

gypsum bas–relief Wall-Slab from
oom C, the north–west Palace of
shurnasirpal II at Kalhu (Nimrud)
3–859 B.C.
2 × 46 in. (183 × 117 cm.), 2½ in.
.4 cm.) thick
old by order of the Governors of
anford School
ondon, 6 July 1994, £7,701,500
11,891,116)

(detail)

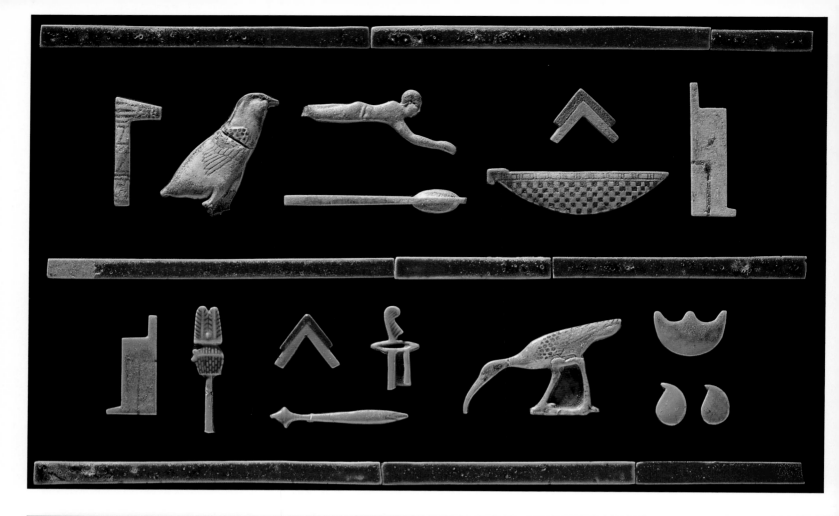

Left:
Hieroglyphic Inlays (selection illustrated)
glassy faience, cast in a mould
circa 4th–3rd Century B.C.
London, 8 December 1993. Sold for a total of
£71,015 ($105,102)

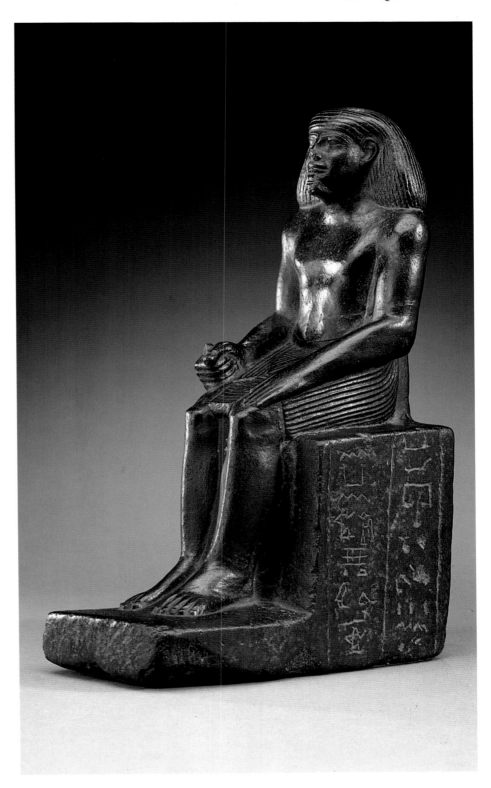

A shallow mosaic glass Bowl
first half 1st Century B.C.
$5\frac{1}{8}$ in. (13.1 cm.) diameter; $1\frac{1}{4}$ in. (3.2 cm.) high
London, 8 December 1993, £59,800 ($88,982)

These glassy 'faience' hieroglyphic inlays and mosaic
glass bowl were part of a magnificent collection of
Ancient Glass and Important Antiquities from
Egypt, which was formed between the 1920s and the
1940s. The collection was sold in three sales from
December 1992 to December 1993. It realised over
£1,700,000, and was the finest and most
comprehensive collection of Egyptian glass ever to
come on the market. The glass reflects the luxurious
life of Ancient Egypt, where the sheen and malleable
property of the glass was more highly prized than
semi-precious stones. Hieroglyphic inlays were cast
in a mould and were probably used to decorate
wooden shrines and furniture. Mosaic glass bowl
was formed by laying numerous slices of multi-
coloured glass canes side by side, then heating and
fusing them together. This bowl was in the Henry
Oppenheimer Collection which was sold at
Christie's in July 1936. It fetched 30 guineas.

An Egyptian Statue of a seated Man
black basalt
Middle Kingdom, Late Dynasty XII, circa 1897–1783 B.C.
$11\frac{13}{16}$ in. (30 cm.) high
New York, 15 December 1993, $299,500 (£201,277)

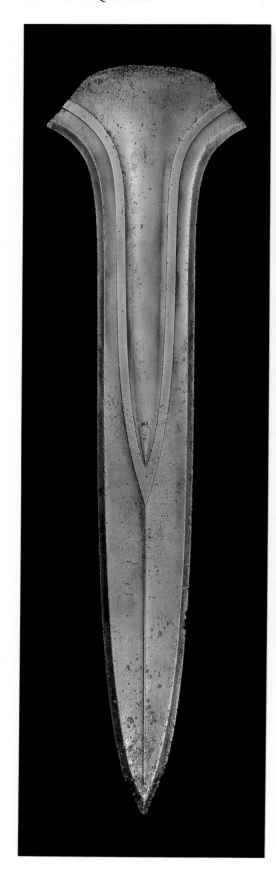

The Oxborough Ceremonial Dirk
bronze
British, Middle Bronze Age,
circa 1500–1350 B.C.
27$\frac{7}{8}$ in. (70.9 cm.) long; 7$\frac{1}{8}$ in. (18.1 cm.)
wide
London, 6 July 1994 £51,000 ($78,744)

An Etruscan Cista
bronze
probably from Praeneste
circa 300 B.C.
16$\frac{1}{4}$ in. (41.3 cm.) high
London, 8 December 1993, £106,000 ($157,728)

A Bust of the Emperor Gaius Caesar, called
Caligula
bronze
Roman, circa 37–41 A.D.
$7\frac{7}{8}$ in. (20 cm.) high
London, 8 December 1993 £265,500 ($394,320)

A Hellenistic Figure of a Goddess
gilt-bronze
circa 1st Century B.C.
$9\frac{7}{8}$ in. (25.1 cm.) high
New York, 10 June 1994, $222,500 (£147,546)

ISLAMIC ART

AN ISLAMIC BRONZE LION

by Jochen Artur Sokoly

In the autumn sale of Islamic Works of Art a bronze lion sculpture was sold for £2,421,500 ($3,608,035), a world record auction price for an Islamic Art object. This record reflected the excitement aroused by the appearance of so remarkable an object. For it is not often that such a piece, unnoticed for many centuries, comes on the market. Very few early Islamic bronze sculptures have survived. The lion has to be counted among the rarest surviving objects that represent the sumptuous courtly civilisation of the Muslim rulers during the medieval period.

Comparison with a number of early Islamic bronzes suggests that the lion originates from eleventh/twelfth-century Spain. Until the middle of the eleventh century Spain was ruled by members of the Umayyad dynasty, who claimed the caliphate, the leadership over the whole of the Muslim world. Archaeological finds of related bronze objects have been made from the caliphal palace of Madinat al-Zahra, close to the city of Cordova, the Umayyad capital of Spain. Other sites that have yielded similar material are the Islamic fortress in Monzon, in the province of Palencia, and the city of Cordova itself. The lion is comparable in execution and in the treatment of the incised decoration to these finds. However, the most important related object is the well-known large bronze griffin formerly crowning the gable of Pisa cathedral. They share similar details of decoration and interior construction. Tradition has it that the griffin arrived in Pisa as booty from a raid of Mahdiyya, in Tunisia, by the Pisans in 1087. A Spanish origin seems likely on stylistic grounds from its similarity to the smaller animals from archaeological sites. That the Pisans gave the griffin such a prominent place in their town suggests that it must have been of great significance to the people from whom it was captured.

Scientific analysis of samples taken from the lion at the Oxford Research Laboratory suggests that the areas of corrosion were caused by water. It is possible that the lion served as a spout for a fountain; details of the interior and the fairly large opening of the animal's mouth could support this assumption. Fountains and water-pools have always been an integral part of Islamic palatial architecture. Some of the most spectacular examples can be found in Spain, for example at the Spanish-Umayyad palace, Madinat al-Zahra. Here the arrangement of pavillions, gardens and fountains feeding water-pools gave an impression of utmost luxury, into which an impressive object like this would have fitted very well. The Lion-court at the Alhambra with its lion-supported fountain in the centre, although much later than Madinat al-Zahra, gives us one possible idea of this lion's environment.

Although the fountain theory is very attractive there are problems with it. The lion's legs are closed at the top so a waterpipe could not have led through them but would have had to pass through the hole in its belly, which would have been unattractive. The Pisa griffin has a similar but perhaps even more problematic feature. Its mouth opening is too small to have served as a spout nor is it connected to the head.

An alternative theory is suggested by an unexplained feature in both objects: an integrally cast bladder-like container in the body with a flaring mouth. It is possible that these 'bladders' might have contained incense. However, there is a better explanation which tells us why the objects had assumed so much prestige in their original context. There is an entry in the chronicles of the tenth-century author Isa bin al-Rafi describing an embassy of the Spanish-Umayyad Caliph 'Abd al-Rahman III at the court of the Byzantine emperor in Constantinople. In it he describes the ambassador who was seated between carved animals which were roaring. The 'bladders' of this lion and the Pisa griffin might essentially be the remains of some sound-making device inside the animals and both figures might have been used in similar ceremonial contexts.

It has been debated that the lion's eyes and their surroundings were inlaid with precious stones, a suggestion supported by the deep panels on the lion's face. This would certainly have added to the luxuriousness of the object. If the figures had had a ceremonial function at the court, not necessarily as a pair, these would have reflected caliphal power and glory. They were prime pieces to be looted by rival Christian troops which is why the Pisa griffin was given such a prominent place on the East gable of the cathedral, above the high altar, while its sister piece, the lion, became a prized possession of an important European princely family.

An Islamic bronze Lion
probably Andalusia, 11th/12th Century
37 in. (94 cm.) high including additional lower legs
London, 19 October 1993, £2,421,500 ($3,608,035)
Record auction price for an Islamic Work of Art

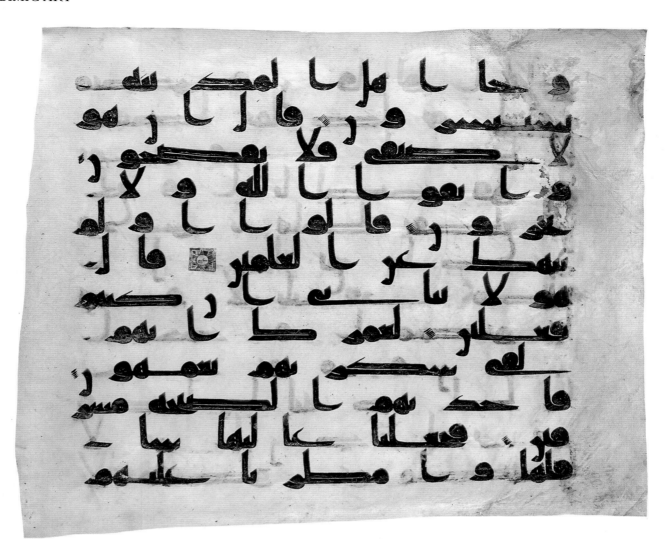

A Qur'an Folio
comprising *sura* xv, *al-Hajar*, pt.v.62–pt.v74
North Africa, early 8th Century
folio 21 × 25¾ in. (53.6 × 65 cm.)
London, 19 October 1993, £32,200 ($47,978)

Right:
A vaulted octagonal wooden Ceiling
Andalusia, circa 14th Century
approx. 66 in. (170 cm.) high; approx. 168 in. (430 cm.) wide
London, 26 April 1994, £210,500 ($313,645)

The prohibition of the depiction of figural forms in a number of Islamic cultures led in the medieval period to a great exploration of the possibilities of geometric interlace. This is evident throughout Islamic Spain, where such forms were to be found in brick, in stucco, in textiles and in tile revetments. The design of a ceiling, by its very nature dependent on wooden supporting beams, is ideally suited to this type of design. This ceiling was purchased from an unknown building in Spain, probably in the 1930s, by that supreme hoarder of architectural elements from all countries and periods, William Randolph Hearst.

A Mamluk silver-inlaid brass Bowl
Egypt or Syria, early 14th Century
12⅝ in. (32.2 cm.) diameter
London, 26 April 1994, £31,050 ($46,265)

Left:
MUHAMMADI (Iranian, circa 1580)
A young Archer
signed, 'Muhammadi'
gouache heightened with gold on buff paper
6 × 3 in. (15.1 × 8.5 cm.)
London, 19 October 1993, £38,900 ($57,961)

Although a few works by are known, little has been discovered
about his life. References within Iranian literature are rare, and
even then, with the simplicity of his name, difficult to tie up with
any certainty to this particular artist. His life has however recently
been somewhat fleshed out, with a list of 34 works by or
attributed to him. His career was based in the eastern Iranian city
of Herat, away from the court at Qazvin. Although his style is
broadly in line with that of the court artists, it demonstrates his
individuality, in particular in the delicacy of line and the
simplicity of composition.

A Seljuk ivory Chesspiece
Iran, circa 12th Century
$2\frac{7}{8}$ in. (7.3 cm.) high
London, 26 April 1994, £32,200 ($47,978)

The game of chess probably came to Iran prior to the seventh
century from India where it is thought to have originated. It is
documented as having been established long ago in the writings
of the tenth-century Arab author, Masudi. Until recently it was
thought that the Iranian version of the game was only played with
pieces of abstract form, of which examples are well-known in
ivory, rock-crystal and pottery. This was challenged by the
discovery of a complete figural set during archaeological
excavations near Samarkand. With the exception of this set
however, the number of figural pieces is well below ten, of which
this is arguably the most ambitious and complete.

Right:
An Iznik pottery Dish
Turkey, circa 1530
$14\frac{3}{4}$ in. (37.4 cm.) diameter
London, 26 April 1994, £43,300 ($64,517)

A silk and silverthread brocaded calligraphic Panel, made to
decorate the Ka'aba (detail)
Ottoman, 18th/19th Century
35 × 249 in. (89 × 631 cm.)
London, 26 April 1994, £38,900 ($57,961)

A decorated calligraphic Panel by Isma'il Jalayir
Persia, circa 1860
$20\frac{1}{4} × 42\frac{3}{4}$ in. (51.5 × 108.6 cm.)
London, 26 April 1994, £26,450 ($39,411)

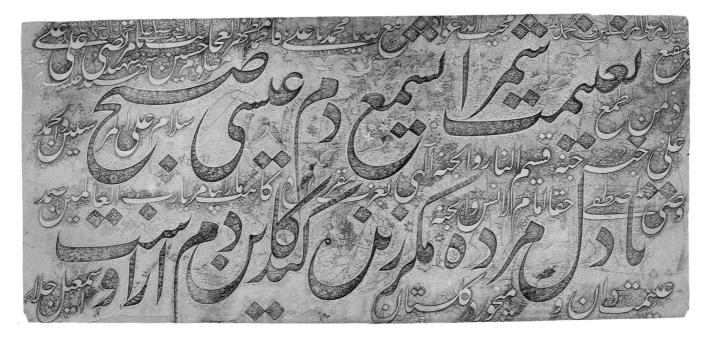

An Isphahan Carpet
Central Persia, first half 17th Century
168 × 134 in. (455 × 341 cm.)
Sold from the Estate of Beatrice Lagrave Maltby
New York, 20 April 1994, $145,500 (£98,311)

A silk Heriz Carpet
Northwest Persia, circa 1870
153 × 112 in. (389 × 285 cm.)
New York, 17 December 1993, $101,500 (£68,258)

Left:
An antique Bidjar Carpet (detail illustrated)
Iran, circa 1880
296 × 175 in. (750 × 442 cm.)
London, 19 May 1994, £23,000 ($34,661)

An Agra corridor Carpet
India, 1890–1900
840 × 86 in. (2,128 × 218 cm.)
London, 19 May 1994, £29,000 ($43,703)

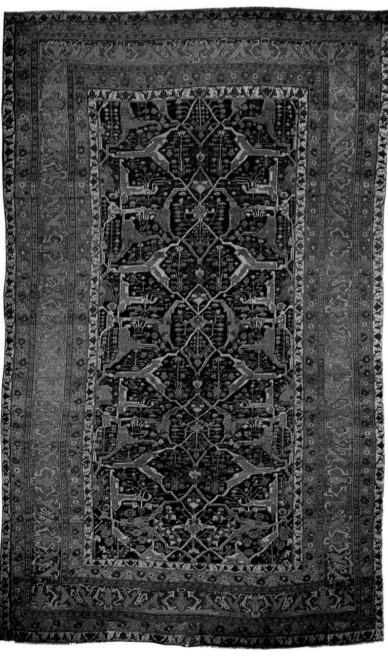

Right:
An East Tibetan bronze Figure of Vajrabhairava and
his female Consort
17th Century
$8\frac{1}{4}$ in. (21 cm.) high
Amsterdam, 12 April 1994, Fl.63,250 (£22,350)

A Nepalese gilt-copper Figure of Avalokitesvara
late 13th Century
$8\frac{1}{2}$ in. (21.5 cm.) high
Amsterdam, 12 April 1994, Fl.51,750 (£18,286)

RADEN SARIEF BASTAMAN SALEH
(Indonesian, 1807–1880)
The Lion Hunt
signed and dated 'Raden Saleh 184(?)'
oil on canvas
16 × 22 in. (40.5 × 56 cm.)
Amsterdam, 21 April 1994, Fl.178,250 (£63,209)

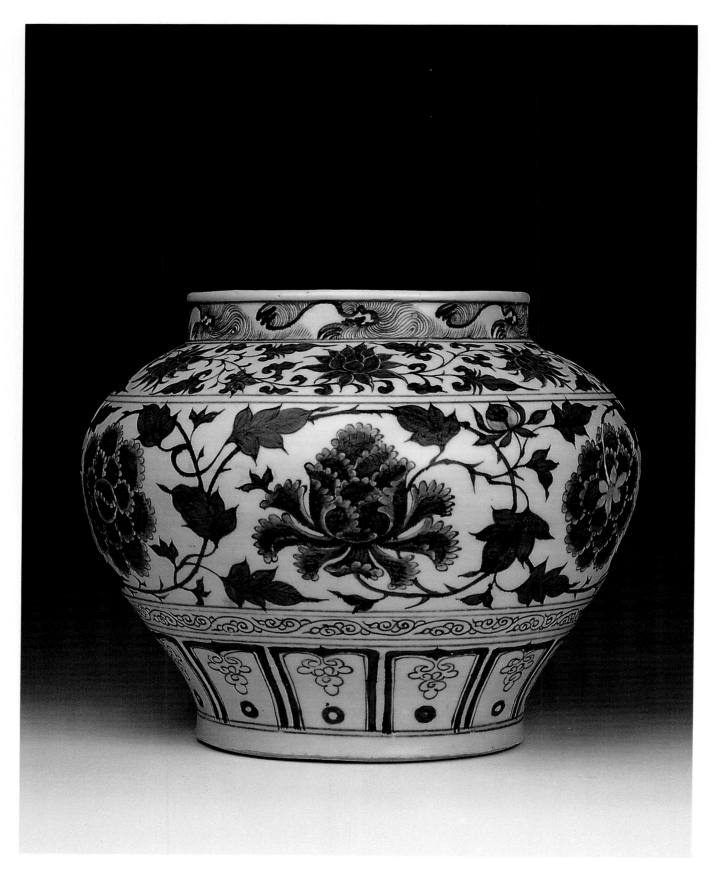

A Yuan blue and white Jar, *guan*
Yuan Dynasty (1279-1368)
13⅜ in. (34.3 cm.) diameter
Hong Kong, 25 October 1993,
H.K.$9,040,000 (£790,141)

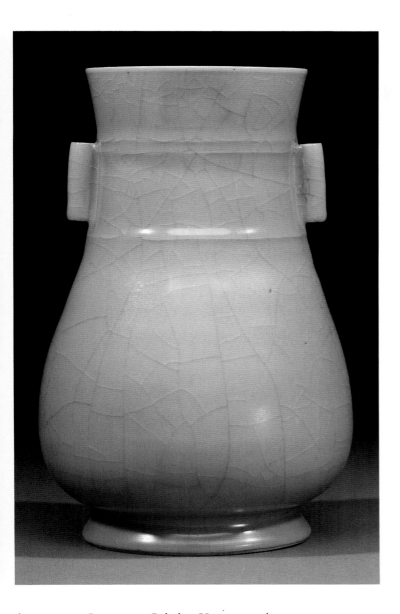

A guan-type Longquan Celadon Vase, *guanerhu*
Southern Song Dynasty (1128-1279)
10¼ in. (26.1 cm.) high
New York, 2 December 1993, $288,500 (£194,015)

There are two varieties of *guan*-type Longquan ware. The first
imitates both the body and glaze of classic *guan* ware, with thinly
potted dark bodies and blue-green crackled glaze. In the second
category, the body material of *guan* ware is not imitated and the
emphasis is on the form of the usually thickly-potted vessel and its
glaze colour and craquelure. The body material is the usual pale
grey Longquan ware that is burnt a reddish brown where
unglazed and exposed to the oxygen-scarce reducing atmosphere
in the kiln. This *guanerhu* belongs to the second category.

An archaic bronze Wine Vessel and Cover, *guang*
Shang Dynasty (circa 1600-circa 1100 B.C.)
7⅛ in. (18 cm.) high
London, 6 June 1994, £73,000 ($109,865)

The bronze has a rich green patina and areas of red cuprite,
malachite, and azurite encrustations. One of the few plain archaic
vessel types of the period, this piece is a very important example
of the transition from late Shang to early Zhou Dynasty art,
showing the transformation of the horned dragon image to a
more deer-like representation.

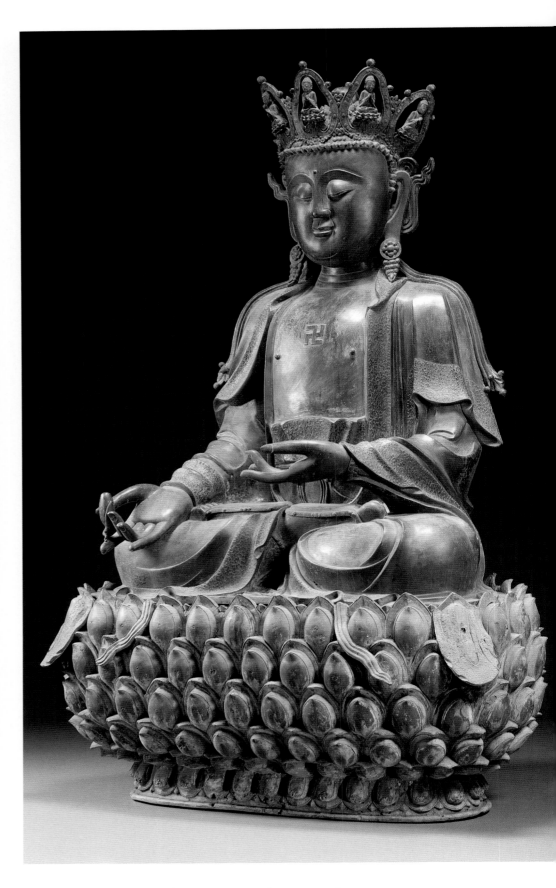

A polychrome marble Figure of a Luohan
Liao Dynasty (907–1125)
69 in. (175 cm.) high
Hong Kong, 24 October 1993,
H.K.$3,650,000 (£318,277)

A massive bronze figure of a Guanyin seated on a Lotus Base
Ming Dynasty (1368–1643)
84 in. (213.5 cm.) high
New York, 2 June 1994, $332,500 (£219,327)

A massive bronze Figure of Guandi
Ming Dynasty (1368–1643)
16th Century
76 in. (193 cm.) high
New York, 2 December 1993, $420,500 (£284,506)

Left:
A large white jade Bowl and Cover
Qianlong period (1736-95)
8⅜ in. (21.2 cm.) diameter
New York, 2 December 1993, $167,500 (£113,329)

The bowl is carved in shallow relief with four of the Buddhist emblems separated by the character *xiang*. The other four Buddhist emblems are carved into the cover and separated by the character *ji*. The two characters *ji xiang* may be translated as 'good fortune'.

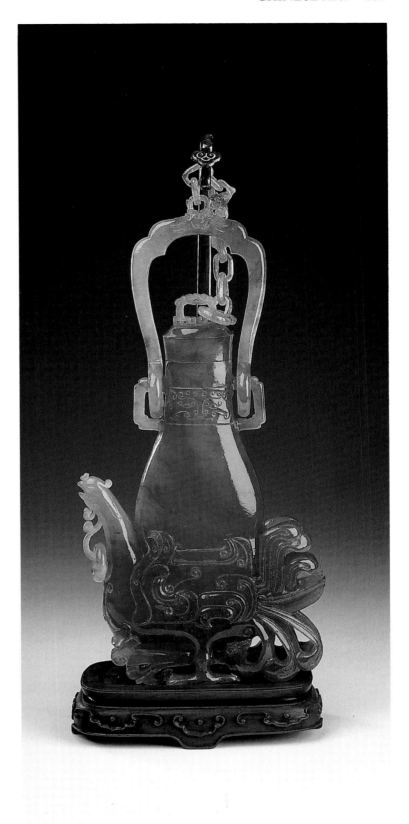

A jadeite hanging Vase and Cover
circa 1880–1930
10⅜ in. (26.4 cm.) high extended
Hong Kong, 25 October 1993, H.K.$6,950,000 (£607,464)

A brilliant green jadeite archaistic covered Vessel
circa 1880–1930
5⅞ in. (15 cm.) across handles
Hong Kong, 25 October 1993, H.K.$5,410,000 (£472,861)

This vessel and others like it are in the style of archaic vessels, usually of bronze, used to hold artists' materials; coloured pigments were kept in the tubular compartments at each corner closed by wooden stoppers, while the central compartment held a saucer and water for mixing the colours.

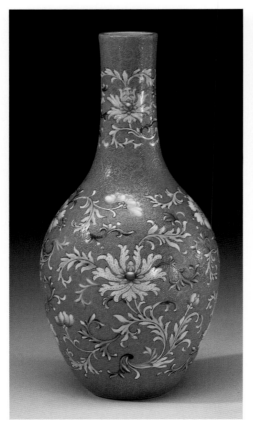

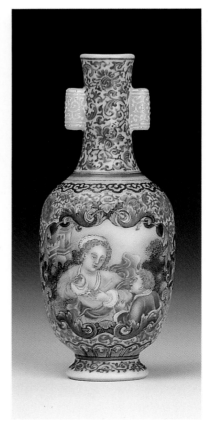

Left:
A large *famille rose* 'peach' Dish
Yongzheng six-character mark and of
the period (1723-35)
19$\frac{7}{8}$ in. (50.5 cm.) diameter
Hong Kong, 2 May 1994,
H.K.$4,420,000, (£377,391)

A *famille rose* scraffiato blue-ground
Vase
Qianlong four-character seal mark in
blue enamel and of the period
(1736-95)
8$\frac{3}{8}$ in. (21.3 cm.) high
New York, 2 December 1993,
$217,000 (£145,931)

A small *famille rose* Beijing enamel
Bottle
Qianlong four-character mark in blue
enamel and of the period (1736-95),
Beijing Palace workshops
1$\frac{15}{16}$ in. (5 cm.) high
New York, 2 June 1994, $79,500
(£52,441)

An Imperial *famille rose* 'European-
subject' miniature Vase
blue enamel Qianlong four-character
mark and of the period (1736-1795)
3$\frac{3}{8}$ in. (9 cm.) high
Hong Kong, 25 October 1993,
H.K.$2,220,000 (£194,039)

A large Imperial embroidered silk Thanka
Yongle six-character presentation mark, Da Ming Yongle Nian Shi, and of the period (1403-24)
132 × 84 in. (335.3 × 213.5 cm.)
New York, 2 June 1994, $1,014,500 (£669,195)
Record auction price for a Chinese textile

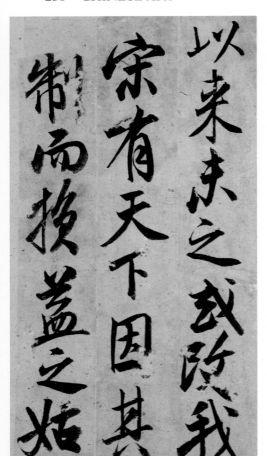
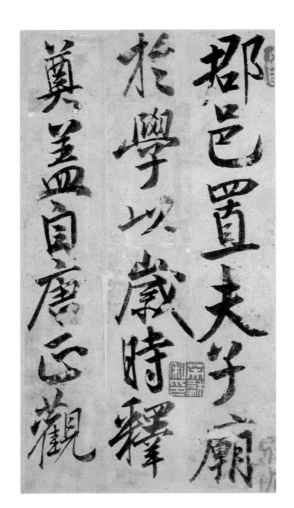

MI YOUREN (1086-1165)
Running Script Calligraphy (*xing shu*)
an album of forty-two leaves (two illustrated)
ink on paper
each leaf measuring 8 × 3¾ in. (20.5 × 9.5 cm.)
New York, 1 June 1994, $310,500 (£205,221)

YAO WENHAN, ZHOU KUN, ZHANG WEIBANG (all
18th Century)
The Dispatch and Victory of the Suppression of Jinchuan (detail),
Sichuan
two handscrolls
ink and colour on silk
20½ × 191½ in. (52 × 486.4 cm.) and 20½ × 208 in (52 × 528.3 cm.)
New York, 1 December 1993, $706,500 (£477,043)
Record auction price for Qing Dynasty Imperial Academy
painting

Above:
LIN LIANG (circa 1430-1490)
Birds and Flowers
one of a pair of hanging scrolls
signed and with seal of the artist
ink on paper
52½ × 13 in. (133.5 × 33 cm.)
Sold from the Jean-Pierre Dubose Collection
New York, 1 December 1993, $244,500 (£165,091)
Record auction price for the artist

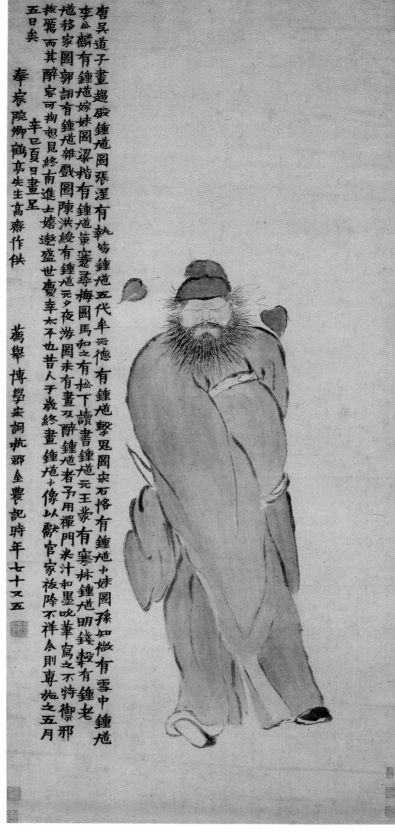

HEN HONGSHOU (1598-1652)
mmortals and the Search for Longevity
nging Scroll
scribed and signed 'In the mid-summer of wuyin year (1638),
ishan Hongshou painted 'Immortals and [the Search for]
ongevity' at Daozhuang Lou (Studio for Collecting Daoist
criptures)'
k and colour on silk
$3\frac{3}{4} \times 38\frac{3}{4}$ in. (200 × 98.5 cm.)
ew York, 1 June 1994, $607,500 (£402,318)
ecord auction price for the artist

JIN NONG (1687-1764)
The Drunken Zhongkui
hanging Scroll
ink and colour on paper
$48\frac{7}{8} \times 22\frac{3}{8}$ in. (124 × 57 cm.)
New York, 1 December 1993, $299,500 (£202,228)
Record auction price for the artist

KOREAN ART

by Sebastian Izzard

An early Choson dynasty (1392–1911) Korean porcelain dish was sold at Christie's New York on 27 April 1994 for a record price. The flat, thinly potted, dish was painted in the well in underglaze cobalt blue with Chinese-style scrolling arabesques surrounded by a narrow band of undulating waves. The underside was decorated with a ring of eight symbols, a mixture of the 'eight buddhist emblems' and the 'eight precious things'.

The fall of the Koryo dynasty (918–1392) and the rise of the Choson dynasty under the General Yi Song-gye (r. 1392–98) and his immediate successors, strengthened the power of the central government while reducing the wealth of both Buddhist temples and noble families who had been associated with the Koryo court. A vigorous new elite dominated Korean society and ruthlessly removed political opposition either by assassination or banishment. The dynamic intellectual atmosphere of the early Choson era is exemplified by the reign of the fourth King, Sejong (r. 1418–50). A man of renowned intelligence, Sejong was responsible for Korea's golden age which saw the invention of *han'gul*, the Korean alphabet, and moveable type – many years before Gutenberg – among other notable achievements.

Fifteenth-century Korean ceramics reflect the new dynamism. These are of two types and replaced the celadons associated with the fallen Koryo dynasty. The first type was a robust stoneware called *Punch'ong*. Decoration was carved or inlaid, or was brushed on with white slip or iron brown and covered with a clear, crackled glaze. (A superb example of *Punch'ong* ware was sold in New York in our 17 November 1993 sale, for the record sum of $376,500 [£254,564]) see page 242. The second type was a fine white porcelain, either plain white or – much more rarely – decorated with underglaze painting, as in the porcelain dish illustrated here.

Not only was the 1994 price a record for a Korean work of art but it was also the highest price ever paid for any piece of porcelain, both Asian and European. Korea was frequently invaded and fought over and has lost many of its treasures, either through destruction or looting. The high price paid for this dish reflects the premium placed on works from the early part of the Choson era. Korean museums and collectors, backed by a supportive government, are determined to retrieve what masterpieces they can. There is, moreover, a widespread fascination with the past in Korea today and a desire to place Korean culture on the world stage.

This beautiful dish is one such rare treasure that has now returned to its native land. It is a product of the earliest period of Korean blue and white porcelain, and clearly displays a debt to China in its shape and decoration. Evidence that blue and white ware was being produced in Korea in the fifteenth century can be found in a document written in 1464 which states that Korean domestic blue cobalt was being used for underglaze painting because there was a shortage of Chinese pigments. In a document of 1481, a Korean official says that artists from the Academy of Painting frequently painted on porcelain made for the royal house.

This dish was probably a product of the Doma-ri kiln in Kwangju, Kyonggi Province, up the Han river from Seoul. Sherds from this site, similar in shape, glaze and decoration, were excavated in 1986. Although the form and cobalt blue are clearly derived from Chinese models dating from the Yongle (1403–24) and Xuande (1426–35) periods, the scrolling flower design is closer to Chinese examples from the Chenghua period (1465–87). Only two other intact dishes of this type are known, both now in Japanese museums. Several other dishes of similar shape, thought to date from the early sixteenth century, are more freely embellished with quintessentially Korean motifs. Thus the decoration of the dishes soon evolved from Chinese models to a purely native aesthetic, losing the formality of Chinese pattern-making in the process.

Although the dish was illustrated in the 1956 edition of *Sekai Toji Zenshu* (The Encyclopedia of World Ceramics), it then disappeared from view. Its re-appearance naturally caused a stir. It was obvious from the beginning that a record price was possible. At our previews in Seoul and Tokyo figures higher than the previous record for a Korean ceramic – set at $990,000 in our New York Rooms in 1990 – were freely discussed. It was clear that a new record would be made. In the event the saleroom battle settled down to a duel between two telephone bidders on either side of the room. Like the audience at a tennis match, all eyes followed the bidders as they doggedly fought it out from $1,600,000 to $2,800,000 – a resounding burst of applause broke out when the final hammer fell.

Clearly prices for the best of Korean art have reached a new threshold. As the economy of South Korea continues to grow in tandem with a drive to recover the national patrimony, it is likely that high prices for the best pieces will be sustained.

A blue and white porcelain Dish
Choson Dynasty, 15th Century
$8\frac{1}{2}$ in. (21.9 cm.) diameter
New York, 27 April 1994, $3,082,500 (£2,044,098)

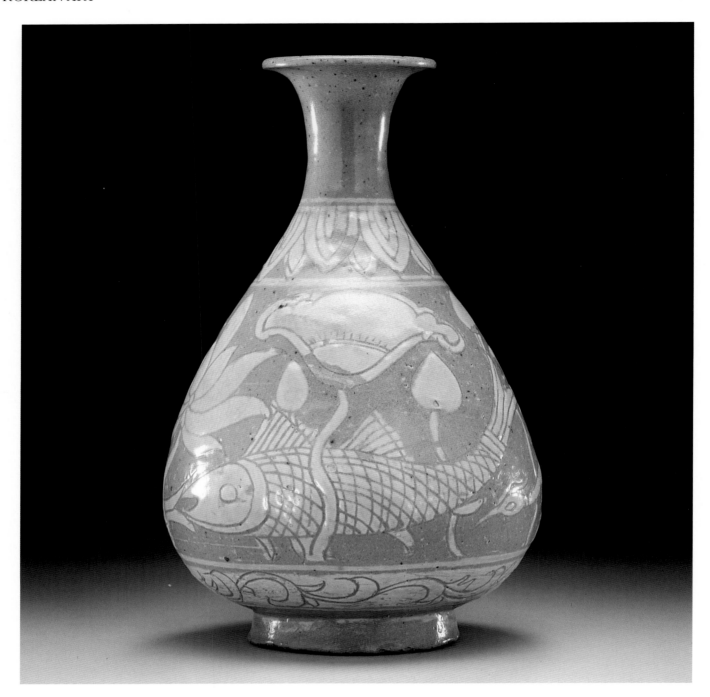

A punch'ong Bottle
Choson Dynasty, early 15th Century
10½ in. (26.7 cm.) high
New York, 17 November 1993, $376,500 (£254,564)
Record auction price for a piece of *punch'ong*

With the advent of *punch'ong* (literally 'powder green') – a
greyish stoneware brushed with white slip – a vigorous and
robust new era of ceramic design was ushered in by the early
Choson potters. This bottle has a band of incised lotus petals
around the neck and a band of scrolling vines around the bottom.
The central area is decorated with two fish and two long-legged
birds in a lotus pond. The birds are presumably preying on the
fish, but the fish are nearly twice as large as the birds. This
humorous, whimsical approach is typical of Choson potters, as is
the preference for bold, asymmetrical design and spontaneous,
freehand effects.

Right:
KOREAN SCHOOL, circa 1830
Celebration of the 40th Birthday and Thirty Year Rule of King
Sunjo
Choson Dynasty
59 × 164 in. (150 × 416.9 cm.)
New York, 17 November 1993, $575,500 (£388,776)

PARK SOO-GUN (Korean, 1914–1965)
Dancers
signed 'Soo-Gun'
oil on board
8¼ × 11¾ in. (21 × 30 cm.)
New York, 17 November 1993, $200,500 (£135,565)

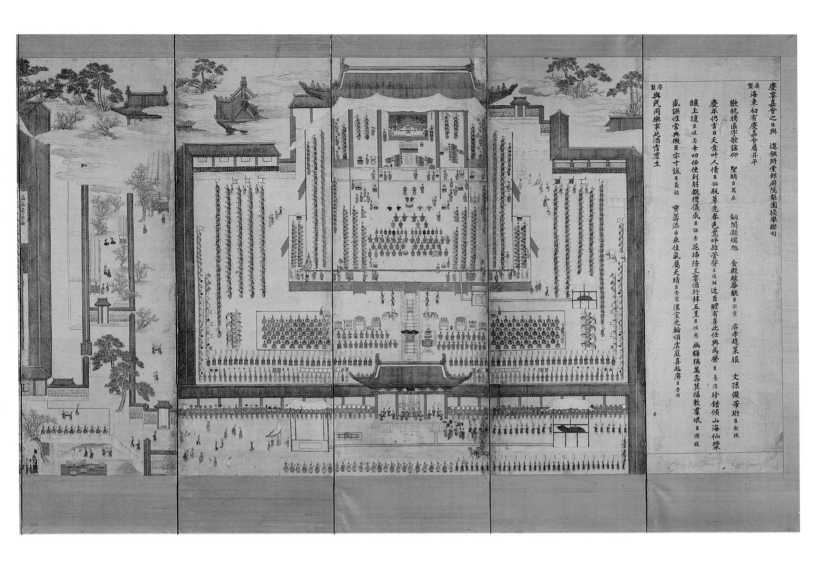

JAPANESE ART

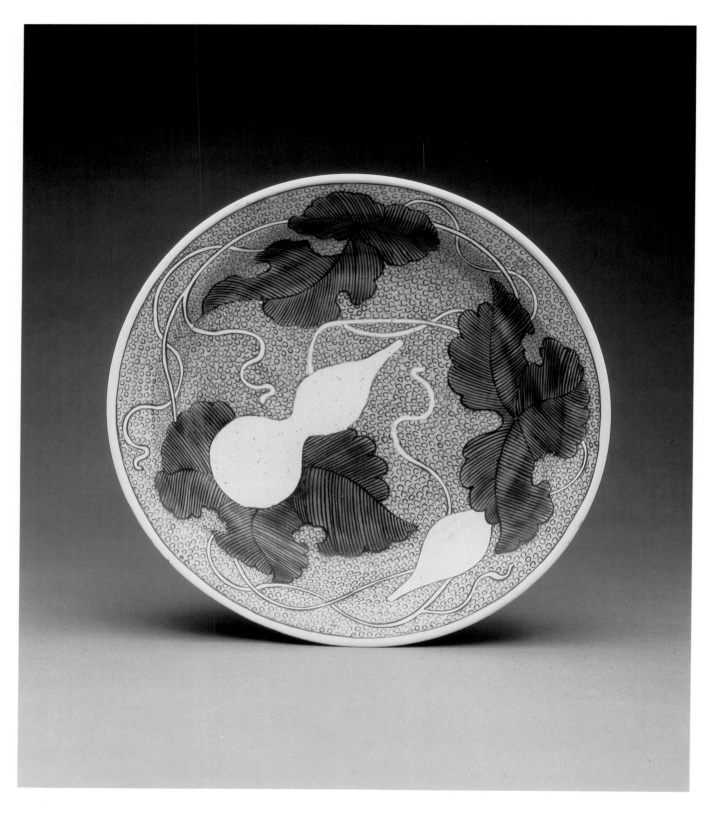

A large Ko-Kutani Bowl
Edo period, late 17th Century
15$\frac{11}{16}$ in. (39.9 cm.) diameter
Sold from the Estate of Blanchette H. Rockefeller
New York, 27 April 1994, $497,500 (£329,576)

Ko-Kutani ware is prized for its rich, dark green enamel colours
and its bold designs. Examples such as this which use green
enamel are called *Aode* or 'Green' Kutani. The Rockefeller
shallow bowl is a masterpiece of its type. Vine grounds and leaves
create a fluid, rhythmical pattern perfectly harmonised with the
circular shape of the bowl. A striking feature of this lush design is
the impact of the white reserve patterns against a yellow ground
densely covered with small black circles.

Kutani is said to have been produced during the seventeenth
century at kilns in Kutani village in Daishoji fief, now in
Yamanaka-cho, Ishikawa prefecture. On the evidence of three
surviving written records, only one of which is roughly
contemporary with Ko-Kutani production, the Kutani kiln began
in about 1655. The founder of the kiln is thought to have been
the metalsmith Goro Saijiro. Three old kiln sites have been
discovered and were excavated between 1970 and 1974. Because
almost no enamelled sherds were found at these sites there is still
scholarly debate as to the place of origin of Ko-Kutani ware. The
term Ko-Kutani (Old Kutani) is used to distinguish seventeenth
century pieces from those produced at the Yoshidaya kiln in
Kutani in the nineteenth century.

A Nabeshima Dish
late 17th/early 18th Century
8$\frac{1}{4}$ in. (20.6 cm.) diameter
London, 20 June 1994, £254,000 ($389,128)

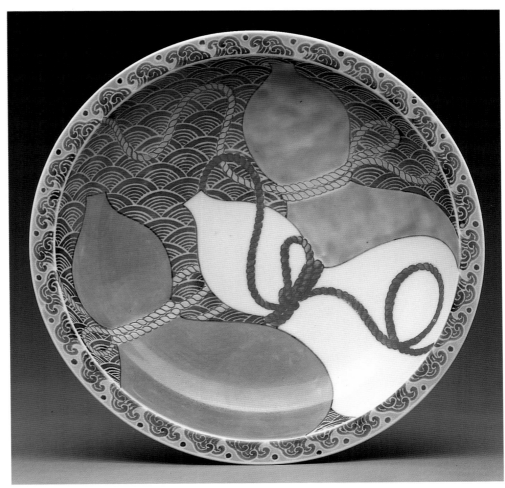

A Kakiemon Vase and Cover
late 17th Century
10$\frac{1}{8}$ in. (25.7 cm.) high
London, 28 March 1994, £69,700 ($104,341)

An inlaid lacquer Table
late 16th/early 17th Century
33¾ in. (86 cm.) high; 16½ in. (42 cm.) wide; 22⅝ in. (57.5 cm.) deep
London, 20 June 1994, £80,000 ($122,560)

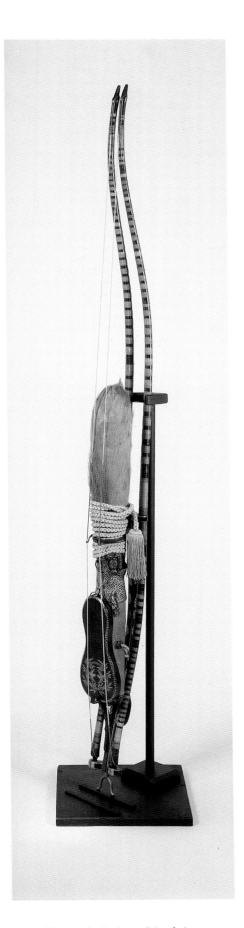

A Nobleman's Quiver *(Utsubo)*
complete with a Pair of matching
Bows and a Set of twenty-five Arrows
with a display Screen
17th Century
twenty-one arrows each 36 in. (91.5 cm.),
four arrows each $36\frac{7}{8}$ in. (93.6 cm.)
London, 28 March 1994, £73,000
($109,281)

A White-laced Suit of Armour of *kozane*
construction
19th Century
London, 16 November 1993, £34,500 ($51,371)

A Katana Blade in fine
mounts
17th Century
$28\frac{3}{8}$ in. (72.1 cm.)
London, 20 June 1994,
£24,000 ($36,768)

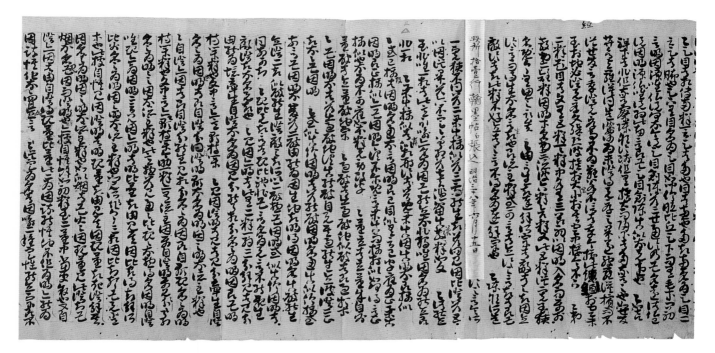

KOBO DAISHI (774–835) and his Circle
Inmyosho, no colophon, n.d. (early 9th Century); *kansubon*,
3 volumes in two handscrolls
manuscript in ink with red notations on paper, with unidentified
seal
$11 \times 288\frac{1}{8}$ in. (28 × 732 cm.) and $11 \times 199\frac{1}{4}$ in. (28 × 506 cm.)
New York, 27 April 1994, $530,500 (£351,179)

KATSUSKI IKA HOKUSAI (1760–1849)
Gaifu kaisei, 'Fine wind, clear weather' ('Red Fuji')
from the series *Fugaku sanjurokkei*, 'Thirty-six views of Mt. Fuji'
signed *Hokusai aratame Iitsu hitsu*, published by Eijudo
$10 \times 14\frac{3}{4}$ in. (25.4 × 37.6 cm.)
London, 20 June 1994, £46,000 ($70,472)

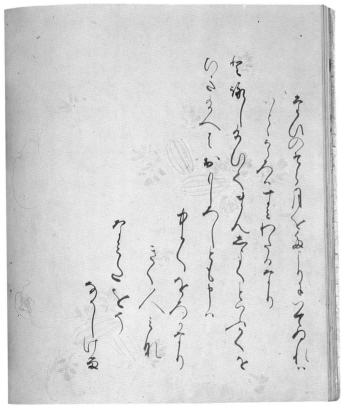

ANONYMOUS
Bishamon no honji, no colophon
late 17th/early 18th Century
fukurotojibon, 5 volumes complete
manuscripts with painted illustrations on gold-decorated paper
11¾ × 9⅞ in. (29.9 × 25 cm.)
London, 15 November 1993, £47,700 ($31,992)

UTAGAWA TOYOKUNI (1769–1825)
Beauty with a Hand-Mirror
signed 'Toyokuni ga', sealed 'Ichiyosai'
hanging scroll, ink and colour on silk, mounted on brocade
36⅝ × 13⅜ in. (93 × 34 cm.)
Sold from the Estate of Blanchette H. Rockefeller
New York, 27 April 1994, $156,500 (£103,780)

CONTEMPORARY JAPANESE ART FROM THE ESTATE OF BLANCHETTE H. ROCKEFELLER

by Sebastian Izzard

In the 1950s, Japanese contemporary art emerged onto the international stage. American abstract expressionists looked to Zen calligraphy and early Japanese ink painting for both spiritual and emotional inspiration. Conversely, their counterparts in Japan were stimulated by the artistic freedom they found available to them in Paris and New York.

Japanese twentieth-century painting has followed two main courses. Some artists have chosen to paint traditional Japanese subjects using traditional materials, a style known as *nihonga* (literally Japanese painting). Others have adopted techniques of oil painting learned in Paris and New York, introducing every major movement or school of twentieth-century art including abstract and avant-garde painting. Their style is known as *yoga* (Western painting). Both schools were initially organised on a rigid structure based on seniority, giving young artists very little opportunity to break through.

The Rockefeller family's interest in Asian art, beginning with Abby Aldrich Rockefeller, has been well documented, as has Blanchette Rockefeller's devotion to modern and contemporary art. Mrs. Rockefeller served as the founding chairman and co-chairman of the Museum of Modern Art's Junior Council (now the Contemporary Art Council) from 1949 to 1955, and from 1955 to 1959 was a founding president of the museum's International Council. In November 1959 she was elected president of the Museum of Modern Art and served in that capacity until 1962. Between 1962 and 1972 she was a board member, and from 1972 to 1985 she served a second term as president. Mrs. Rockefeller served as Chairman of the board of the museum from 1985 until 1987 when she was elected president emeritus.

Her association with M.O.M.A. provided her introduction to contemporary Japanese art. Her mentors included William S. Lieberman, M.O.M.A.'s curator of drawings and prints, and the architect Philip Johnson, a M.O.M.A. trustee. Her aim was to form a comprehensive and representative collection of Japanese contemporary art and to encourage and promote young Japanese artists. Her main purchasing activities took place in the late 1950s and early 1960s, but she continued to build the collection until 1985, the year she purchased *Image of Gate: Black* by Kawabata Minoru (b. 1911) from the Jack Tilton Gallery. At one point her collection included such international luminaries as Okada Kenzo (1902–1982), Arakawa Shusaku (b. 1936) and Isamu Noguchi (1904–1988). Many works were later given to Vassar College, M.O.M.A. and the Japan Society, New York. Her collection encompassed work by nearly all the major artists of the day.

In 1965 M.O.M.A. organised a touring exhibition of contemporary Japanese artists entitled *The New Japanese Painting and Sculpture*: many of Mrs. Rockefeller's paintings were included. The selections were made by Dorothy C. Miller and William S. Lieberman, and served to introduce these artists across America. This ground-breaking exhibition was the largest show of Japanese contemporary art as yet assembled. A reciprocal exhibition of recent art from the United States was held in Tokyo and Kyoto simultaneously with the exhibition's New York showing.

Why then, after a gap of almost thirty years, did the paintings in Mrs. Rockefeller's collection arouse such interest, especially among Japanese museums? One reason is that many of the best works of these artists are no longer available in Japan. These were painted with an American audience in mind and were sold in America. There was a rush of museum building on the prefectural level in Japan during the 1980s and younger curators are intent on building well-rounded, fully representative collections of twentieth century Japanese art. Our sale answered their needs.

Another reason for the interest in the Rockefeller sale was the unusual range of artists and mediums that she assembled: sculptures, ceramics, experimental calligraphy and paintings in both Japanese and Western styles. There were many works by artists who have only recently received popular acclaim in their own country. Mrs. Rockefeller was ahead of her time.

Her holdings included two major paintings by Saito Yoshishige (b. 1904), a leading member of the avant-garde and a pioneer of abstract art. Saito is thought to have reached a creative peak in the late 1950s and early 1960s, just at the time Mrs. Rockefeller was buying. His *Untitled (Red)* (right) was the most expensive painting in our sale. With its thickly applied, brilliant red oil pigments, gouge marks, and machine-made bore holes, the picture is typical of Saito's work. He began to use these techniques and materials in 1930 and they remained a key element in his work throughout his career. At first his paintings were not readily accepted by the Japanese public as these seem neither painting nor sculpture, but international recognition changed matters. In 1961 his *Work No.10* won the international painting award at the Sao Paulo Biennale and the inclusion of four works in the M.O.M.A. exhibition confirmed his international status.

Another experimental and avant-garde artist collected by Mrs. Rockefeller was Yoshihara Jiro (1905–1972), a self-taught painter who in 1954 founded the Gutai association, a group formed of experimental artists active in the visual arts as well as in theatrical and outdoor performances. Gutai artists relied on the physicality of paint itself to express emotion, rather than on representational subject matter. Abstractions by Hasegawa Sabro (1906–1957) in ink on paper were keenly pursued during the sale. Hasegawa, together with his friend and colleague Isamu Noguchi, was influential in the introduction of avant-garde Japanese art to the West and frequently participated in international meetings discussing the role of abstract art in contemporary life.

Younger abstract artists in the Rockefeller sale included Kazuki Yasuo (1911–1974), whose experiences as a Russian prisoner-of-war in Siberia provided him with artistic inspiration.

Experimental works were not the only area of Japanese contemporary art represented in Mrs. Rockefeller's collection. There were examples from the *mingei* (folk-art) movement which has been very influential in twentieth-century Japanese applied arts. Ceramics by the masters Hamada Shoji (1894–1978) and Kitaoji Rosanjin (1883–1959) were represented, as was calligraphy by both Rosanjin and Munakata Shiko (1903–1975), the great twentieth-century print-maker and painter. *Nihonga* was represented by famous artists such as Takeuchi Seiho

(1864–1942), Kobayashi Kokei (1883–1957), Maeda Seison (1886–1977), and Kayama Matazo (b. 1927).

Many of the artist's included in the sale had never been offered at auction in either Europe or America. The success of the sale (only one lot was unsold) was the result of the mix of paintings from various schools. It was an encyclopedic representation of Japanese art from the 1950s and 1960s, a period that has only recently come under scrutiny. That the sale was such a success is a testament to the taste of Mrs. Rockefeller and her advisors, and to the burgeoning interest in contemporary art and culture by young Japanese curators and collectors. American collectors also played a part. A surprising percentage of works in the sale remained in this country, to the dismay of the many Japanese dealers who attended the sale.

SAITO YOSHISHIGE (b. 1904)
Untitled (red)
signed on reverse *Saito Yoshishige* in Japanese and in Roman script 'Y. Saito', dated '62'
oil on wood
$71\frac{3}{4} \times 47\frac{3}{4}$ in. (182.2 × 121.3 cm.)
Sold from the Estate of Blanchette H. Rockefeller
New York, 27 April 1994, $376,500 (£249,668)
Record auction price for a work by the artist

TRIBAL ART

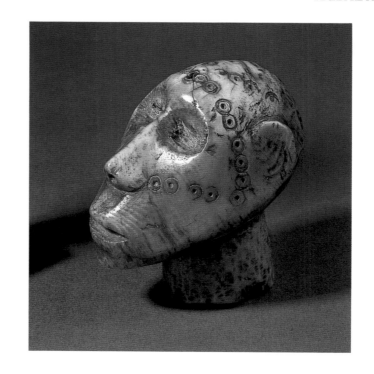

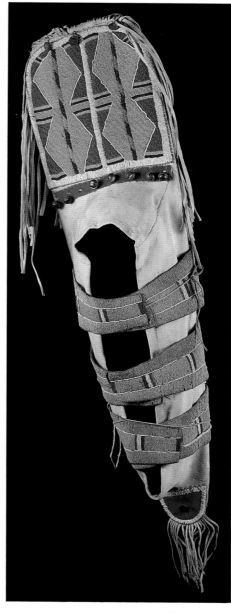

Left:
A Navajo Chief's Wearing Blanket
Southwest United States, circa 1850−60
51¾ × 70 in. (131.5 × 177.8 cm.)
New York, 23 May 1994, $200,500 (£129,188)

An Arapaho painted hide Shield
Plains Indians, circa 1840−60
18¾ in. (47.7 cm.) diameter
New York, 23 May 1994, $41,000 (£26,418)

A Cheyenne beaded and fringed hide Pipe Bag
Plains Indians, circa 1840−60
18 in. (45.8 cm.) long without attachments
New York, 23 May 1994, $32,200 (£20,747)

Above:
A Sioux quilled and fringed hide Warrior's Shirt
Plains Indians, circa 1840−50
39¼ in. (99.7 cm.) long without attachments
New York, 23 May 1994, $74,000 (£47,680)

A crow-beaded hide Cradleboard
Plains Indians, circa 1870−90
39¾ in. (101 cm.) long without attachments
New York, 23 May 1994, $50,600 (£32,603)

PRINTED BOOKS AND MANUSCRIPTS

THE REAPPEARANCE OF SCALIGER'S ARISTOTLE AND BESSARION'S APULEIUS IN THE BERIAH BOTFIELD SALE

by Felix de Marez Oyens

The practice of selling literary property by auction reached medieval Europe from the Islamic world. Several early sales are recorded through the survival of manuscripts listing their contents, but how exactly they were conducted is unknown. In Italy and England bids could be made on substantial lots for as long as it took to burn a candle, a rule which not surprisingly caused frequent disputes. The modern manner of knocking lots down to their successful bidders, i.e. by the strike of a hammer, was common in the Southern Netherlands. The first sale for which a printed catalogue is extant took place at Leyden in 1599, the unmentioned auctioneer being Louis Elzevier. It comprised part of the second library formed by Philips van Marnix, Lord of St. Aldegonde, a pivotal figure in the Dutch revolt against Spain; the venue was his widow's house, where according to a laconic announcement in the catalogue some paintings by Albrecht Dürer would also be auctioned.

Some half dozen years before the date of the Marnix sale, which he may well have attended, and after long negotiations Leyden University was able to engage Europe's greatest classical scholar Joseph Justus Scaliger. He had to leave most of his books behind in France, but quickly built up another highly important collection. At his death in 1609, he bequeathed 170 oriental manuscripts, as well as all his Greek and Latin codices, to the University Library. His closest friends, including his distinguished pupil Daniel Heinsius, were allowed to select a number of printed books for themselves. The *beau reste* of the library was consigned to Elzevier for auction, who charged 5% of the proceeds for his services. Petrus Scriverius's copy annotated with prices and names of purchasers, formerly at Kiel, was destroyed in the Second World War, but it is known that Daniel Heinsius, librarian, latinist and poet, was the major buyer at the sale, acting both for himself and on behalf of the University. Heinsius marked the books he acquired in the sale as coming from Scaliger's library, and it is this happy decision that two centuries later alerted the English bibliophiles Richard Heber and Beriah Botfield to the important association attached to their set of the Aldine Aristotle.

Daniel's library was inherited by his even more talented son, Nicolaus Heinsius, the most encyclopaedic book collector of the seventeenth century and agent for the greatest female bibliophile ever, Queen Christina of Sweden. After Nicolaus died in 1681, the sale of his library was organized by the Leyden publisher and bookdealer, Johannes de Vivie, who compiled a catalogue of more than 13,000 lots and had it printed by Abraham Elzevier. Several issues are known of this famous catalogue: the first is the auction issue with a title stating place and date of sale, while the others omit all references to the sale and were evidently marketed after the event as an enumerative bibliography and price-guide (with the results supplied in manuscript). The entries were still of the briefest kind but showed a marked improvement on those in the Scaliger catalogue, and most editions listed are easily identified. The celebrated *editio princeps* of Aristotle's works, printed in Greek by Aldus Manutius at Venice in 1495–98, fetched just over six florins, a derisory price considering that Fl.200 per annum were needed to support a family of four (according to a recently published calculation). Contemporary Amsterdam editions of the same author reached ten times that figure in the same sale; today such seventeenth-century editions would bring no more than £100 at auction, whereas the Scaliger-Heinsius-Heber set of the Aldine edition fetched £144,500 in the Botfield sale last March.

As an early member of the Roxburghe Club and future author of *Prefaces to the First Editions of the Greek and Roman Classics*, Beriah Botfield was well aware of the importance of a Scaliger provenance, and when he bought his Aldine Aristotle in the mid-1830s for 30 gns. from the Pall Mall booksellers, Payne and Foss, he spent another 21 gns. on getting it lavishly rebound by Charles Lewis and £1 10s. on 'thirty hours cleaning.' The book was only one of nineteen remarkable Greek *editiones principes* in the Botfield sale, a small selection made by Christie's from this extraordinary but until recently little-known collection and consigned from Longleat House by order of the Trustees of the Bath Settled Estates. The buyer was Bernard Quaritch, London's leading house of antiquarian booksellers, who have established a kind of monopoly on the Aldine Aristotle bound in gold-tooled morocco: over a period of seven years they acquired complete sets in the Doheny (1987), Spencer (1988), O'More (1989) and Botfield (1994) sales.

Botfield was not aware of the other and even greater association copy he owned, this one hiding among his Latin first editions; nor for that matter were Payne and Foss, who in 1830 sold him the book for 40 gns. It was Cardinal Bessarion's reading copy on paper of Apuleius's works, edited by Johannes Andreae de Buxiis, Bishop of Aleria, and printed at Rome by Conrad Sweynheym and Arnold Pannartz, the first Germans to spread the art of typography from Mainz to Italy; also included in the edition are Latin translations of *Asclepius*, traditionally ascribed to one Hermes Trismegistus, and the epitome of Platonic philosophy by Albinus. Bessarion's arms, symbolizing the union of the Greek and Roman Churches, are emblazoned on the first page, and his discreet reading marks and red interlinings occur particularly in the neo-Platonic texts. The editor's dedicatory letter to Pope Paul II is mostly written in praise of Cardinal Bessarion whose patronage was probably instrumental in bringing the Sweynheym and Pannartz press from the Benedictine monastery at Subiaco to the house of the brothers de Maximis in Rome. Among the twenty-two printed books from Bessarion's library still preserved in the Biblioteca Marciana at Venice, there is another copy of the Apuleius, printed on vellum and illuminated, but without any evidence of having been read. It was no doubt presented to Bessarion as a *de luxe* copy, whereas that on paper will have served as his humbler, but now more interesting, working copy. The New York booksellers H.P. Kraus paid £95,000 for Botfield's unsuspected treasure, no more than three times the current market value of an ordinary copy.

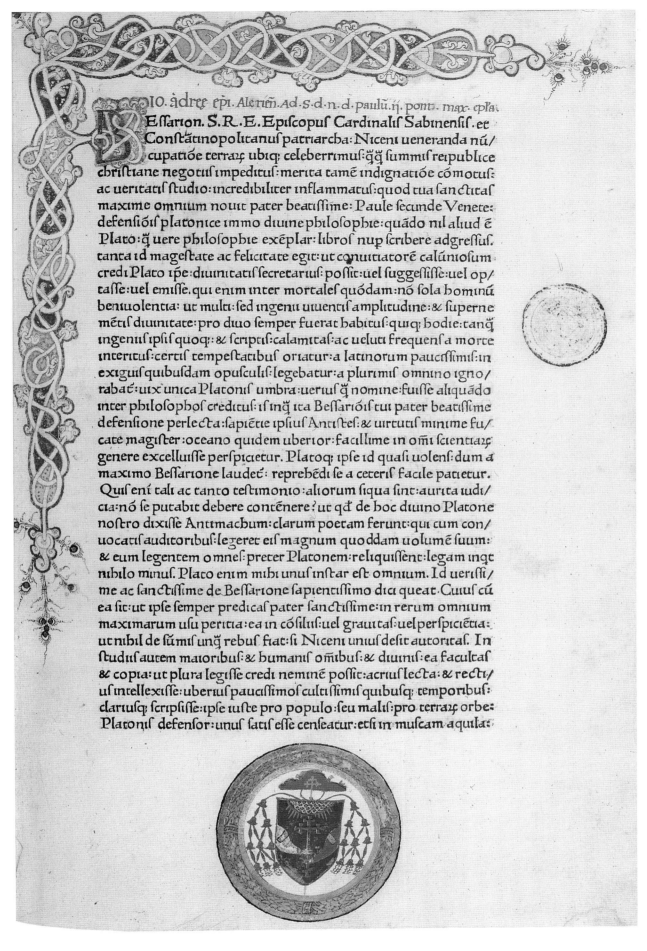

Lucius Apuleius Madaurensis, *Opera*, Hermes Trismegistus, *Asclepius*, Albinus Platonicus (active 2nd century A.D.), *Epitoma disciplinarum Platonis*, Rome, [Conradus Sweynheym and Arnoldus Pannartz], 28 February 1469, folio 12½ × 8⅜ in. (31.6 × 21.3 cm.), illuminated initials by a Roman artist, with white-vine decoration opening most works and both dedications, gold-tooled green morocco over pasteboard, Botfield arms on covers, by Charles Lewis, first edition of all texts, from the library of Cardinal Bessarion

London, 30 March 1994, £95,000 ($141,265)

VNDVM ET HOC QVOD NOMINE
alio Cęlum appellari libuit:cuius circúflexu tegunt̄
cuncta:numen esse credi par est:ęternum:inmensum
neqʒ genitū:neqʒ interituʒ umǭ·Huius extera ídaga/
re:nec interest hominū:nec capit humanę coniectura
mentis.Sacer est:ęternus:imensus:totus í toto:ímo
uero ipse totūm infinitus:ac finito similis.Omnium
reʒ certus & similis incerto.Extra intra cuncta com/
plexus in se idemqʒ reʒ naturę opus & reʒ ipsa natu/
ra:furor est:mensuram eius animo quosdam agitasse
atqʒ pdere ausos.Alios rursus occasione hinc sumpta
aut bis data ínumerabiles tradidisse mundos:ut toti/
dem reʒ naturas credi oporteret.Aut si una omnes incubarent:totidē tamē soles:toti
demqʒ lunas:et cętera etiam in uno:& inmensa & ínumerabilia sydera:ǭsi nó eadem
quęstióe semp in termino cogitationis occursura desiderio finis alicuius.Aut si hęc
infinitas naturę oím artifici possit assignari.Non illud idē in uno facilius sit ítelligi
tanto pręsertim opere:furor est:pfecto furor egredi ex eo.Et tanǭ interna eius cuncta
plane iam sint nota ita scrutari extera quasi uero mensuram illius rei possit agere:qui
sui nesciat aut homíes possint uidere quę mūdus ipse non capiat.

Ormam eius in spetié orbis absoluti globatam esse nomen inprimis & cósensus
in eo mortalium orbem appellantium.Sed & argumēta reʒ docent nó solú quia
talis figura oíbus sui partibus uergit in se se:ac sibi ipsa tolleranda est:seque includit
et continet nullaʒ egens compagū:nec finem aut initiū ullis sui partibus sentiēs:nec
quia ad motum quo subinde uerti mox apparebit:talis aptissima est.Sed oculorum
quoqʒ pbatione qʒ connexus mediusqʒ quacúqʒ cernatur:cum id accidere in alia non
possit figura.
    Anc ergo formam eius ęterno & irrequieto ambitu inenarrabili celeritate.xxiiii.
horaʒ spatio circúagi solis exortus et occasus haud dubium relíquere an sit imē/
sus:& ideo sensum uariū facile excedēs tantę molis rotata uertigine assidua sonitus nó
equidē facile dixerim:non hercle magis ǭ circumactoʒ simul tinnitus sydeʒ suosque
uoluétium orbes.An dulcis quidam & incredibili suauitate concętus nobis qui intus
agimur iuxta diebus noctibusqʒ tacitus labit̄ mundus:esse innumeras ei effigies ani/
malium reʒqʒ cunctaʒ impressas.Nec ut in uolucrum notamus ouis leuitatem cóti/
nuam lubricū corpus:quod clarissimi quidē auctores dixere:uerū argumētis indicat̄
quoniam inde deciduis reʒ omniū seminibus in numerę in mari precipue:ac pleʒqʒ
confusis monstrificę digenerantur effigies:Pręterea uisus probatione alibi ursi tauri
alibi:alibi:litterę figura & candidiore medio super uerticem circulo

    Quidem & consensu gentium moueor.Namque.Cosmos gręci nomine orna/
menti appellauerunt eum & nos a perfecta absolutaqʒ elegantia mundum:Cęlū
quidem haud dubie cęlati argumēto diximus:ut interpretat̄.M.Varro.Adiuuat reʒ
ordo descripto circulo qui signifer uocat̄ in.xii.aíaliū effigies:& per illas solis cursus
congruens tot sęculis ratio.
    Ec de elementis uideo dubitari ǭtuor esse ea.Ignitum summo:inde tot stellarū
collucētium illos oculos:pximū spiritus:quē gręci nostriqʒ eodē uocabulo aera
appellant.Vitalē hunc:& per cuncta reʒ meabilē totoqʒ cósertum:cuius ui suspēsam
cum quarto aquaʒ elemēto librari medio spatii tellurē ita mutuo cóplexu diuersitatis

Gaius Plinius Secundus, *Historia naturalis*, Venice,   One of the first three books printed at Venice
Johannes de Spira, 1469, folio $16\frac{1}{2} \times 11$ in.
(42×28 cm), first edition, very large copy, from
the library of Pierre-Henri Larcher
London, 30 March 1994, £177,500 ($263,943)

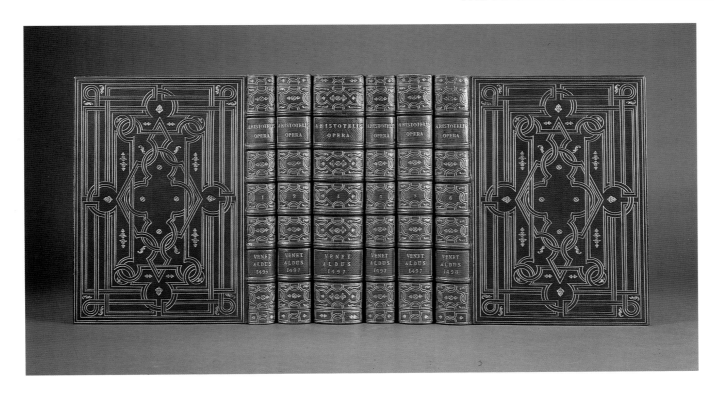

Aristotle, *Opera*, in Greek, Venice, Aldus Manutius, 1 November 1495–June 1498, folio 12 × 8⅛ in. (30.7 × 20.7 cm.), five parts bound in 6 volumes, *editio princeps* of Aristotle and of all other texts included, an important association copy from the library of Joseph Justus Scaliger
London, 30 March 1994, £144,500 ($214,872)

Richardus de Bury (1281–1345), *Philobiblon*, Cologne, [Printer of Augustinus, *De fide*], 1473, quarto 7⅛ × 5 in. (18.2 × 12.6 cm.), first edition of the first printed book on bibliophily
London, 30 March 1994, £100,500 ($149,444)

Hemerocallis Fulva   *Hemerocalle Fauve.*

Pierre-Joseph Redouté (1759–1840), *Les Liliacées*, text by
Augustin-Pyramus de Candolle, François Delaroche and Alire
Raffeneau-Delile, Paris, Imprimerie de Didot jeune for the
author, 1802–16
8 volumes, folio 20 × 13⅜ in. (50.8 × 34 cm.), 487 stipple-
engraved plates printed in colours and finished by hand,

contemporary red straight-grained morocco, bound for the
Duchesse de Berry, with her arms blocked in gilt in the centre of
the covers, by F. Doll, first edition, limited to 280 copies, of
Redouté's masterpiece and an outstanding association copy from
the library of one of his patrons
London, 30 March 1994, £210,000 ($312,270)

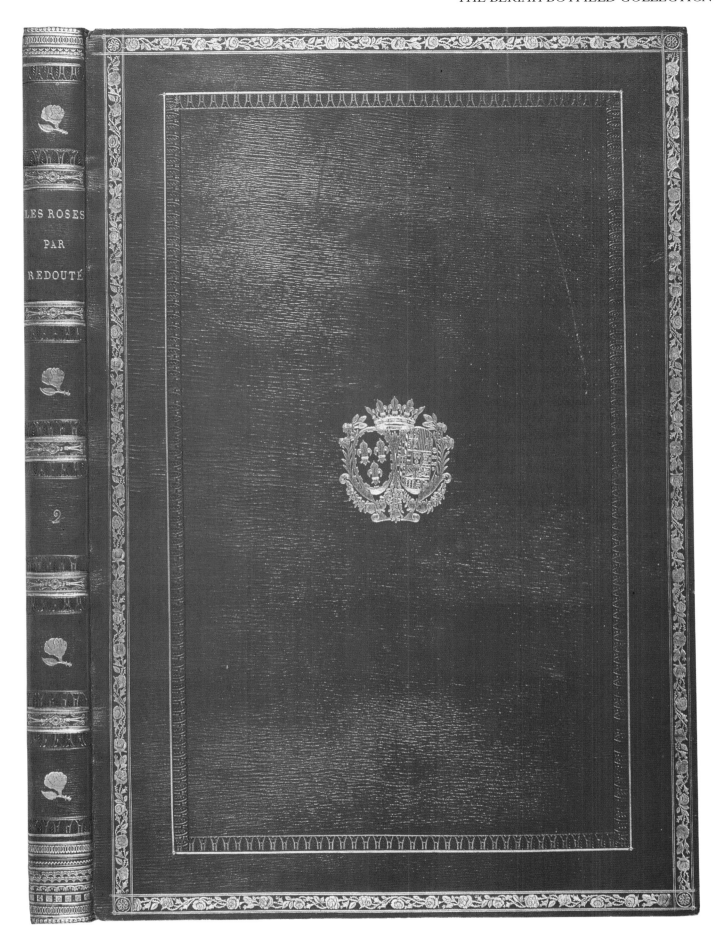

Pierre-Joseph Redouté (1759–1840) and Claude-Antoine Thory, (1759–1827), *Les Roses*, Paris, Firmin Didot, 1817–24, 3 volumes, folio $20\frac{7}{8} \times 13\frac{5}{8}$ in. (52.9 × 34.7 cm.), floral wreath and 169 stipple-engraved plates printed in colours and finished by hand, contemporary red straight-grained morocco, bound for the Duchesse de Berry, with her arms blocked in gilt in the centre of the covers by René Simier, first edition, limited large-paper issue of Redouté's most famous work and an outstanding association copy from the library of one of his most influential patrons London, 30 March 1994, £260,000 ($386,620)

BOOKS FROM THE BURTON LIBRARY

by Nina Musinsky

The 1930s witnessed an outpouring of magnificent and rare books from major collections on the Continent and in the United States – those of Edouard Rahir, Lucien Gougy and Henri Beraldi in Paris, of Cortlandt Field Bishop and Mortimer L. Schiff in New York, to name but a few of the most prominent sales, which coincided with rather than were occasioned by the great Depression. The overall success of these sales demonstrated the hardiness of a small international group of booksellers who were able to marshal their curtailed resources and pay record prices for exceptionally fine copies of extremely rare books. Of all the decade's sales, the extended dispersal (in 1930–38) of the private collection of the great bibliophile-bookseller Edouard Rahir, successor to Damascène Morgand, was perhaps the most brilliant, and a Rahir provenance quickly joined the constellation of French names – the Comte d'Hoym, Baron Jérôme Pichon and Ambroise Firmin-Didot among them – which bring to a book the distinction that only truly blue blood can confer on a title.

Through astute bidding at the Rahir sale alone a knowledgeable bookseller could fill a collector's shelves with books the likes of which would bring the most distinguished booksellers and collectors flocking from every corner of the Common Market and the United States today. Such was the relationship between the

bookseller Henri Lardanchet, the Lyonese collector Henri Burton (d. 1971) and the highly cosmopolitan audience who competed for the portion of his library offered by Christie's New York on behalf of his three American grandchildren on 22 April 1994.

M. Burton, a resident of Geneva from the early thirties until his death, appears to have acquired his fine collection of predominantly French illustrated printed books of the fifteenth to twentieth centuries almost exclusively from or through the agency of his fellow-townsman Lardanchet, and the majority of his most important books had in fact crossed Rahir's shelves. Those which had not were graced with equally illustrious provenances, including all of the aforenamed and Nicolas Yemeniz, Horace de Landau, Robert Hoe, Hector de Backer, A. Brölemann, Antoine-Augustin Renouard, among others. In spite of his fondness for great names, Henri Burton was a reserved collector, and only a few of the mutedly excited attendees of the New York sale professed to have heard of his collection, while no more than two had actually visited it. A group of his books had been sold in the seventies, a few others bearing his green or red morocco bookplate had surfaced since, but this was the most substantial group of books from his library to come up at auction since his death, and one of the finest collections of French Renaissance literature to have appeared at auction within memory.

The 104 lots offered in April, of which all but three minor lots were sold, fetched a total of over $1,684,000, nearly twice their high estimate. The sale was not surprisingly dominated by the European and mainly French book trade. Nevertheless, although most of the books have returned to France (two of them to the Bibliothèque Nationale to fill gaps in the collection), the high prices fetched by nearly all of them were made possible by a strong showing by the American and British book trade – H. P. Kraus, Martin Breslauer, Quaritch, Maggs, Ursus and others competing vigorously and occasionally successfully against their Gallic colleagues, whose appetite had been whetted by pre-sale exhibitions in Paris and Geneva of thirty of the finest books from the collection. The fundamental vivacity of the European book trade was made hearteningly evident to all present, as were the advantages of selling a major collection in a truly international arena.

Henri Burton was an exacting bibliophile who rejected all but the finest and most complete copies of significant editions, but the taste of his time differed radically from the present ethic in book-collecting. While today's collectors prefer the challenge of hunting for books in unsophisticated 'original' condition, amateurs of M. Burton's time still appreciated early printed books whose blemishes had been carefully washed away or whose defects had been ever so delicately restored by an earlier generation, and whose gleaming morocco bindings were the work of the greatest French bookbinders of the nineteenth or early twentieth centuries. With a few remarkable exceptions, M. Burton's books reflected this fashion, but even the most fastidious modern collector would hardly sneer, for example, at one of the earliest incunable editions of the first French almanac, the highly influential and copiously illustrated *Kalendrier des Bergirs*, for its washed and mended leaves and nineteenth-century morocco binding. Indeed, the copy of Guy Marchant's April 1493 edition (illustrated right) was the third of eight incunable editions and the only one to come on the market since its own appearance in the Rahir sale, it was one of two lots in the April sale to fetch the top price of $189,500, nearly doubling its high estimate. It shared this honour with another Rahir book, a copy of an undated incunable edition of Aesop's *Fabulae* (illustrated right), printed in Augsburg by Anton Sorg in about 1480 (according to the standard bibliographies; a more likely date is circa 1485–93), which is adorned with the original woodcuts from Johannes Zainer's Ulm circa 1476–77 edition, the first illustrated edition of what may be the most frequently illustrated work in Western literature. The Burton copy, bound in red morocco and one of two owned by Rahir, was purchased by a French private collector.

The same collector paid $83,900 for one of a small but hotly competed for group of sixteenth century books in the Burton collection still in their original bindings: M. Burton's copy of the first edition of Hugues Salel's French translation of the first ten books of Homer's *Iliade* (illustrated left) (Paris 1545), one of the rarest of the many masterpieces of French sixteenth century book design, was appropriately clothed in a contemporary painted strapwork and arabesque goatskin binding from one of the Parisian ateliers of the 1550s (possibly the anonymous "Grolier Cuspinianus" binder). M. Burton's Homer was again, astonishingly, one of two copies owned by Rahir; the other, in a delicate contemporary parchment binding, is now at Harvard.

Left:
Homer, *Les dix premiers livres de l'Iliade*, Paris, Jehan Loys for Vincent Sertenas, 1545, folio $11\frac{9}{16} \times 7\frac{11}{16}$ in. (29.4 × 19.5 cm.), title woodcut of Homer represented as the fountain of poetry, 10 large woodcuts at the head of each chapter within woodcut ornamental borders, contemporary Parisian gold-tooled and painted entrelac goatskin binding, first edition of Hugues Salel's translation of the *Iliad*, from the library of Edouard Rahir
Sold from the Estate of Henri Burton
New York, 22 April 1994, $83,900 (£56,384)

Right:
Aesop, *Vita et fabulae*, Augsburg, Anton Sorg, circa 1485, Chancery folio $10\frac{5}{8} \times 7\frac{1}{2}$ in. (27 × 19 cm.), 194 woodcuts, morocco by Chambolle-Duru, from the library of Edouard Rahir
Sold from the Estate of Henri Burton
New York, 22 April 1994, $189,500 (£127,352)

Le compost et kalendrier des Bergiers, Paris, Guy Marchant, 18 April 1493, Chancery folio $10\frac{1}{8} \times 7\frac{1}{4}$ in. (25.7 × 18.5 cm.), calendar with 24 woodcuts, 65 woodcuts in the text, morocco by Bauzonnet-Trautz, arms of Baron Jérôme-Fréderic Pichon on sides. One of four known copies, from the libraries of Baron Pichon, Jean-Baptiste Huzard, Ambroise Firmin-Didot, Thomas Brooke, Edouard Rahir and Grace Whitney Hoff
Sold from the Estate of Henri Burton
New York, 22 April 1994, $189,500 (£127,352)

Above, from Left:

Bible, *in Latin*, with prologues attributed to St. Jerome and the interpretation of Hebrew names, Paris, circa 1250,
illuminated manuscript on vellum, 728 leaves, $6\frac{1}{8} \times 4\frac{1}{8}$ in. (15.5 × 10.3 cm.), 88 historiated initials, 66 illuminated initials, 15th Century blind-stamped calf over wooden boards, a signed binding by Livinus Stuvaert of Ghent and Bruges
Sold from the Lord's New Church, Pennsylvania
New York, 22 April 1994, $68,500 (£46,035)

The Miracles of Saint Hildegard, in Latin, illuminated manuscript on vellum, Southern Germany, Benedictine monastery of Kempten, second quarter of the 15th Century, $6\frac{1}{2} \times 4\frac{1}{2}$ in. (16.6 × 11.5 cm.), 65 leaves, 9 large historiated initials, 27 full-page miniatures, bound in early 16th Century South-German blindstamped calf over wooden boards
London, 29 June 1994, £155,000 ($240,560)

Right, from Top Left:

Sir Isaac Newton (1642–1727), *Philosophiae Naturalis Principia Mathematica*, London, Joseph Streater for the Royal Society, 1687, quarto, first edition, first issue with two-line imprint on title page, folding engraved plate, woodcut diagrams
London, South Kensington, 2 July 1994, £52,000 ($79,820)

Frederick DuCane Godman and Osbert Salvin, editors, *Biologia Centrali-Americana; or, contributions to the knowledge of the fauna and flora of Mexico and Central America*, London, for the editors by R.H. Porter and Dulau and Co., 1879–1915, 66 volumes, quarto $12\frac{1}{4} \times 9\frac{7}{8}$ in. (31 × 25 cm.) and oblong folio $12\frac{3}{8} \times 19\frac{5}{8}$ in. (31.5 × 50 cm.) approximately 1,657 lithographic and autotype plates of the fauna, flora and archaeology of Central America, including 890 hand-coloured lithographs, uniform contemporary gold-tooled red morocco, original wrappers and *Botany* indices bound in 3 separate volumes in contemporary red half cloth, Frederick DuCane Godman's copy
London, 3 November 1993, £111,500 ($165,020)

John James Audubon (1785–1851) and Rev. John Bachman (1790–1874), *The Viviparous Quadrupeds of North America*, New York, J.J. and V.G. Audubon, 1845–54, 6 volumes, comprising plates, 3 volumes, atlas folio, $27 \times 20\frac{7}{8}$ in (68.5 × 53 cm.) and text: 3 volumes, royal octavo, $10\frac{3}{8} \times 6\frac{7}{8}$ in. (26.4 × 17.4 cm.), atlas with 150 finely coloured lithographed plates after John James and John Woodhouse Audubon, text with 6 coloured plates after J.W. Audubon by W.E. Hitchcock, atlas bound in 19th Century English green half morocco gilt by J. Wright, text in American purple half morocco gilt
New York, 29 October 1993, $222,500 (£149,075)

PHILOSOPHIÆ
NATURALIS &
PRINCIPIA
MATHEMATICA.

Autore *JS. NEWTON*, *Trin. Coll. Cantab. Soc.* Matheseos
Professore *Lucasiano*, & Societatis Regalis Sodali.

IMPRIMATUR·
S. PEPYS, *Reg. Soc.* PRÆSES.
Julii 5. 1686.

LONDINI,

Jussu *Societatis Regiæ* ac Typis *Josephi Streater*. Prostat apud
plures Bibliopolas. *Anno* MDCLXXXVII.

GUSTAVIA. SUPERBA. *Berg. var.* SALVINIÆ, *Hemsl.*

LYNX CANADENSIS, GEOFF.

John James Audubon (1785–1851), *The Birds of America; from Original Drawings*, London, published by the author, 1827–38, 4 volumes, double elephant folio, $38\frac{3}{4} \times 25\frac{7}{8}$ in. (98.5 × 65.5 cm.), engraved titles and 435 hand-coloured etchings with aquatint engraving by William Home Lizars of Edinburgh, Robert Havell, Sr. and Robert Havell, Jr. of London, after Audubon's original life-size watercolours, on J. Whatman and J. Whatman Turkey Mill paper with watermarks dated 1827–38, bound in light brown pigskin by Zaehnsdorf
New York, 29 October 1993, $3,027,500 (£2,028,250)

MACROCERCUS HYACINTHINUS.

Hyacinthine Macaw

3/4 Nat Size

Edward Lear (1812–1888), *Illustration of the Family of Psittacidae, or Parrots*, London, published by E. Lear 1830-32, large folio, $21\frac{1}{2} \times 14\frac{1}{2}$ in. (54.7 × 37.3 cm.), 42 hand-coloured lithographed plates, all but one signed by Lear, printed by Charles Hullmandel, bound in contemporary English red half straight-grained morocco preserving five pictorial lithographed front wrappers from the original instalment parts
New York, 29 October 1993, $112,500 (£75,375)

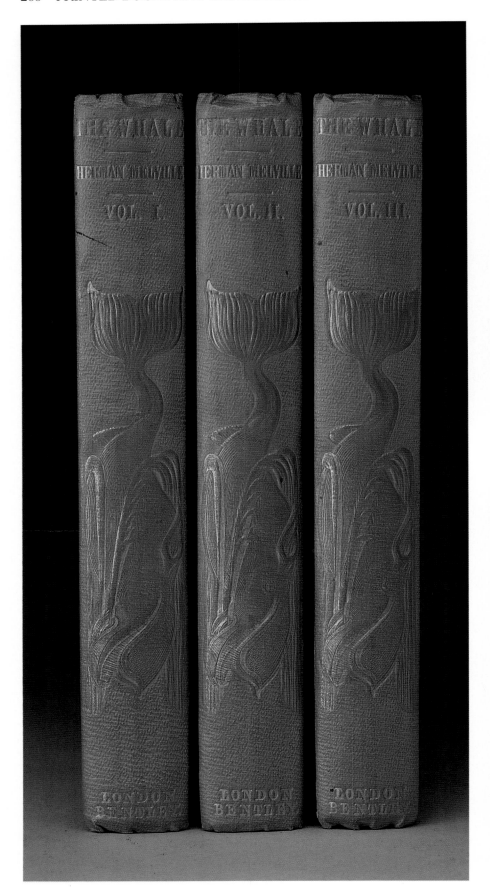

Herman Melville (1819–1891), *The Whale*, London, Richard Bentley, 1851, 3 volumes, octavo, original binding of blue cloth sides and cream cloth spines gilt-stamped with a sounding whale and gilt-lettered, first edition of *Moby Dick*
New York, 9 December 1993, $75,100 (£50,317)

John Steinbeck (1902–1968), *The Grapes of Wrath*, New York, 1939, octavo, original pictorial beige cloth, pictorial dust jacket, first edition, presentation copy, inscribed by Steinbeck on the front free endpaper
New York, Christie's East, 20 April 1994, $11,270 (£7,574)

John Steinbeck (1902–1968), *Cup of Gold*, New York, Robert M. McBride, 1929, octavo, original yellow cloth, top edge stained blue, pictorial dust jacket, quarter morocco slipcase, first edition, first issue, inscribed by Steinbeck on the front free endpaper
New York, Christie's East, 20 April 1994, $12,650 (£8,501)

Georges Rouault (1871–1958), *Cirque de l'étoile filante*, Paris,
Ambroise Vollard, 1938, folio $18 \times 13\frac{3}{4}$ in. (45.5 × 35 cm.),
17 aquatint plates printed in colours by Rouault, 82 wood-
engraved illustrations by Georges Aubert after Rouault, edition
limited to 280 copies (20 of which *hors-commerce*), this one of
215 on *Vergé de Montval*
London, 29 June 1994, £47,700 ($74,030)

John Adams.

Philadelphia Novr 15th 1775.

Dear Sir.   The Course of Events, naturally turns the Thoughts of Gentlemen to the Subjects of Legislation and Jurisprudence, and it is a curious
Problem what Form of Government, is most readily & easily adopted
by a Colony, upon a Sudden Emergency. Nature and Experience
have already pointed out the Solution of this Problem, in the Choice
of Conventions and Committees of Safety. Nothing is wanting in
Addition to these to make a compleat Government, but the Appoint-
ment of Magistrates for the due Administration of Justice.

Taking Nature and Experience for my Guide I have made the following Sketch, which may be varied in any one particular
an infinite Number of Ways, So as to accommodate it to the
different, Genius, Temper, Principles and even Prejudices of different
People.

A Legislative, an Executive and a judicial Power, comprehend the
whole of what is meant and understood by Government. It is
by Ballancing each of these Powers against the other two, that the Effort
in humane Nature towards Tyranny can alone be checked and
restrained and any degree of Freedom preserved in the Constitution.

Let a full and free Representation of the People be chosen for an
House of Commons.

Let the House choose by Ballott twelve, Sixteen, Twenty four
or Twenty Eight Persons, either Members of the House, or from
the People at Large as the Electors please, for a Council.

John Adams (1735–1826), a signed autograph Letter to Richard
Henry Lee of Virginia, Philadelphia, 15 November 1775
New York, 9 December 1993, $409,500 (£274,280)

James Monroe (1758–1831), autograph
Manuscript, the Draft of his First Inaugural
Address, delivered 4 March 1817
New York, 9 December 1993, $332,500
(£222,706)

Abraham Lincoln (1809–1865), a signed
autograph Letter to George Clayton Latham,
a classmate of Robert Todd Lincoln at
Phillips Exeter Academy; Springfield, Illinois,
22 July 1860
New York, 9 December 1993, $728,500
(£487,944)

PHOTOGRAPHS

LEWIS HINE (American, 1874–1946)
Mechanic and Steam Pump
titled in pencil and 'Interpretive Photography' stamped on the
verso
gelatin silver print, 1920s
$9\frac{5}{8} \times 6\frac{7}{8}$ in. (24.4 × 17.5 cm.)
New York, 20 April 1994, $90,500 (£61,149)
Record auction price for a photograph by the artist

ALFRED STIEGLITZ (American, 1864–1946)
The Terminal (1892)
signed, titled and dated twice in the margin
photogravure, circa 1910
$10 \times 13\frac{1}{8}$ in. (25.4 × 33.3 cm.)
New York, 8 October 1993, $107,000 (£70,302)
Sold by the family of Aline and Charles Leibma
Record auction price for a single photogravure

PETER HENRY EMERSON (British, 1856–1936)
Life and Landscape on the Norfolk Broads, London: Sampson
Low, Marston, Searle and Rivington, 1886, ordinary edition with
text by Emerson and T.F. Goodall, with forty platinum prints
printed by Valentine of Dundee
ranging in size from approximately $5\frac{1}{4} \times 9\frac{1}{4}$ in. (13.3 × 23.5 cm.)
to $8 \times 11\frac{1}{4}$ in. (20.3 × 28.6 cm.)
London, 12 May 1994, £23,000 ($34,339)

ALFRED STIEGLITZ (American, 1864–1946)
Georgia O'Keeffe: A Portrait – Hands with Thimble
signed, inscribed 'Photograph' and dated in pencil on the original
overmat
solarised palladium print, 1920
$9\frac{1}{4} \times 7\frac{5}{8}$ in. (23.5 × 19.4 cm.)
New York, 8 October 1993, $398,500 (£261,827)
Sold by the family of Aline and Charles Leibma
Record auction price for a photograph

MAN RAY (American, 1890–1976)
Noire et Blanche
signed and dated in pencil on the recto
gelatin silver print, 1926
$8\frac{3}{8} \times 10\frac{3}{4}$ in. (21.3 × 27.3 cm.)
New York, 20 April 1994, $354,500 (£239,527)
Record auction price for a photograph by the artist

This picture was formerly in the collection of Jacques Doucet

In the world of Parisian *couture*, design and art in the 1920s, the name Jacques Doucet was synonymous with impeccable taste. Doucet, a leading couturier and art patron, was known for his adventurous eye and provocative stance on collecting. Having collected eighteenth-century paintings, drawings and furniture, he decided in 1912 to sell his entire collection at auction. After the war, Doucet's appetite for collecting reached grand proportions, as he developed his eye for the twentieth-century avant-garde. In painting, he preferred Matisse and Picasso. He acquired this photograph from the artist.

Doucet was no stranger to Man Ray – or Kiki of Montparnasse, the model in this photograph – and the circles of Dada and Surrealism. Man Ray, in a rare portrait sitting of the collector, photographed Doucet.

Man Ray's quiet, elegant and dreamy study, *Noire et Blanche* would have naturally appealed to Doucet complementing his own vision which combined an appreciation of the ancient and primitive arts with a sophisticated, modern taste.

TINA MODOTTI (American, 1896–1942)
Two Callas
initialled and dated in pencil on the tipped mount
platinum print
$9\frac{1}{4} \times 7$ in. (23.5 × 17.8 cm.)
Record auction price for a photograph by the artist
New York, 8 October 1993, $189,500 (£124,507)

Right:
EDWARD WESTON (American, 1886–1958)
Cloud, Mexico
signed, titled and dated in pencil on the verso
platinum print, 1926
$5\frac{7}{8} \times 9\frac{1}{2}$ in. (15 × 24.1 cm.)
New York, 20 April 1994, $156,500 (£105,743)
Sold by the J. Paul Getty Museum
Record auction price for a photograph by the artist

ALVIN LANGDON COBURN (British, 1882–1966)
Self Portrait
titled and dated in pencil on the verso
platinum print, 1905
$8\frac{1}{2} \times 6\frac{1}{4}$ in. (21 × 15.9 cm.)
London, 12 May 1994, £36,700 ($54,793)

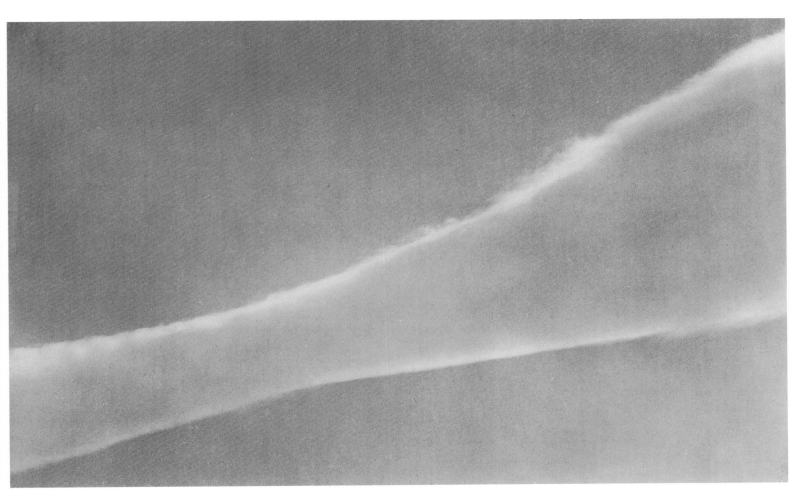

Left:

A Sassanian Empire, Varham II (274–293) gold Dinar
Spink, 12 October 1993, £5,500 ($8,393)

A Henry VII Testoon
Spink, 6 July 1994, £5,830 ($9,002)

A Jahangir, Mughal Emperor of India (1605–28) gold Mohur
dated A.H. 1023, showing the sign of the Zodiac Leo
Spink, 2 March 1994, £8,800 ($13,077)

A George V Proof Crown struck in gold, 1935, one of 25 issued
Spink, 24 November 1993, £8,580 ($12,776)

An Elizabeth I Ryal
Spink, 6 July 1994, £5,720 ($8,832)

A Victoria Proof Five-Pounds, 1839
Spink, 2 March 1994, £13,200 ($19,615)

A Bank of England One Pound, 2 March 1797, signed by
Abraham Newland and numbered 'No. 2', the earliest known
Bank of England note
Spink, 7 October 1993, £57,200 ($87,230)

A Government of the Straits Settlements Five-Dollars,
1 September 1898, serial number A/1 00001, the first note issued
for the Straits Settlements
Spink Singapore, 25 June 1994, S.$46,200 (£19,585)

Right:

A China, Yuan Shi K'ai (1912–16) Pattern Dollar, 1916, struck in
gold
Spink Singapore, 25 June 1994, S.$15,400 (£6,528)

A China, Ts'ao K'un (1923–24) Pattern Dollar, 1923, struck in
gold
Spink Singapore, 25 June 1994, S.$20,900 (£8,860)

A United States gold Ten-Dollars or 'Eagle', 1795, the first gold
coin struck by the United States, only 5,583 pieces were made in
total
New York, 22 March 1994, $35,200 (£23,689)

A gold Fifty-Dollars, 1855, made by the private minting
company Kellogg & Co., San Francisco at the height of the gold
rush, one of eleven to survive
New York, 22 March 1994, $88,000 (£59,219)

A historically important diamond set Badge of the Order of
Westphalia attributed to Jérôme Bonaparte, King of Westphalia
1807–13, by Gibert, Paris
Spink, 12 July 1994, £25,300 ($39,721)

A diamond set Imperial Presentation Badge of the Russian Order
of the White Eagle, circa 1900
Spink, 29 March 1994, £22,000 ($32,934)

THE RYOHEI ISHIKAWA COLLECTION OF UNITED STATES POSTAGE STAMPS, 1847–69

by Colin Fraser

A new auction record was set at Christie's New York on 28–29 September when the Ryohei Ishikawa Collection of United States stamps and covers realised a total of $9,540,359 (£6,318,119). This represented the highest price achieved at auction for a single collection of United States stamps.

The Ryohei Ishikawa Collection was generally considered to have been the most important collection of United States classic issues formed in recent years. Its importance was widely recognised, most notably at various international stamp exhibitions. In 1981, the International Philatelic Jury at *WIPA '81* (Vienna International Postage Stamp Exhibition) awarded the collection the International Grand Prix: at the presentation of this award in Vienna, the Ishikawa Collection was described as 'the most impressive and important display of United States classic issues ever formed'. Subsequent awards included the National Grand Prix, earned at *AMERIPEX '86* (American International Postage Stamp Exhibition), an international exhibition in Chicago in 1986. The following year at *CAPEX '87* (Canadian International Philatelic Exhibition), in Toronto, the collection was given the highest award – the Grand Prix d'Honneur.

In assembling so exceptional a collection, Mr Ishikawa brought together many of the highlights and showpieces from the finest collections of United States philately. From 1976 to 1981 he acquired privately and at auction property once owned by such notable philatelists as Alfred H. Caspary, Col. E. H. R. Green, Josiah K. Lilly and George Worthington. While these acquisitions formed the core of his collection, later additions were made, including selected covers from the Louis Grunin collection of 1851–7 stamps on cover which were sold at Christie's in 1987–8.

Mr Ishikawa's interest in philately began in 1970 and he quickly distinguished himself as a true philatelist. From the start, he was completely devoted to his subject, immersing himself in all the available literature and travelling the world to discuss his interests with leading specialists. During these early travels, Mr Ishikawa read and studied Stanley Ashbrook's book, *The U.S. One Cent* which had been lent to him by Dr. S. Ichida, one of the foremost students of Japanese philately during the 1950s and 1960s, and author of many handbooks on the early stamps of Japan. Ashbrook's book led Mr Ishikawa to form an outstanding collection of this single stamp.

From his original focus on the 1c, Mr Ishikawa's imagination was quickly captured by United States classic issues – those from 1847 until 1869 – perhaps to the challenge they posed for collectors. Intriguing to Mr Ishikawa was the technical mastery and exquisite detail of these stamps; designed by the most skilled engravers of the time, their tiny compositions offered endless features for study and appreciation.

Mr Ishikawa began exhibiting his collection of 1847–69 at an early stage. The enthusiastic reception he enjoyed from the start further encouraged his efforts. He soon formed a firm resolution: to acquire all the best examples of U.S. classic issues.

These classic issues of the United States provide a fascinating insight into the historical development of mid-nineteenth-century America. The stamps played an integral role in the country's economic, social and cultural evolution. Many of them are decorated with such iconic images as George Washington, Abraham Lincoln, the Declaration of Independence and the Pony Express. The pictorial issue of 1869 helped to unify the emerging nation by transporting both mail and American symbols among citizens east and west. Their beautifully detailed motifs captured the spirit of an entire age, when manifest destiny, rapid commercial expansion and extraordinary technological developments shaped the face of a new nation.

The highest price in the two-day sale was $717,500 (£475,166) for the May 1851 combination cover from Montreal to England via New York bearing a horizontal strip of five of the 1847 5c used in combination with a Canada 3d 'Beaver'. This is one of only two known covers bearing such a combination franking and could only have been used for 38 days in 1851, between April, when the stamp was issued, and June, when the U.S. stamp was invalidated.

George Washington is inextricably tied to the meaning of America, his image serving as a permanent symbol to this day. The general, hero, founding father and first President embodied the values of this new country: prudence, reason, self-discipline, selflessness, and benevolence. Washington became a symbol of national stability and unity, carrying the country through the turbulent divisions which ultimately erupted in civil war.

Washington's features were best described as classical. He was often compared to Roman heroes, not surprising, since eighteenth-century America cherished classical history, hence the eagle, olive leaf and Latin motto of the great seal. Painters and poets flocked to Washington's home, Mount Vernon, to record the legendary figure. Many of them, such as Houdon, portrayed him as the ideal 'citizen soldier', as industrious with his plough as with his sword. It was Houdon's famous sculpture, now in the State Capitol, Richmond, Virginia, that inspired the 1851 3c stamp of the United States. But the image of Washington that would predominate was Gilbert Stuart's portrait, used initially as the model for the 1847 10c and subsequently for numerous other denominations; this image was repeated on patriotic songsheets,

broadside poems, bank notes, coins and other postage stamps.

Washington was by far the most popular image on stamps in the nineteenth century. In the 1861 issue, a total of six different denominations showed his portrait. The Ishikawa collection included a spectacular Washington item, the mint block of six of the 1847 10c, the largest multiple of its kind, which realised $464,500 (£307,616).

Benjamin Franklin, an undisputed Renaissance man, is recalled as a distinguished scientist, statesman, philosopher, inventor and one of the authors of the Declaration of Independence. He exercised his cunning wit on the widely-read *Poor Richard's Almanac* (written under the pseudonym of Richard Saunders). His negotiating skills in France, and his revolutionary ideas about technology – in his famous kite experiment and the eponymous stove – are equally memorable. As an academic, he helped to found the Academy of Philadelphia which later became the celebrated University of Pennsylvania.

This Founding Father's effort had a single underlying theme: colonial unity. It should come as no surprise that Franklin served as Deputy Postmaster General from 1753 to 1774, for he saw the postal roads as centralising elements in the emerging republic.

Franklin is represented in every classic series of United States stamps. The 1847 5c stamp was modelled after a drawing by Longacre. The Ishikawa Collection included an unused block of sixteen which realised $255,500 (£169,205).

Left:
United States: 1847 10c Black, unused block of six
New York, 28 September 1993, $464,500 (£308,433)

Right:
United States: 1847 5c Red Brown, unused block of sixteen
New York, 28 September 1993, $255,500 (£169,656)

United States: 1860 30c Orange, used on Pony Express Patriotic Cover addressed to Germany
New York, 28 September 1993, $222,500 (£147,742)

United States: 1847 5c Red Brown and Canada 1851 3d 'Beaver' combination Cover to England
New York, 28 September 1993, $717,500 (£476,428)

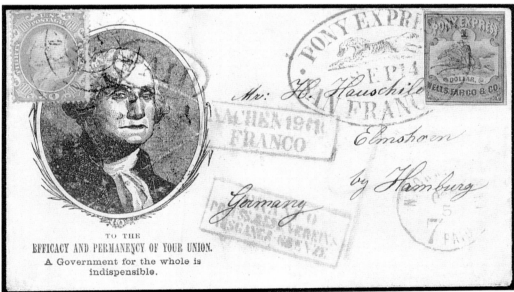

MUSICAL INSTRUMENTS

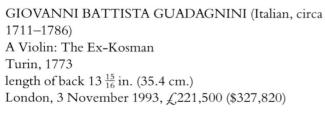

GIOVANNI BATTISTA GUADAGNINI (Italian, circa 1711–1786)
A Violin: The Ex-Kosman
Turin, 1773
length of back $13\frac{15}{16}$ in. (35.4 cm.)
London, 3 November 1993, £221,500 ($327,820)

FERDINAND GAGLIANO (Italian, active circa 1770–1795)
A Violin
Naples
length of back $13\frac{7}{8}$ in. (35.2 cm.)
London, 3 November 1993, £56,500 ($83,620)

JEAN BAPTISTE VUILLAUME (French, 1798–1875)
A Violin
Paris
length of back $14\frac{1}{16}$ in. (35.7 cm.)
London, 23 March 1994, £54,300 ($80,744)

PIETRO GUARNERI OF MANTUA (Italian, 1655–1720)
A Violin
Cremona, 1715
length of back $14\frac{1}{6}$ in. (35.7 cm.)
London, 22 June 1994, £221,500 ($338,895)

CLOCKS AND WATCHES

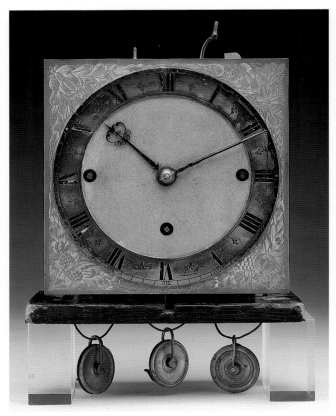

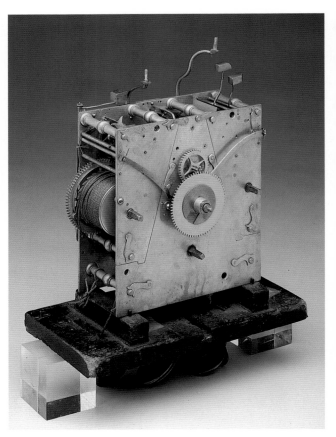

SAMUEL KNIBB (British, 1629–circa 1670)
A Charles II kingwood small Longcase Clock
72½ in. (184 cm.) high
New York, 29 January 1994, $233,500 (£155,459)

MATTHEW BOLTON (British, 1728–1809)
A George III ormolu Minerva Mantle Clock, the movement
by Justin Vulliamy
$18\frac{1}{2}$ in. (47 cm.) high
London, 23 June 1994, £177,500 ($271,575)

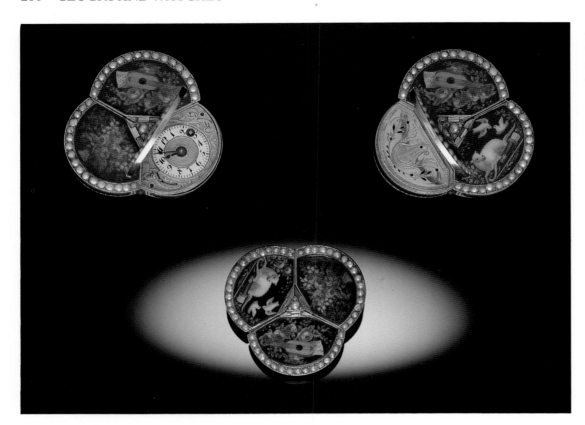

A small Swiss trefoil-shaped gold and
enamel and pearl-set musical
automaton Vinaigrette with Watch
unsigned, circa 1820
1½ in. (3.8 cm.) overall width
Geneva, 18 May 1994, S.Fr.135,500
(£63,496)

BREGUET & SONS
A silver-cased astronomical, calendar
and alarm Carriage Timepiece,
No. 2940/1624
Paris, 1928
6¼ in. (16 cm.) high
London, 24 November 1993, £34,500
($51,371)

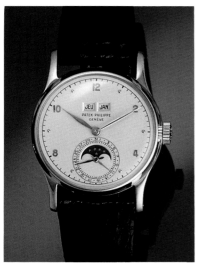

Top, from left:
PATEK PHILIPPE & CO.
A gold openface jump hour Chronograph, No. 80549
Geneva, circa 1896
2 in. (5.1 cm.) diameter
New York, 20 October 1993, $79,500 (£53,284)

C. MARCKS & CO.
An 18 carat gold enamel and diamond-set Hunter-cased keyless
lever Watch with independent centre-seconds and flying
5th-seconds Chronograph, made for the Indian market
signed 'C. Marcks & Co., Bombay & Poona, N. 34882'
circa 1890
$2\frac{1}{8}$ in. (5.5 cm.) diameter
Geneva, 18 May 1994, S.Fr.55,200 (£25,867)

PATEK PHILIPPE & CO.
An 18 carat pink gold perpetual calendar openface keyless lever
Watch with moonphases
signed 'Patek Philippe & Co., Geneve, No. 931091'
Geneva, circa 1950
Geneva, 18 May 1994, S.Fr.52,900 (£24,789)

Above, from left:
PATEK PHILIPPE & CO.
An 18 carat pink gold perpetual calendar Wristwatch with
moonphases
signed 'Patek Philippe & Co., Geneve, No. 962290'
Geneva, circa 1949
Geneva, 18 May 1994, S.Fr.100,300 (£47,001)

JULIUS ASSMANN
An 18 carat gold Hunter-cased minute repeating keyless lever
Watch with Chronograph and Recorder
signed 'J. Assmann, Glasshutte u/Sachsen'
circa 1900
Geneva, 18 May 1994, S.Fr.50,600 (£23,711)

PATEK PHILIPPE & CO.
An 18 carat pink gold world time Wristwatch
signed 'Patek Philippe & Co., Geneve, No. 921709'
Geneva, circa 1944
Geneva, 17 November 1993, S.Fr.72,450 (£32,606)

ARMS AND ARMOUR

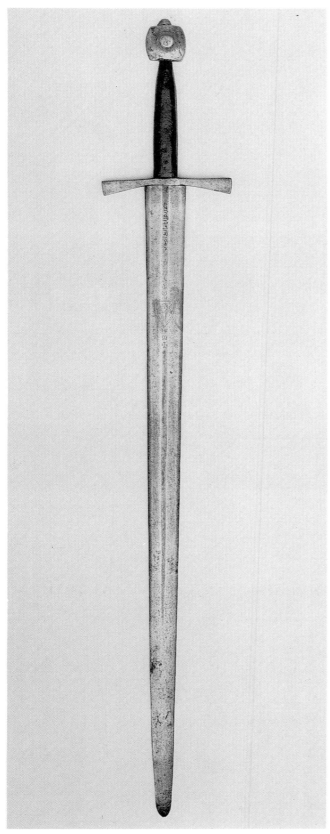

A Medieval Sword
probably Italian
late 14th Century
the blade 34 in. (86.4 cm.)
London, 18 May 1994, £28,750 ($43,125)

Right:
DURS EGG (British, 1748–1831)
A pair of silver-mounted Flintlock Duelling Pistols made
for George, Prince of Wales, later King George IV
1788
14¾ in. (37.5 cm.)
Sold from the Wilfrid Ward Collection
London, 27 October 1993, £54,300 ($80,201)

JOHN COOKSON (British, late 17th Century)
An English Flintlock breech-loading repeating Gun on the
so-called 'Lorenzoni system'
circa 1685
33 in. (83.8 cm.) barrel
Sold from The Wilfrid Ward Collection
London, 27 October 1993, £47,700 ($70,452)

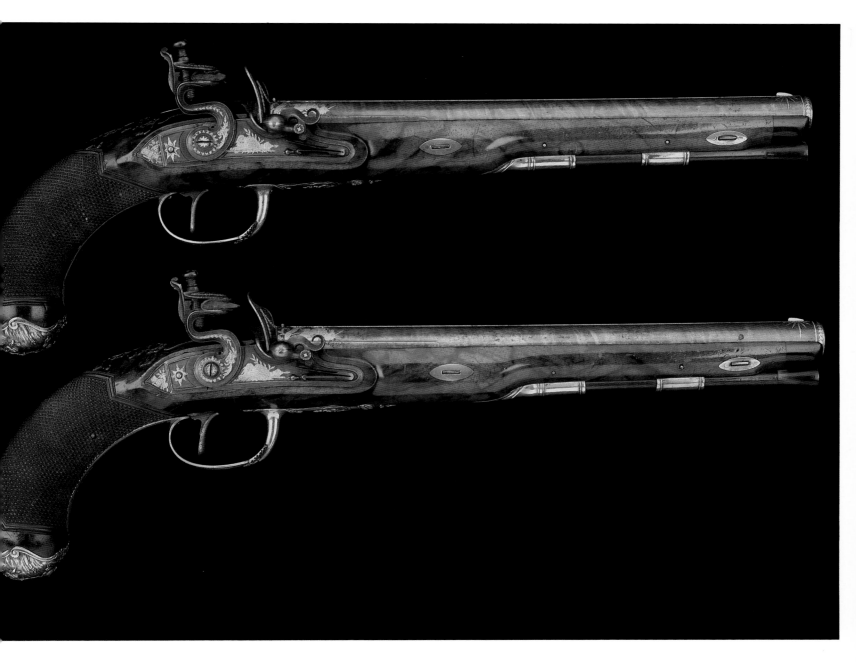

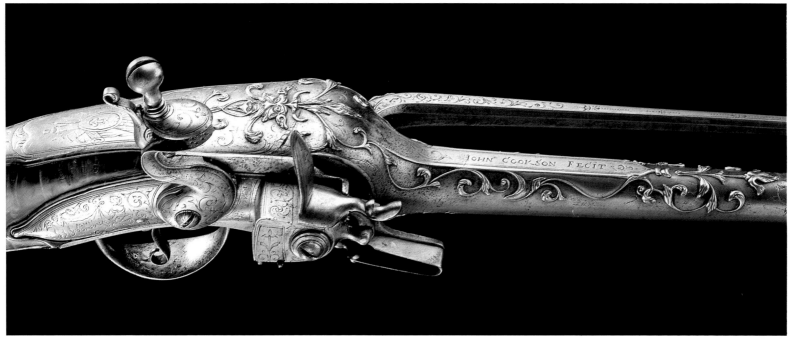

SPORTING GUNS

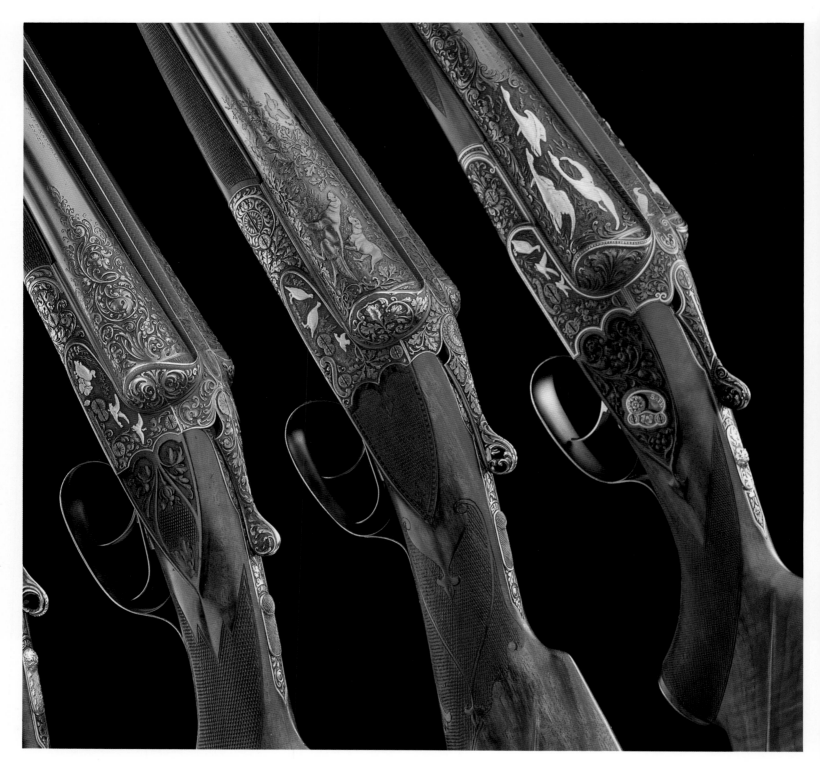

J.P. SAUER (German)
A set of De-luxe engraved presentation Guns (detail of three
illustrated), circa 1910–30, comprising:
20-bore Gun, No. 162597; 16-bore Gun, No. 133019;
12-bore Gun, No. 133643; and 10-bore Gun, No. 169160
London, 23 March 1994, £41,100 ($61,116)

Right, from top:
BOSS (British)
A 28-bore over-and-under sidelock ejector Gun, No. 7254
(detail illustrated) circa 1925
weight 4 lb. 15 oz. (2.24 kg.); the stock 14¼ in. (36.2 cm.);
the barrels 28 in. (71.1 cm.)
London, 23 March 1994, £47,700 ($70,930)

HOLLAND & HOLLAND (British)
A .500/.465 D.B. hammerless 'Royal' sidelock ejector Rifle,
No 35551 (detail illustrated)
London, circa 1988
weight 10 lb. (4.54 kg.); the pull 15 in. (38.1 cm.);
the barrels 24 in. (61 cm.)
London, 20 July 1994, £36,700 ($56,812)

L. DOUARD (French)
A .410 D.B. hammerless sidelock ejector Pistol, No. 1580 (detail
illustrated)
circa 1930
weight approx. 1lb. 12 oz. (0.79 kg.); the barrels 7¼ in. (18.4 cm.)
London, 23 March 1994, £10,925 ($16,245)

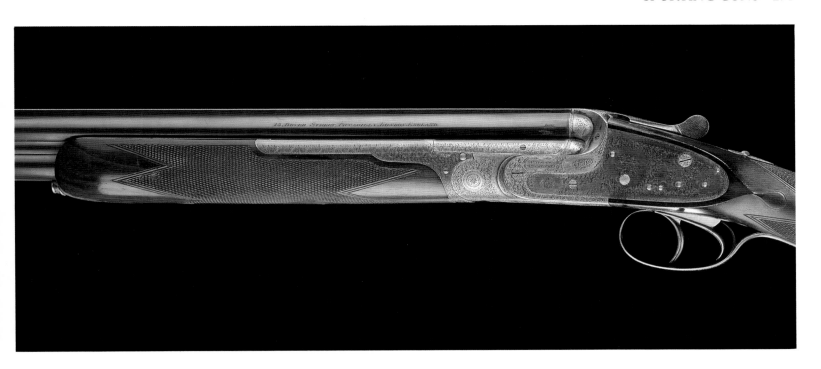

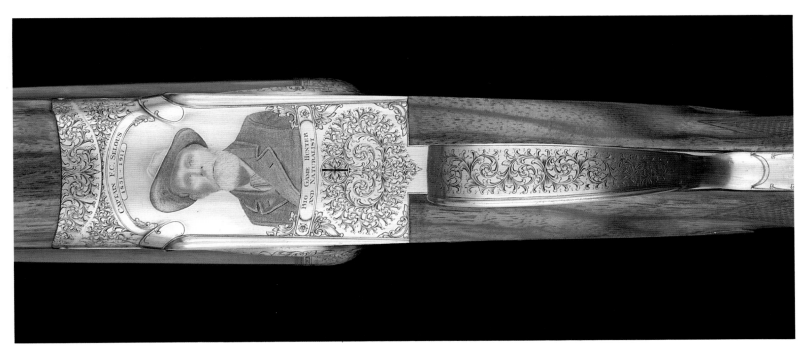

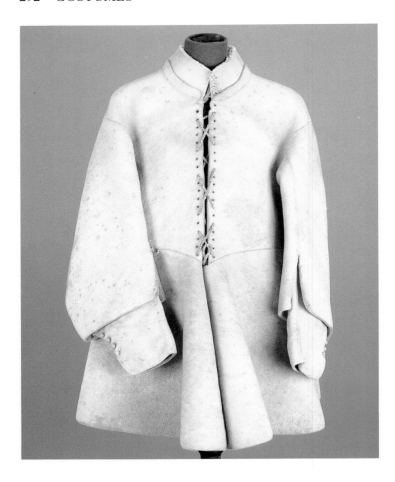

Above:
A Fortuny silk velvet 'Domino' Cape
1930s
Sold from the Collection of Tina Chow
New York, 21 September 1993, $34,500 (£22,490)

Left, from top:
A buff Coat of grey leather, with front lacing and buttoned inner
cuff: worn by Sir John Gell (1593–1671), parliamentary colonel
circa 1643
Sold by Order of the Executors of the late Lt. Colonel John
Chandos-Pole, C.V.O., O.B.E.
South Kensington, 21 June 1994, £15,400 ($23,639)

A bell shaped Evening Coat of black grosgrain and a Hat of tulle
and chiffon
mid–1950s
labelled 'Eisa', Balenciaga's Madrid Salon
Sold from the wardrobe of the late Mrs Heard De Osborne
South Kensington, 21 June 1994, £1,430 ($2,195)

The collection totalled £134,668 ($207,042)

FANS
by Susan Mayor

The sale of fans at Christie's, South Kensington, on 12 May was the second most valuable ever held. It realised £213,373 in total. The record is still held by Christie's, South Kensington's sale of June 1991.

Like the 1991 sale, this was an anonymous collection. It had been assembled comparatively recently and the quality was generally very high. Occasionally it was superb, notably the enchanting silk fan painted by Marin Marie in 1929 and presented to his friend Madame Virginie Heriot by the Yacht Club of France. It depicts her Bermudian-rigged eight metre racing schooner *L'Aile VI*. Marin Marie (Marin Durand Coupel de Saint Front, 1901–1987) was a single-handed trans-Atlantic yachtsman as well as a famous marine artist. The sticks of this fan are mother of pearl richly carved with Amphitrite, dolphins and putti and are signed 'Jorel, Sculpt'. The assembled serious collectors recognised the fan's quality and it fetched £8,250, the second highest price in the sale.

There was also a fine selection of Grand Tour fans. Some were well-known with a long provenance, such as a mid-eighteenth-century example painted with a peregrinic theatre in the Piazza de San Marco after Canaletto, possibly by Joseph Baudin. First recorded in the Robert Walker Collection in 1882, it fetched £6,250.

Two rare Dutch signed fans, one by F. Xavery, 1762, realised £4,180. Frans Xavery was the son of Jean-Baptist Xavery, the sculptor. He trained as a decorative painter under de Wit. Only three other fans and a fan leaf by him are recorded.

A Fan, the silk leaf painted with *L'Aile VI*
signed 'Marin Marie'
1929
12 in. (30.5 cm.)
South Kensington, 12 May 1994, £8,250 ($12,317)

The top lot, which realised £11,000 was a mid-eighteenth-century fan in the style of Pillement, with a hidden message 'Le Bonheur'. It has some of the finest carved ivory sticks ever seen. There were several unusual fans such as 'The Map of Affections' circa 1740, a brise fan painted with an allegorical chart of an imaginary continent – £3,080, as well as a rare Jacobite fan, possibly painted by Sir Robert Strange, with a portrait of Prince Charles Edward which realised £5,500.

The collection also contained seven Cantonese fans which we held back for the following fan sale on 14 June which coincided with Christie's, South Kensington's Asian Week. The June sale included the rarest fan sold this season (£9,350), a Renaissance or Elizabethan fan dating from circa 1580. It had belonged to the Strachey family of Saffron Walden and later Somerset. There is only one other fan of this type recorded, in the Musée de la Renaissance at the Château d'Ecouen, near Paris. The fan is ten inches long and is made of pierced vellum, delicately painted in pink, blue, green and gold, with bone sticks. The upper portion is bound with green silk thread which slots through the leaf, alternate folds slot with mica painted with blue and gold flowers (only fragments remain); the guardsticks are each trimmed with seven green silk pompoms.

The success of the 12 May sale did not depend on provenance; it was an anonymous and recently assembled collection. The high prices were the result of a familiar auctioneer's equation: price is the product of quality plus demand.

'Elliot', a blue plush covered Teddy Bear by Steiff
German, circa 1908
South Kensington, 6 December 1993, £49,500 ($73,854)

Helen Beatrix Potter (English, 1866–1943)
The Guinea Pig Gardeners
signed with initials 'HBP'
pencil, pen and ink and watercolour
$3\frac{1}{2} \times 6\frac{3}{4}$ in. (8.9 × 17.1 cm.)
South Kensington, 21 July 1994, £24,200 ($37,413)
Record auction price for a single-sided Beatrix Potter illustration

A tinplate Marklin Ferris Wheel
circa 1890s
21 in. (53.3 cm.) high
New York, 15 June 1994, $55,200 (£36,388)

A Kyser & Rex Co. Mikado Bank
5 in. (12.7 cm.) base length
New York, 18 December 1993, $63,000
(£42,367)

THE SALE OF THE BRITAINS ARCHIVE

by Hugo Marsh

William Britain and Company was founded in London by William Britain Sen. (1826–1906), and trades today, as successfully as ever, as Britains Petite Limited of Nottingham.

In 1993 Britains celebrated the centenary of their perfecting the technique for hollow-casting toy soldiers and other figures in lead alloy; this contributed to their domination of the market until lead figure production ceased in 1964, under pressure from the health lobby. This centenary was commemorated in an Exhibition at The Guards Museum in 1993 which Christie's sponsored.

It was with great pride that Christie's South Kensington undertook the sale of the extensive Britains Archive. Probably the most historically important toy figure collection ever to come to auction, the Archive had been built up by the company over the past century. It included unissued prototype figures, special sample cards from the factory Paint Room as 'controls' for outworkers, early mechanical novelty toys, individual figures, sets and 'premiums' made for other companies.

The high level of pre-sale interest stimulated astonishing prices and the Archive doubled its expected pre-sale total, achieving £119,341 with 100% sold.

Britains' entry into the toy market was achieved by William Britain Sen., who from the middle of the last century manufactured lead toys from his North London home. A rare 'Blondin' Cyclist from the 1880s, one of a handful known, realised the top price in the sale, £7,150, a world record for a Britains item. The toy represents the intrepid tight-rope walker, with finely pomaded moustaches and original clothing, perched on an Ordinary or Penny-Farthing bicycle; powered by clockwork, he rides smartly round in circles.

The need to widen the range of customers drove the founder's innovative son, William Britain Jun., to conceive and perfect the hollow-cast method of lead soldier production.

Over the years, using this technique, Britains modelled hundreds of British regiments in different variants, from an 1898 Set 84, small-size 2nd Life Guards (£715), to a 1962 Set 9321 Grenadier Guards (£385). Exceptional rarities included a factory prototype from 1934 of a Marching Guardsman, with pin-jointed swinging leg, that sold for £3,080, a world record for any toy soldier. A part set of four Miniature Guardsman, with tiny box, made by Dennis Britain himself in 1924 for the Queen Mary's Dolls' House, realised £825.

While most production up to 1921 was devoted to military figures, as shown by the bulk of the Paint Sample Cards in the sale, Britains responded to war fatigue by introducing the Model Home Farm range in 1921. The figures are heavily nostalgic, conjuring up a non-existent rural idyll, and the sale offered examples of most of the range. Queen Mary is alleged to have observed a lacuna in the British Empire Exhibition of 1924 – "Where is the Village Idiot?" – so he was duly created; the Archive included two previously unknown colours, which realised £1,155 on a Paint Sample Card with other items.

The very last item in the sale provided a fitting end to an auspicious day: a figure of Her Majesty the Queen on the Coronation Throne, one of only 85 made in 1993 to celebrate the 40th Anniversary of her Coronation and the Britains Centenary. It realised £2,750 – a remarkable sum for a modern piece, and a reflection of the huge popularity of the products of Britains Petite Limited as it marches into the next century.

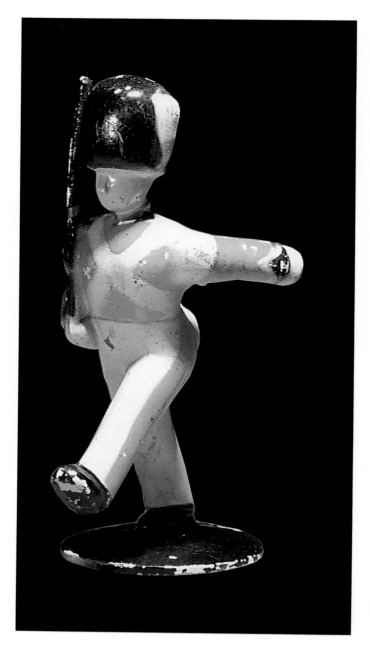

No. 1299 Marching 'Toytown' Figure
1959
South Kensington, 27 June 1994, £374 ($576)

A 50/54 gun Navy Board box and fruitwood rigged model of an
English fourth rate of 1702, representing the Establishment of
1703
early 18th Century
29 × 36 in. (73.7 × 91.5 cm.)
Sold by order of the Trustees of the Edward James Foundation
South Kensington, 7 October 1993, £154,000 ($100,984)

WILLIAM OSMOND DOYLEND (English, 1913–1992)
Bristol Brabazon I G-AGPW
38¼ in. (97.1 cm.)
South Kensington, 25 February 1994, £3,300 ($4,884)
Record auction price for a scratch-built model

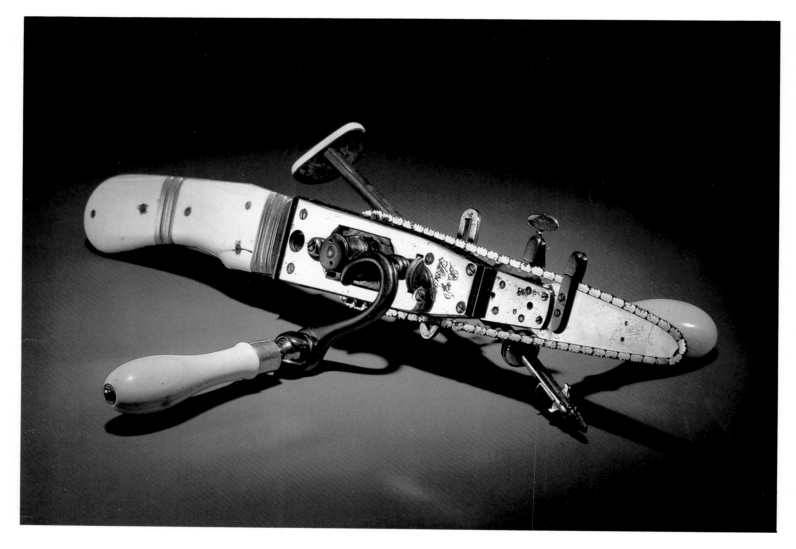

Left:
HEINE OF WURZBURG
A mechanical steel and ivory Chainsaw
14 in. (40 cm.) overall length
South Kensington, 19 August 1993, £23,100 ($34,904)
Record auction price for a medical instrument

A. ADAMS AND CO., London
A quarter-plate De Luxe hand Camera with red-leather covered
body, 18 carat gold fittings hallmarked London, 1901
made for the Sultan Abdul Aziz, ruler of Morocco from
1894–1912
South Kensington, 25 November 1993, £39,600 ($26,649)
Record auction price for a Camera

NEMET SIMON
A bowler hat and cane used by Charlie Chaplin throughout his
career; the inside leather hatband stamped with manufacturer's
details Nemet Simon, Budapest, V11 Jöhöly-utz; and original
studio label blindstamped THE CHAPLIN STUDIOS Inc.
CALIFORNIA and inkstamped CHARLES CHAPLIN FILM
CORPORATION, Alfred Reeves, General Manager;
the bamboo cane $32\frac{1}{2}$ in. long; accompanied by two letters of
authenticity from Ted and Betty Chaplin Tetrick.
South Kensington, 17 December 1993, £55,000 ($81,785)

UNITED ARTISTS
The Gold Rush
1925, one-sheet poster, linen backed
41 × 27 in. (104.1 × 68.6 cm.)
New York, 13 December 1993, $70,700 (£47,354)

Right:
WALT DISNEY STUDIOS
Alice's Day at Sea
1924, one-sheet poster, stone
lithograph, linen backed,
and five stills of Virginia Davis starring
in the *Alice Comedies*, each 8 × 10 in.
(20.3 × 25.4 cm.)
41 × 27 in. (104.1 × 68.6 cm.)
South Kensington, 18 April 1994,
£22,100 ($32,509)
Record auction price for a Disney
Poster

FRANK FRAZETTA (American,
b. 1928)
A Princess of Mars commissioned for
the hard cover book-club edition of
Edgar Rice Burrough's classic
futuristic Mars adventure, 1970
oil on canvas board
16 × 20 in. (40.6 × 50.8 cm.)
New York, 30 October 1993, $90,500
(£60,861)

WALT DISNEY STUDIOS
When the Cat's Away
A complete storyboard for the short
featuring Mickey and Minnie Mouse,
drawn by director Bert Gillett
1929, graphite on animation paper
12 × 9½ in. (30.5 × 24.1 cm.)
New York, 18 June 1994, $55,200
(£36,316)
Record auction price for a Disney
Drawing

WALTER LANTZ
PRODUCTIONS
Mount Rushmore, Woody
Woodpecker immortalised in stone
1978, oil on canvas by Walter Lantz
15½ × 19½ in. (39.4 × 49.5 cm.)
New York, 18 June 1994, $29,900
(£19,671)
Record auction price for the artist

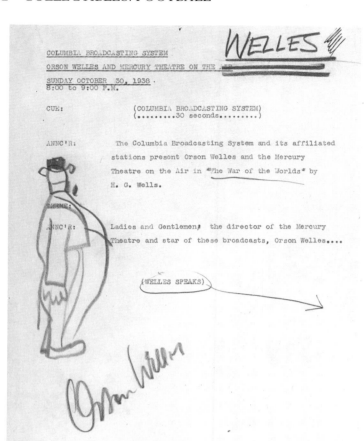

Orson Welles's typescript Radioplay 'The War of The Worlds',
some pages with original drawings by Welles
New York, 2 June 1994, $32,200 (£21,240)

Right:
Joe Dimaggio's 1940s Yankee Road Jersey
size 44
New York, 2 October 1993, $41,400 (£27,711)

1930–31 Babe Ruth Contract with New York Yankees
New York, 26 March 1994, $29,900 (£20,000)

Six Medals from the Ray Kennedy Collection
Glasgow, 20 October 1993, collection £88,407 ($131,903)

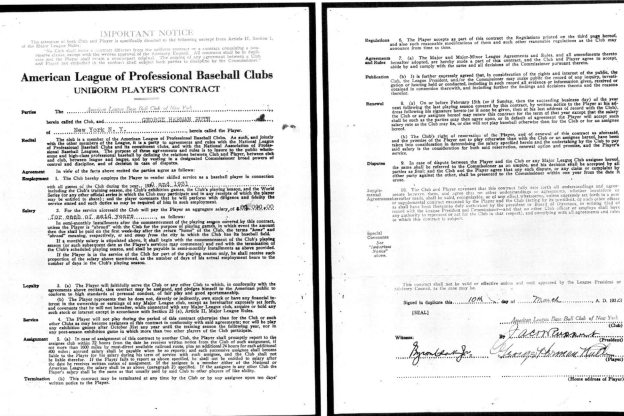

WINE

A MAGNIFICENT PRIVATE CELLAR

by Paul Bowker

Among the (increasingly) multifarious categories regularly sold by Christie's, wine is perhaps the least likely to surprise, a degree of predictability indeed is almost inherent in the nature of wine sales at auction. Wine is after all, a commodity, and yet, every now and then, an event in the world of wine auctions proves so momentous that it is talked about for decades afterwards. One such event was the sale by Christie's in 1985 of the Jefferson 1787 Château Lafitte (*sic*) which shattered by a factor of ten the previous record price for a bottle of wine, selling to the late Malcolm Forbes for £105,000.

A second, but very different event took place in Christie's Ryder Street Room on 16 June 1994; the sale of 'A Magnificent Private Cellar', an extraordinary collection of wines of the very highest quality, accumulated (for drinking) over a period of some thirty years by a highly respected English wine authority, Master of Wine, sometime wine merchant and wine writer. Achieving the extraordinary total of £1,560,000, it almost doubled the previous existing record for a single wine auction. Individual prices realised within the 847 lots were at a quite unprecedented level, and the sale attracted more interest than any in living memory. Over five hundred bidders from 24 countries registered for the sale, and some six thousand individual commission bids were received. Major buyers had flown in especially for the sale from as far afield as the USA, Hong Kong and Japan.

The reason for this degree of worldwide interest was not the size, or the value of the cellar, but rather the sheer range, breadth and depth of wines on offer, and the quantities offered of wines previously rarely ever seen.

The Bordeaux section, always the centre-piece of English cellars, commenced with four cases of Château La Mission-Haut-Brion 1945 (£6,380-£7,480 per case) and ended with no less than fifty-two cases of Château Cheval Blanc 1982 (£1,485-£1,760 per case). The 1947 vintage of the same property produced one of the most spectacular results: acknowledged as one of the greatest Clarets, it is a rare visitor to the salerooms even in single bottles. In this sale were seven cases, all in pristine condition. Offered with a bold estimate of £10,000-£15,000, they attracted fierce bidding and finally sold for between £17,600 and £19,800 per case. Other superb Clarets also achieved impressive prices: Château Lafite 1953, £4,290 per 6 magnums; Château Mouton Rothschild 1959, £5,280 per 6 magnums; Château Haut Brion 1961, £6,820 per 6 magnums. Even younger (and therefore less scarce) vintages achieved extraordinary prices. 1982 Château Lafite £2,310 and Château Mouton Rothschild £3,410.

The Rhône, of which the vendor is an acknowledged expert (and lover) was represented by arguably the greatest collection ever, and included over one hundred cases of the magnificent 1978 vintage from all the top Domaines, including Chave, Guigal, Jaboulet and Château Rayans. All sold in excess of their estimated prices. The famous Hermitage La Chapelle 1961, of which a unique six and a half cases were offered, achieved record prices of between £5,940 and £6,380 per case. Also rarely seen at auction, the renowned sweet wines of Alsace were present in abundance.

A unique feature of the sale, at the request of the vendor, was the offering of two 'Super-lots'; effectively ready-made cellars of some of the most celebrated wines that money can buy, comprising roughly two hundred cases each including, Claret, White Bordeaux, Red and White Burgundy, Rhônes, Alsace, Champagne, Port, Madeira etc. Both were estimated at £200,000 to £300,000 which in both cases was no more than the sum of the values of the component wines. The first sold to London art dealer David Mason, Chairman of MacConnal-Mason for £374,000 after a competitive bidding battle against two Hong Kong and one American bidders. The second was acquired for £220,000 by the underbidder of the first.

One of the most appealing elements of this sale was the uniquely broad spectrum of wine origins. In a market normally totally dominated by the wines of Bordeaux, it was most encouraging also to be able to achieve spectacular prices for Australian wines (Grange Hermitage, 1971 £2,650 per case) and Monbazillac (£902 for twelve bottles of mixed vintages). Equally the lot in the sale which surpassed most spectacularly its estimate was that with three bottles of the Italian Sassicaia. Being 1968, the first vintage ever produced, the three bottles attracted highly competitive bidding, selling for £1,375 against a pre-sale estimate of £200-£300.

This sale was unhesitatingly described as 'The Finest Private Cellar ever to appear at auction'. It may be that none will ever surpass it in terms of sheer quality, and quantity. However, with one buyer having acquired almost 50% by value of it, it is nice to know that the cellar, so carefully accumulated, has preserved much of its integrity.

Largely because of this auction, Christie's Wine Department has had a record season, with the thirty-seven United Kingdom sales achieving over £8,100,000.

Top, from left:
A Jeroboam of Romanée-Conti, Vintage 1966
London, 16 June 1994, £3,960 ($6,031)

One Magnum each of Château Lafite, Vintage 1953,
Château Latour, Vintages 1953, 1955 and 1964,
Château Haut-Brion, Vintage 1953 and Château
Mouton-Rothschild, Vintage 1961
(four illustrated)
London, 16 June 1994, £3,520 ($5,361)

Above:
Four Bottles of Whisky, circa 1940 (VAT 69, Haig
Dimple and two of James Martin & Co. Ltd.)
Sold by S.S. Politician PLC
Glasgow, 24 November 1993, £3,570 ($5,316)

MOTOR CARS

Left
A 1915 Locomobile Model 48
Touring Car
Chassis No. 9197
Engine No. 9998
Pebble Beach, 22 August 1993
$90,000 (£59,484)

A 1956 Mercedes-Benz 300S
Convertible
Chassis No. 1880100001152
Engine No. 0001052
Pebble Beach, 22 August 1993
$140,000 (£92,532)

Right
The Ex Works 1956 O.S.C.A.
Tipo MT4–2AD 1500
Coachwork by Carrozzeria
Fratelli Morelli
Chassis No. 1182
Engine No. 1536TN
Olympia, 25 February 1994
£133,500 ($90,203)

A 1963 Aston Martin DB4
Convertible Series V
Chassis No. DB4C/1091/R
Engine No. 370/1085
Beaulieu, 11 September 1993
£78,500 ($50,579)

A 1964 Aston Martin DB5
Convertible
Chassis No. DB5C/1502/R
Engine No. 400/1589
Beaulieu, 14 May 1994
£65,300 ($43,362)

A HOUSE SALE AT MERE HALL

by Anthony Browne

The 1993/4 Season was another successful one for sales on the premises. During the autumn of 1993 five were held, totalling over £3.8 million. The contents of Myles Place in the Close at Salisbury, sold on behalf of the Executors of the late Sir Philip Shelbourne, attracted interest from around the world and included a splendid George II mahogany bookcase which fetched the then highest price ever for an individual lot in a sale on the premises of £221,500. During the summer of 1994 there were sales at Mere Hall, Cheshire; at The Mill House, Sonning-on-Thames, where a fascinating and varied collection formed by Count and Countess Csáky, fetched £1,746,209, and at Newnham Hall, Daventry, the contents of which were sold on behalf of the Executors of the Late Lt. Colonel John Chandos-Pole, CVO, OBE, for a total of £469,099.

Mere Hall was the largest sale of the Season doubling the pre-sale estimate at £2,744,302. The varied accumulation of objects at Mere reflected the changing fortunes and taste of generations of the Brooke family. Two members of the family in particular had made their mark with purchases made on Grand Tours of the Continent: Jonas Brooke (c.1758-1784) and Peter Langford-Brooke (1793-1840). By coincidence each of their lives ended in tragedy. Jonas died in Milan and never saw his purchases installed in his native Cheshire and Peter died falling through ice while skating on the Mere.

Although the Brookes had been squires of Mere since 1652, a marriage a century later led to the enrichment of the house and its collection. In 1756, Peter Brooke married Elizabeth Langford, the heiress of Jonas Langford of Theobalds, Hertfordshire. It was probably she who asked Samuel Wyatt to rebuild Mere Hall in the classical style. The album of Wyatt's designs for a grand palladian house was included in the sale (£5,750). Although these designs were never carried out, Mere was to be rebuilt by Samuel Wyatt's nephew, Lewis Wyatt in about 1813.

Elizabeth Langford-Brooke also commissioned the firm of Gillows of London and Lancaster to furnish the house. No doubt she was influenced in her choice both of architect and furniture maker by her neighbours, the Egertons of Tatton Park. Among her purchases was the splendid set of twenty four dining chairs, bought in June 1803, which fetched £210,500.

The Langford-Brooke's association with Gillows was continued by Elizabeth's son Thomas (d.1815) and by her grandson Peter. Thomas commissioned the library bookcases which were supplied in 1815 under the direction of his architect Lewis Wyatt. They are recorded in Gillows' Estimate Sketch Books for May 1815 at a cost of £300. These sold for £200,670. Peter Langford-Brooke added the grand folio cabinet, a popular design by Gillows, at a cost of £13 2s 6d. In 1994 it fetched £32,200. He also ordered the unusual suite of ebonised bedroom furniture (£43,792).

The fact that so much was known of the origin of the contents of Mere can largely be attributed to Peter Langford-Brooke's meticulous account books in which he recorded his purchases. The prolonged tour that he and his wife Elizabeth made between 1828 and 1831 added greatly to the collection at Mere and their purchases were noted in the accounts. The copies of Sir William Hamilton's vases, attributed to Johann Heinrich Wilhelm Tischbein, were bought in Naples on 10 March, 1829. The engravings, published between 1791 and 1803 provided a record of Sir William Hamilton's collection lost with the wreck of the *Colossus* in 1798. Brooke recorded the purchase of the five pairs of large engravings and ten pairs of smaller ones for a total of 66 ducats. These sold, with an additional pair, for a total of £49,220.

The Langford-Brookes took drawing lessons from Giacinto Gigante to whom numerous payments were made from August 1830 until their departure from Italy in 1831. Three charming watercolours by Gigante of views near Naples, were sold for a total of £12,650.

The account books were also fascinating for the insight they afforded into the life of an eighteenth-century gentleman, both at home and abroad, and even the cost of a haircut in Rome.

It is probable that the most important Old Master picture at Mere, Guido Reni's *Roman Charity* was also purchased by Peter Langford-Brooke on his Italian tour. This newly rediscovered picture, which appears to be that recorded in the inventory of the Chigi collection in Rome in 1693, made £60,900. The portrait busts of Peter Langford-Brooke and his wife commissioned from Richard James Wyatt while in Rome in 1832, provided a visual memorial to the young couple while on their tour of Italy. The account book records the payment of £60 to the sculptor. The busts sold in 1994 for £5,290.

In embarking on the Grand Tour, Peter Langford-Brooke had followed the precedent set by his uncle, Jonas, who visited Italy in 1783-4 and made significant purchases there. His acquisitions were shipped back to Cheshire from Leghorn, following his death in Milan on 19 July 1784. In a touching letter to his mother, the shipping agent wrote of the white marble group of the *Three Graces* that 'No man's urn deserves better to be supported by the Graces than his'. The most poignant memorial to Jonas's premature death, is the portrait of his friend Sir James Graham by Hugh Douglas Hamilton. In it Graham is seen leaning on the tomb of Jonas Brooke on which there is an inscription to their friendship. This exceptional example of a full length pastel by Hamilton fetched £73,000.

Among the numerous works of art acquired by Jonas in Italy, the series of views in and around Naples by Xaverio della Gatta stood out for their exquisite quality and condition. These fine examples of the artist's work were bought in Naples in 1784, and sold for a total of £151,800. While in Rome Jonas commissioned works from the Scottish artist Jacob More. His views of Rome and Tivoli remained at Mere and were sold for £45,000 and £40,000 respectively.

In spite of the detailed records of the collection at Mere, it is not known when the grandest picture, Sir Nathaniel Dance's *Venus appearing to Aeneas and Achates as a Huntress*, was purchased. Commissioned in Rome in 1760 by Sir Henry Mainwaring, 4th Bt. of nearby Peover Hall, the picture is recorded in the inventory

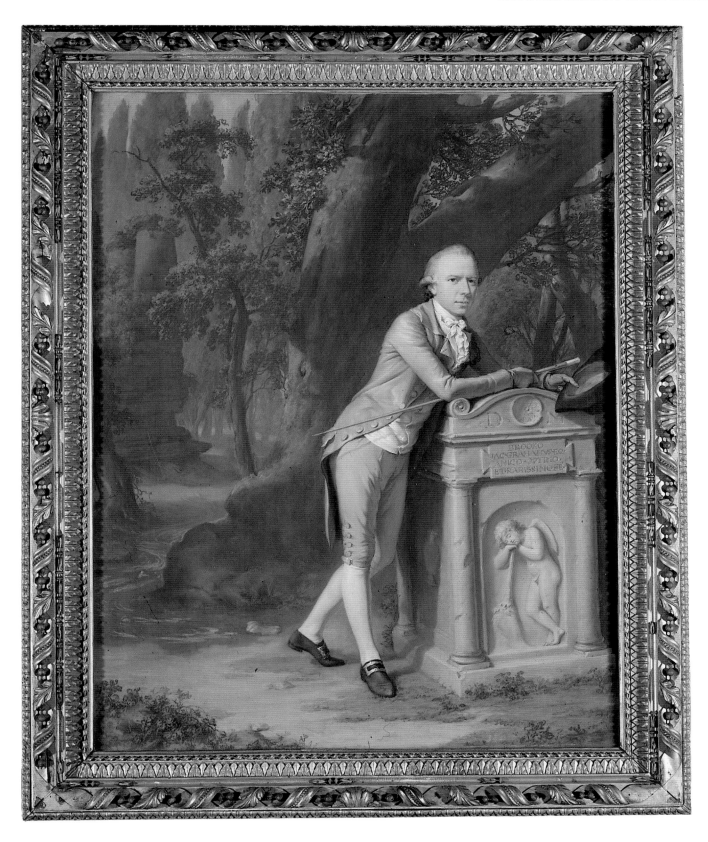

of Mere on Peter Langford-Brooke's death in 1840. Dance painted the scene from the *Aeneid* in Rome in 1762 where he and his brother became familiar with the work of the great Grand Tour artist, Pompeo Batoni, to whom this picture owes so much. The picture sold for £243,500, the most expensive single lot sold in a sale on the premises (see page 38).

Although the collection of the Brookes is now scattered, many of the most notable lots found their way into other British collections: Innocenzo Spinazzi's copy of the *Medici Venus* went to the National Gallery of Scotland and the superb library furniture by Gillows has gone to furnish another library in Britain.

The contents of Mere represented a rare survival from a great age of English collecting and reflected a taste that appeals as strongly to collectors two hundred years later.

HUGH DOUGLAS HAMILTON (1736–1808)
Portrait of Sir James Graham, 1st Bt. leaning on an altar which is inscribed 'D.M. / BROOKO / JAC. GRAHAMUS. E.Q. / AMICO / OPTIMO / RARISSIMO FET.'
pastel
$33\frac{1}{2} \times 25\frac{3}{4}$ in. (85 × 65.3 cm.)
Mere Hall, 23 May 1994, £73,000 ($110,230)

INDEX

International Offices

Salerooms

UNITED KINGDOM

Head Office
Christie, Manson & Woods Ltd.
8 King Street, St. James's
London SW1Y 6QT
Tel: (071) 839 9060. Telex: 916429
Fax: (071) 839 1611
Chairman: The Lord Hindlip

South Kensington
Christie's South Kensington Ltd.
85 Old Brompton Road
London SW7 3LD
Tel: (071) 581 7611. Telex: 922061
Fax: (071) 584 0431
Chairman: W. A. Coleridge, F.R.I.C.S.

Scotland
Christie's Scotland Ltd.
164-166 Bath Street
Glasgow G2 4TG
Tel: (041) 332 8134.
Fax: (041) 332 5759
Chairman: Sir Ilay Campbell, Bt.

Robson Lowe at Christie's
8 King Street, St. James's
London SW1Y 6QT
Tel: (071) 839 9060. Telex: 916429
Fax: (071) 389 2688

UNITED STATES

Christie, Manson & Woods International, Inc.
502 Park Avenue
New York, New York 10022
Tel: (212) 546 1000. Telex: 620721
Fax: (212) 980 8163
Chairman: Christopher Burge
Vice Chairman: Stephen S. Lash
President: David Tyler

Christie's East
219 East 67th Street
New York, New York 10021
Tel: (212) 606 0400.
Telex: 672 0346
Fax: (212) 737 6076
President: Kathleen Guzman

WORLDWIDE

Australia
Melbourne
James B. Leslie, A.C., M.C. *Chairman*
Roger McIlroy *Managing Director*
Christie's Australia Pty. Ltd.
1 Darling Street
South Yarra
Victoria 3141
Tel: (613) 820 4311
Fax: (613) 820 4876

Hong Kong
Baroness Lydia Dunn D.B.E. *Chairman*
Anthony Lin
Christie's Swire (Hong Kong) Ltd.
2804-6 Alexandra House
16-20 Chater Road, Hong Kong
Tel: (852) 521 5396. Telex: 72014
Fax: (852) 845 2646
Regional Marketing and Business
Development (except Japan)
Alice Yuan Piccus

Italy
Rome
Franz Ziegler, *Managing Director*
Francesco Alverà
Christie's (Int.) S.A.
Palazzo Massimo Lancellotti
Piazza Navona 114
Rome 00186
Tel: (396) 687 2787
Fax: (396) 686 9902

Monaco
Humphrey Butler (Paris)
Pascal Bego
Christie's Monaco S.A.M.
Park Palace, 98000 Monte Carlo
Tel: (33) 93 25 19 33
Fax: (33) 93 50 38 64

The Netherlands
Charles André de la Porte *Chairman*
Victor J. E. Moussault *Managing Director*
Christie's Amsterdam B.V.
Cornelis Schuytstraat 57
1071 JG Amsterdam
Tel: (3120) 57 55 255
Fax: (3120) 6 64 08 99
Rotterdam
Coolsingel 93,
P.O. Box 21320
3001 AH Rotterdam
Tel: (3110) 414 3202
Fax: (3110) 412 6896

Switzerland
Geneva
François Curiel, *President*
Dan Klein, *Vice President*
Jocelyne Keller
Franz Ziegler
Christie's (Int.) S.A.
8 Place de la Taconnerie
1204 Geneva
Tel: (4122) 311 1766
Fax: (4122) 311 5559

Representatives

UNITED KINGDOM AND IRELAND

Northumbria
Aidan Cuthbert
Eastfield House, Main Street,
Corbridge
Northumberland NE45 5LA
Tel: (0434) 633181
Fax: (0434) 633891

North-West
Victor Gubbins, F.R.I.C.S.
Eden Lacy, Lazonby, Penrith
Cumbria CA10 1BZ
Tel: (0768) 898800
Fax: (0768) 898020

Yorkshire
Sir Nicholas Brooksbank, Bt.
Mrs. Giles Bilton
192 Huntington Road
York YO3 9BN
Tel: (0904) 630911
Fax: (0904) 644448

North-West Midlands and North Wales
Richard Roundell, F.R.I.C.S.
Dorfold Hall, Nantwich
Cheshire CW5 8LD
Tel: (0270) 627024
Fax: (0270) 628723

South Midlands and South Wales
The Earl Fortescue
111 The Promenade
Cheltenham, Glos. GL50 1PS
Tel: (0242) 518999
Fax: (0242) 576240
Sukie Paravacini (*Consultant for South Wales*)
Rupert de Zoete *Consultant*

East Midlands
The Hon. Lady Hastings
The Stables, Milton Hall
Peterborough PE6 7AA
Tel: (0733) 380781
Fax: (0733) 380979

East Anglia
Charles Bingham-Newland
Sackville Place
44-48 Magdalen Street
Norwich NR3 1JU
Tel: (0603) 614546
Fax: (0603) 633740

Cornwall
Christopher Petherick
Porthpean House, St. Austell
Cornwall PL26 6AX
Tel: (0726) 64672
Fax: (0726) 70548

Devon
The Hon. George Lopes, A.R.I.C.S.
Gnaton Estate Office
Yealmpton, Plymouth
Devon PL8 2HU
Tel: (0752) 880636
Fax: (0752) 880968

West Country and Wiltshire
Richard de Pelet
Huntsman's Lodge
Inwood, Templecombe
Somerset BA8 0PF
Tel: (0963) 370518
Fax: (0963) 370605

South Dorset and Hampshire
Nigel Thimbleby
Wolfeton House, Nr. Dorchester
Dorset DT2 9QN
Tel: (0305) 268748
Fax: (0305) 265090

Essex and Hertfordshire
James Service
Hawkins Harvest
Great Bardfield, Essex CM7 4QW
Tel: (0371) 810189
Fax: (0371) 810028

Hampshire and Berkshire
Richard Wills
Middleton Estate Office
Longparish, Andover
Hampshire SP11 6PL
Tel: (0264) 720211
Fax: (0264) 720271

Sussex & Surrey
Mark Wrey
Keith Middlemas *Consultant*
Wellesley House
Manor Road
Hurstpierpoint, Nr Brighton
West Sussex BN6 9UH
Tel: (0273) 835575
Fax: (0273) 835576

Kent
Christopher Proudfoot
The Old Rectory, Fawkham
Longfield, Kent DA3 8LX
Tel: (0474) 702854

SCOTLAND

North of Scotland
John Douglas-Menzies
Mounteagle, Hill of Fearn
Ross-shire IV20 1RP
Tel: (086283) 2866
Fax: (086283) 2720

Tayside, Fife and Grampian
Roy Miller, F.R.I.C.S.
3/5 Mill Street, Perth PH1 5JB
Tel: (0738) 43088

Edinburgh and the Borders
Roy Miller, F.R.I.C.S.
5 Wemyss Place
Edinburgh EH3 6DH
Tel: (031) 225 4756/7
Fax: (031) 225 1723

South West Scotland
Victor Gubbins F.R.I.C.S.
Eden Lacy, Penrith
Cumbria CA10 1BZ
Tel: (0768) 898 800
Fax: (0768) 898 020

Isle of Man
The Marchioness Conyngham
Myrtle Hill, Andreas Road
Ramsey, Isle of Man
Tel: (0624) 814502
Fax: (0624) 814502

Channel Islands
Richard de la Hey
58 David Place, St. Helier, Jersey
Tel: (0534) 77582
Fax: (0534) 77540

REPUBLIC OF IRELAND
Desmond Fitz-Gerald,
Knight of Glin
Glin Castle, Glin, Co. Limerick
Fax: (35361) 68 34 364
Private Residence
52 Waterloo Road, Dublin 4
Tel: (3531) 668 05 85
Fax: (3531) 668 02 71

NORTHERN IRELAND
Danny Kinahan
Castle Upton, Templepatrick
Co. Antrim BT39 0AH
Tel: (08494) 33480
Fax: (08494) 33410

UNITED STATES

Baltimore
Betsy Gordon Matthai
100 West Road, Suite 300
Baltimore, Maryland 21204
Tel: (410) 832 7555
Fax: (410) 825 9222

Boston
Elizabeth M. Chapin
Perry T. Rathbone *Consultant*
Brigitte Bradford *Consultant*
342 Broadway Cambridge,
Mass, 02139-1843
Tel: (617) 576 0400
Fax: (617) 876 7725

Chicago
Frances Blair, Lisa Cavanaugh
Laura de Frise,
Susan Florence (Jewellery)
200 West Superior Street
Chicago, Illinois 60610
Tel: (312) 787 2765
Fax: (312) 951 7449

Dallas
Carolyn Foxworth
7047 Elmridge Drive
Dallas, Texas 75240
Tel: (214) 239 0098
Fax: (214) 386 6102

Los Angeles
Terry Stanfill, Hannah Shore,
Ursula Hermacinski,
Deborah McLeod (*Contemporary Art*),
James de Givenchy (*Jewellery*)
Nancy Cerbone, (*Collectibles*)
342 North Rodeo Drive
Beverly Hills, California 90210
Tel: (310) 275 5534. Telex: 6711872
Fax: (310) 275 9748

Miami
Mary Hoeveler
110 Merrick Way, Suite 2A
Coral Gables, Florida 33134
Tel: (305) 445 1487
Fax: (305) 441 6561

New Orleans
Susan Gore Brennan
1518 Fourth Street
New Orleans, Louisiana 70175
Tel: (504) 895 4832
Fax: (504) 895 4964

Newport
Betsy D. Ray,
Ralph Carpenter (*Consultant*)
228 Spring Street
Newport, Rhode Island 02840
Tel: (041) 849 9222
Fax: (041) 849 6322

Palm Beach
Helen Cluett, Lucy Ullmann
251 Royal Palm Way
Palm Beach, Florida 33480
Tel: (407) 833 6952
Fax: (407) 833 0007

Philadelphia
Paul Ingersoll
P.O. Box 112, Bryn Mawr
Pennsylvania 19010
Tel: (215) 525 5493
Fax: (215) 525 0967

San Francisco
Ellanor Notides,
Elizabeth Lowsley-Williams
3516 Sacramento Street
San Francisco, California 94118
Tel: (415) 346 6633
Fax: (415) 346 8084

South East
Carol W. Ballard
3950 Carmichael Place, Suite 107
Montgomery, Alabama 36117
Tel: (205) 244 9688
Fax: (205) 244 9588

Washington
John Gardner, Nuala Pell, Mary Itsell
Hamilton Court, 1228 31st Street N.W.,
Washington, D.C. 20007
Tel: (202) 333 7459
Fax: (202) 342 0537

Canada
Suzanne E. Davis
Christie, Manson & Woods
International, Inc.
170 Bloor Street, Suite 210
Toronto, Ontario M5S 1T9
Tel: (416) 960 2063
Fax: (416) 960 8815

Mexico
Patricia Hernandez
Debra Nagao (*Assistant*)
Eugenio Sue 65
Col. Polanco
11560 Mexico, D.F.
Tel: (525) 280 9804/281 0190
Fax: (525) 281 3088

Argentina
Christiana
Erhart del Campo
Arroyo 850, 1007 Capital, Buenos Aires
Tel: (541) 393 4222
Tel: (541) 394 9617
Fax: (541) 394 9578

Brazil
Rio De Janeiro
Maria Thereza de Azevedo Sodré
Consultant
Av. Rui Barbosa, 582
22250 Rio de Janeiro
Tel: (5521) 551 1467
Telex: 213 4285
São Paulo
Paulo Figueiredo
A. Fernao Cardim,
116, Bela Vista
01403-020 São Paulo
Tel: (5511) 283 0775
Fax: (5511) 284 3765

Colombia
Harry M. Hanabergh
Aptdo. Aereo 250670, Calle 71,
No. 13-10, Bogotá, Colombia
Tel: (571) 211 5049
Fax: (571) 255 1442

Venezuela
Alain Jathière
Quinta La Magnolias
Calle Los Olivos
Los Chorros, Caracas
Tel: (582) 238 03 55
Fax: (582) 357613

WORLDWIDE

Australia
Sydney
Janelle Dawes
298 New South Head Road
Double Bay, Sydney N.S.W. 2028
Tel: (612) 326 1422. Telex: 26343
Fax: (612) 327 8439
Adelaide
Ian Bruce
193 Hutt Street, Adelaide S.A. 5000
Tel: (618) 232 2860
Fax: (618) 232 6506

Austria
Dr. Johanna Schönburg-Hartenstein
Christie's Kunstauktionen GmbH
Kohlmarkt 4, 1010 Vienna
Tel: (431) 533 88 12
Fax: (431) 533 71 66

Belgium
Brussels
Bernard de Launoit (*General Manager*)
Sabine Taevernier *Contemporary Art*
Roland de Lathuy (*Old Master Pictures*)
Bernard Steyaert (*Chairman*)
Christie's Belgium S.A.
33 Boulevard de Waterloo
1000 Brussels
Tel: (322) 512 8830
Fax: (322) 513 3279

Denmark
Birgitta Hillingsø
Dronningens Tværgade 10
1302 Copenhagen K
Tel: (45) 33 32 70 75
Fax: (45) 33 13 00 75

Finland
Barbro Schauman
Ulrikagatan 3 A
00140 Helsinki
Tel: (3580) 60 82 12
Fax: (3580) 66 06 87

France
Paris
Nicholas Clive Worms, (*Chairman*)
Humphrey Butler (*Managing Director*)
Betrand du Vignaud
Guy Jennings (*Director of Modern
Pictures*)
Christie's France S.A.
6 rue Paul Baudry, 75008 Paris
Tel: (331) 42 56 17 66
Fax: (331) 42 56 26 01
Aix-en-Provence
Fabienne Albertini (*Consultant*)
Tel: (33) 92 72 43 31
Fax: (33) 92 72 53 65
Bordeaux
Marie-Cecile Moueix
49 Cours Xavier Arnozan
33000 Bordeaux
Tel: (33) 56 81 65 47
Fax: (33) 56 51 15 71
Lyon
Viconte Thiery de Lachaise
36 Place Bellecourt 69002 Lyon
Tel: (33) 78 42 83 82
Fax: (33) 78 42 83 84

Germany
Berlin
Marianne Kewenig
Viktoria von Specht
Barbara Bergdolt
Fasanenstrasse 72, 10719 Berlin
Tel: (4930) 882 7778
Fax: (4930) 883 8768
Düsseldorf
Jorg-Michael Bertz
Birgid Seynsche-Vautz
Christie's (Deutschland) GmbH
Inselstrasse 15
40479 Düsseldorf
Tel: (49211) 498 2986
Fax: (49211) 492 0339
Frankfurt
Charlotte Prinzessin von Croÿ
Julia Pfeffer
Savignystrasse 42
60325 Frankfurt am Main
Tel: (4969) 74 50 21
Fax: (4940) 75 20 79
Hamburg
Christiane Gräfin zu Rantzau
Wentzelstrasse 21, 22301 Hamburg
Tel: (4940) 279 4073
Fax: (4940) 270 4497
Munich
Marie Christine Gräfin Huyn
Residenzstrasse 27, 80333 Munich
Tel: (4989) 22 95 39
Fax: (4989) 29 63 02

Greece
Elisavet Logotheti-Lyra
27 Vassilisis Sophias Avenue
Athens 10674
Tel: (301) 725 3900
Fax: (301) 723 8347

Israel
Mary Gilben
Christie's (Israel) Limited
Asia House
4 Weizmann Street
Tel Aviv 64239
Tel: (9723) 6950695
Fax: (9723) 6952751

Italy
Milan
Clarice Pecori Giraldi
Tito Pedrini
Christie's (Int.) S.A.
Via Manin 3, 20121 Milan
Tel: (392) 29 00 13 74
Fax: (392) 29 00 11 56
Bassano del Grappa
Isabelle von Schoenfeldt
Viale Vicenza, 152
36061 Bassano del Grappa
Tel: (39424) 50 41 61 / 50 32 70
Fax: (39424) 50 32 71
Turin
Conte Sandro Perrone di San Martino
Corso Matteotti 33
10121 Turin
Tel: (3911) 548 819
Bologna
Franco Calarota
Via M. D'Azeglio 15, 40123 Bologna
Tel: (3951) 235 843
Fax: (3951) 222 716

Japan
Sachiko Hibiya (*Deputy Chairman*)
Koji Yamada (*Managing Director*)
Christie's Japan Limited
Ichibankan Building, B1
3-12, Ginza 5-chome
Chuo-ku
Tokyo 104
Tel: (813) 3571 0668
Fax: (813) 3571 5853

Norway
Ulla Solitair Hjort
Christie's
Colbjornsensgt. 1
0256 Oslo 2
Tel: (4722) 44 12 42
Fax: (4722) 55 92 36

Portugal
Antonio M. G. Santos Mendonça
R. Conde de Almoster 44, 1°Esq.
1500 Lisbon
Tel: (3511) 78 63 83
Fax: (3511) 60 95 10

Singapore
Irene Lee
Cecilia Ong *Consultant*
Christie's International
Singapore Pte Ltd.
Unit 3, Parklane,
Goodwood Park Hotel,
22 Scotts Road, Singapore 0922
Tel: (65) 235 3828
Fax: (65) 235 8128

South Africa
Cape Town
Juliet Lomberg
14 Hillwood Road
Claremont
Cape Town 7700
Tel: (2721) 761 2676
Fax: (2721) 762 7129
Johannesburg
Harriet Hedley
P.O. Box 72126
Parkview
Johannesburg 2122
Tel: (2711) 880 6975
Fax: (2711) 880 6926

Spain
Casilda Fz-Villaverde y Silva
Juan Varez
Christie's Iberica S.L.
Antonio Maura, 10
28014 Madrid
Tel: (341) 532 66 26/7
Fax: (341) 523 12 40

Sweden
Stockholm
Lillemor Malmström
Christie's Sweden AB
Sturegatan 26, 11436 Stockholm
Tel: (468) 662 0131
Fax: (468) 660 0725
South of Sweden
Baroness Irma Silfverschiold
230 41 Klagerup
Tel: (4640) 44 03 60
Fax: (4640) 44 03 71

Switzerland
Zürich
Maria Reinshagen *Vice President*
Christie's (Int.) A.G.
Steinwiesplatz, 8032 Zürich
Tel: (411) 262 0505
Fax: (411) 251 0471

Taiwan
Anthony Lin
Bobbie Hu
Christie's Swire Taiwan
6th Floor, 369 Fu-Hsing North Road
Taipei 10483, Taiwan, R.O.C.
Tel: (886) 2 718 1612
Fax: (886) 2 718 3702